100 THINGS
X-MEN FANS
SHOULD KNOW & DO
BEFORE THEY DIE

100 THINGS
X-MEN FANS
SHOULD KNOW & DO
BEFORE THEY DIE

Brian Cronin

TRIUMPH
BOOKS

Library of Congress Cataloging-in-Publication Data

Names: Cronin, Brian, author.
Title: 100 things X-Men fans should know & do before they die / Brian Cronin.
Other titles: One hundred things X-Men fans should know and do before they die
Description: Chicago, Illinois : Triumph Books, 2018. | Series: 100 things... fans should know
Identifiers: LCCN 2018002048 | ISBN 9781629375663 (paperback)
Subjects: LCSH: X-men (Comic strip)—Miscellanea. | X-Men (Fictitious characters) | Comic books, strips, etc.—Miscellanea. | BISAC: PERFORMING ARTS / Film & Video / General. | COMICS & GRAPHIC NOVELS / Nonfiction.
Classification: LCC PN6728.X2 C76 2018 | DDC 741.5/973—dc23
LC record available at https://lccn.loc.gov/2018002048

This book is available in quantity at special discounts for your group or organization. For further information, contact:

Triumph Books LLC
814 North Franklin Street
Chicago, Illinois 60610
(312) 337-0747
www.triumphbooks.com

Printed in U.S.A.
ISBN: 978-1-62937-566-3
Design by Patricia Frey

For my mom, Kathleen Cronin, who bought me my first X-Men comic book, on the spinner rack at a bookstore that no longer exists in a mall that no longer exists. The X-Men are still around, though.

Contents

Introduction

When it comes to the X-Men, it really matters when you started reading the series. If you were a reader who started following the book in the 1960s, you likely recall either the outlandish powers or, if you came around later on in the decade, just how amazing Neal Adams' artwork was (years after the fact, Chris Claremont still remembered the first time he saw Neal Adams' Jean Grey and was instantly smitten). If you started reading the book in the 1980s, when it started to become a sales goliath, you embraced the way that the series spoke to how being a misfit was okay. That there was nothing wrong about being different from everyone else. That's likely the iconic take on the X-Men from a fan perspective.

However, if you picked up the book when I did, at the absolute peak of the X-Men's success in 1991, then the title had a whole other meaning to you. For me, the X-Men were the height of cool. Wolverine was probably the coolest character in all of comics. The books were being drawn by the most popular artists in comics, from Jim Lee to Marc Silvestri to Rob Liefeld. I had read some histories of comic books before actually collecting comic books, so I knew more than most fans, but even with that in mind, I was in for such a shock when I opened up my first issue of X-Men and had the hardest time just keeping track of all of the characters in the book (try to figure out what Forge's powers are without the comic book explicitly telling you—it's not easy).

Still, the X-Men were so cool that I was hooked. By the time I was a teen, I was already working at the comic book store down the street from my house and I was right there for the peak of the overall comic book sales bubble. The week that "The Death of Superman" came out also saw the release of *Bloodshot #1* and at least one part of the X-Men crossover, "The X-Cutioner's Song" (each issue bagged with a trading card, of course). It was nuts. Each of those three books sold at least 500,000 copies and that was just one week!

Years later, while doing an internship after my first year of law school, I first discovered Comic Book Resources' message board. I was soon not only a member, but a moderator there of the X-Men forum. In 2004, few friends and I started a comic book blog called "Comics Should Be Good," back when every third comic book reader was starting a comic book blog. Comics Should Be Good was popular enough that Comic Book Resources brought us in as their official blog in 2006. Over a decade later, I still write Comics Should Be Good as part of Comic Book Resources.

I also still love the X-Men now as much as I did back in 1991, despite the X-Men no longer being quite the king of the mountain as they were back then, when it was somehow a realistic business model to charge $1.99 a minute for fans to call a 1-900 number advertised in the comics to answer trivia questions about the X-Men (I didn't do it, but it was tempting).

Hopefully these next 100 chapters will give you an idea of why the X-Men are still so cool, almost 60 years after they first took on Magneto at Cape Citadel in *X-Men #1*.

—Brian Cronin, 2017

1 The X-Men

In the late 1970s, Stan Lee was less and less involved in the day-to-day managing of Marvel Comics. He would ultimately move to California in 1980 to devote his time solely to adapting Marvel Comics into other media. With Lee's presence on the actual books lessening, Marvel began to do a sort of ceremonial introduction at the start of each issue to make it seem like Lee was still a part of the company (since even back then, Lee was one of the most famous names in comics). It would give a basic description of the comic book and end with Stan Lee presenting it. For the X-Men, after noting the individual team member names, it stated "Children of the atom, students of Charles Xavier, MUTANTS—feared and hated by the world they have sworn to protect. These are the strangest heroes of all! Stan Lee presents: the Uncanny X-Men!"

That's really the X-Men in a nutshell—feared and hated by the world they have sworn to protect. They are the strangest heroes of them all. However, a funny thing happened along the way. For the first decade of their existence (the series debuted in 1963), the X-Men were very much not only outcasts within the Marvel Universe, but they were outcasts to comic book readers as well. *X-Men* was one of Marvel's lowest-selling ongoing titles, and in the early 1970s, the series was canceled. A few months later, it was revived as a reprint-only series, spotlighting Lee and Kirby's original '60s stories. Yes, amazingly enough, the X-Men were actually canceled after less than a decade of existence!

Then, in 1975, a book called *Giant-Size X-Men #1* came out that changed everything. A brand-new team of X-Men made their first appearance, and while even then the book was not a big seller right away (it was practically the end of the decade before the book even sold well enough to be released on a monthly basis), the book was slowly gaining in sales. Then, sure enough, the strangest heroes of them all ended up becoming the most popular heroes of them all.

Beginning in the 1980s, the X-Men were not only the most popular comic book series that there was, but it wasn't even close. *X-Men* sold twice as many copies as any other Marvel Comics title during most of the '80s. The only other titles that rivaled it in sales were the inevitable spinoffs from the *X-Men* series, like *New Mutants* and *X-Factor*. What began as a comic book series eventually became practically its own imprint at Marvel Comics.

During the '90s, when comic book sales were exploding, the popularity of the X-Men grew to new heights, complete with a hit animated television series, a best-selling action figure series, and a series of popular video games.

In 2000, Fox's *X-Men* was the first major Marvel superhero film to be released, and it was a hit. It paved the way for all the other superhero films to follow, eventually leading to Marvel forming their own film studio to make their own movies. However, in that regard, the X-Men almost became a victim of their own success. Once Marvel began to produce their own films, the fact that they did not own the movie rights to the X-Men made it a difficult situation for Marvel. They could push a comic book series which they did not own all of the rights for *or* a series in which they did own all of the respective rights (specifically the Avengers). Thus, by the end of the decade, the Avengers were ascendant and the X-Men found themselves eclipsed.

Nowadays, Marvel has recommitted itself to their X-Men comic book line and we're in the midst of a second wave of X-Men films, following a 2011 reboot of the film franchise. X-Men film spinoffs are starting to become more popular, with 2016's *Deadpool* being one of the biggest film hits of the year. This looks like it will lead to more and more X-Men-related films from Fox, with *New Mutants* and *Deadpool 2* both on the horizon.

In this book, we'll look at the comic book characters and creators that are most responsible for the X-Men becoming pop culture institutions, and we will examine the ups and downs along the way of how the X-Men went from being canceled in 1970 to eventually starring in the highest-selling single comic book issue in comic book history just 21 years later.

2 Chris Claremont

When you look to the most important people involved in the success of a particular piece of popular culture, you are almost always going to be looking at the people who were the creators of the character and/or series. When you look to the history of Spider-Man, for instance, the most important people involved with the character are his two creators, Steve Ditko and Stan Lee. However, in the case of the X-Men, it is someone who did not come aboard the series until it had been around for over a decade. Writer Chris Claremont is the main reason that the X-Men became as popular as they have been in history.

Claremont began working at Marvel Comics in the late 1960s as an intern while he was still in college. Amazingly enough, it was during this point that he had his first connection with the X-Men, as Claremont was credited with a plot assist on *X-Men #59* (Claremont gave writer Roy Thomas an idea for the ending of the issue) and after graduating college in 1972, Roy Thomas gave Claremont some writing gigs. By 1974, Claremont was writing one-off issues of a number of Marvel titles, as well as being the regular writer on the horror/war comic book, *War is Hell.* When the All-New, All-Different X-Men debuted in 1975's *Giant-Size X-Men #1,* writer Len Wein (who had recently worked with Claremont on *Giant-Size Fantastic Four #4*) could not continue on the series when it became an ongoing series, so Claremont scripted over Wein's plots for *X-Men #94–95* and then took over the series as the sole writer with *X-Men #96.*

Since Claremont took over the series so early in the run, he was able to have a greater deal of control over the characterizations of the heroes in the series than most writers do when taking over a series. Therefore, in general terms, what we think of when we think of the characterizations of the All-New, All-Different X-Men are what Claremont came up with during his time on the series. Claremont is well known for his willingness to give his artists a say in how the series goes, and since X-Men artist Dave Cockrum was already on the series when Claremont took over the book, Cockrum had a lot of say in what happened in the book.

When Cockrum was unable to keep up with the deadlines on the series (even when the series was only released once every two months), he left the book and was replaced by artist John Byrne, who had worked with Claremont already on both *Iron Fist* and *Marvel Team-Up.* Claremont soon began to include Byrne in the plotting of the series and the two creators (along with inker Terry Austin) soon went on a hot streak of classic stories, culminating with the back-to-back successes of "The Dark Phoenix Saga" and "Days of Future Past." Byrne, though, chafed under the writing arrangement, since Claremont, as the scripter on the book, often had final say over what would actually make it into the comic book, despite Byrne doing the bulk of the plotting in the later issues.

X-Men #96 marked the start of Chris Claremont's run as the sole writer. (Cover art by Marie Severin, Sal Buscema, and Annette Kawecki)

With the book now a hit, Cockrum returned as the regular artist and the book continued its rise to the top of the charts, which was solidified when Cockrum left for a second time and was replaced by an up-and-coming artist by the name of Paul Smith. Smith only stayed on the book for a year, but by the time he left, *Uncanny X-Men* was solidly Marvel's number one seller.

What people loved the most about Claremont's work was the way that he mixed deeply personal characterizations with striking melodramatic story lines. Essentially, Claremont used the classic soap opera approach—a never-ending serialized story complete with a large cast who all had interesting personalities. Claremont's stories were as complex as his characters and it really paved the way in the 1980s for other comic book series to tell similarly modern and mature superhero stories. There is no Marv Wolfman and George Perez *New Teen Titans* or Paul Levitz and Keith Giffen *Legion of Super-Heroes* if not for Chris Claremont's *X-Men* run.

After Paul Smith left the series, John Romita Jr. stayed on the book for three years. Romita Jr. was followed by Marc Silvestri (the series had become so popular that they often shipped two issues a month, making it too much for a single artist to draw, so Silvestri was joined by Rick Leonardi as an alternate artist). In 1990, Claremont was joined by a new artist, Jim Lee.

Lee was a superstar artist at a time when superstar artists were selling more comic books than ever, as a speculator's market had led to a gigantic boom in comic book sales. Claremont began to co-plot the series with Lee, just like he had done with Cockrum and Byrne, but soon it became clear that Lee and Claremont had different ideas of where to take the X-Men. Ultimately, *X-Men* editor Bob Harras chose Jim Lee over Claremont and Claremont's final issue of his original *X-Men* run came in the third issue of a newly launched second X-Men series. Seventeen years later, Claremont was no longer the regular writer of the X-Men.

In 2000, Claremont had been working in an editorial position at Marvel when he was lured back to the X-Men to take over both *Uncanny X-Men* and *X-Men*. The return proved to be a disappointment and Claremont was off of both books within a year. Marvel then launched a third X-Men series, *X-Treme X-Men*, and gave that to Claremont. When that series ended, Claremont returned one last time to write *Uncanny X-Men #444–474*. Marvel has Claremont under a unique exclusive contract where they pay him whether he writes something or not. He has done a handful of X-Men-related series in the last decade, including a series called *X-Men Forever* that was based on the notion of "What if Claremont had never left the X-Men in 1991?" and most recently, a 2014 Nightcrawler series that lasted less than a year.

Whether he ever writes another X-Men issue again, Chris Claremont has forever changed the history of the X-Men in comic books and in the films based on his epic run on the series.

3 Wolverine

One of the things that people often forget about Wolverine is that it was not like he was pulled out of the scrap heap when he was made a part of the X-Men in *Giant-Size X-Men #1* in 1975. His debut appearance a year earlier in *Incredible Hulk #181* (by Len Wein, Herb Trimpe, and Jack Abel—with a costume designed by Marvel's art director, John Romita Sr.) was well received at the time. It was very likely that Wolverine would have ended up in some comic book series if he had not ended up as part of the X-Men. Marvel tended to be very good at eventually using good characters like Wolverine. That said, it was still very impressive to see Wolverine go from being "Oh, that guy is kind of interesting" to Marvel's most popular character.

The first step toward superstardom for Wolverine came when Wein added him to the cast of the All-New, All-Different X-Men in *Giant-Size X-Men #1*. The X-Men were all from different parts of the world and the Canadian Wolverine fit right in to the theme. The cover for the issue turned out to be a major change in Wolverine's history. Gil Kane, one of the industry's most popular artists, had become a sort of go-to cover artist for Marvel in the mid-1970s. He drew the cover for *Giant-Size X-Men #1*, changing Wolverine's mask on the cover, giving him a straight cowl instead of the original Romita mask that had little whiskers on it. Dave Cockrum liked the change so much that he went through the issue and redrew all of the pages to make the mask fit the cover.

Wolverine was not an automatic star in the series. Cockrum and Claremont even talked about writing the character out of the book, as neither creator had a great handle on the feisty mutant who seemed like he might stab you at any moment. At one point, Cockrum and Claremont planned to reveal that Wolverine was actually not a mutant, but rather a mutated Wolverine created by the High Evolutionary (Cockrum caused a lot of confusion over the years when he mistakenly referred to that idea as something he worked with Wein on, when it really wasn't until after Wein left the book). They quickly dropped that idea.

When John Byrne joined the series, that's when things changed for Wolverine. Byrne was a Canadian, as well, and he took a shine to his countryman and made a point to make Wolverine more and more of a central figure in the series. One of the things Byrne did was to play up the fact that Wolverine was a dangerous guy who was not against killing if the need arose. This was a guy who was covered in unbreakable adamantium metal and had sharp claws burst out of his forearms, after all. Byrne also gave Wolverine a cool new costume soon before leaving the X-Men, a brown and tan costume that Wolverine wore for the rest of the 1980s.

The next big step for Wolverine was when he got his own miniseries, written by Chris Claremont and drawn by Frank Miller and Joe Rubinstein. Miller and Claremont plotted the series together and they came up with the idea of making Wolverine basically a samurai. Miller famously used ninjas a lot in his Daredevil work and shockingly enough, Wolverine fought a lot of ninjas in his miniseries. The miniseries was a massive success and within a few years, Wolverine graduated to his own ongoing series. He was the first member of the All-New, All-Different X-Men to achieve such an honor.

Wolverine became so popular that the comic book boom of the 1990s also saw a boom in Wolverine appearances in other comic book series. Besides appearing regularly in X-Men and his own solo series, Wolverine also was the regular lead feature in the anthology series, *Marvel Comics Presents*, and guest starred in pretty much every Marvel comic book ever published. Wolverine literally guest starred in at least one non-X-related comic book every month from January 1991 through December 1993.

After he became a movie star with Hugh Jackman's portrayal in 2000's *X-Men*, Wolverine only became even more prolific in that decade, as he joined the Avengers in 2005's relaunch of the *New Avengers*. He did so while still being a member of the X-Men and appearing in all three then-current X-Men series. Things were so crazy that there was even a Wolverine story that made fun of Wolverine's schedule by showing how he was spending each day of the week with a different superhero team.

While he has traditionally been a loner, Wolverine eventually took on a greater leadership role when he broke from Cyclops in an X-Men story line called "Schism," where Wolverine decided that the X-Men needed to get back to teaching young mutants and not just training them to become soldiers. He reopened Xavier's School for Mutants and renamed it the Jean Grey School for Higher Learning, becoming the headmaster of the school.

Tragically, after being attacked by an alien virus, Wolverine's famous healing factor, which allowed him to recover from any number of attacks (and stay alive despite being born in the 19th century), was eliminated. In 2014, Marvel published "Death of Wolverine" by Charles Soule and Steve McNiven, which saw

Wolverine get captured by one of the scientists who worked on the Weapon X project that gave Wolverine his adamantium skeleton. The scientist was trying to replicate the experiment on others, but needed Wolverine's healing power for it to work. Wolverine, of course, did not have it any more. He then killed the scientist and freed the other subjects, but not before the scientist encased Wolverine in molten adamantium, killing him.

His young female clone, Laura Kinney, has taken over as the All-New Wolverine, but recently, the original Wolverine has made a comeback.

4 The Original Five

Naturally, if there were never any X-Men to begin with, then the X-Men could never have become a pop culture phenomenon, but it's still surprising to see how little respect the original five X-Men get when it comes to the history of the X-Men. It's almost as if X-Men history began in 1975 with *Giant-Size X-Men #1*, while obviously there already had been an X-Men team going back to 1963.

When the X-Men debuted in 1963, the first issue saw Professor Charles Xavier welcome a new female student to join his four male students. Naturally, the four boys were falling over themselves to impress the new girl, who turned out to be Jean Grey, a beautiful red-headed teen girl who took on the code name of Marvel Girl. The established members of the team were Scott Summers (Cyclops, the group leader), Warren Worthington III (The Angel), Hank McCoy (The Beast), and Bobby Drake (Iceman), who was the youngest of the group.

Jean barely had time to get acclimated to living in the X-Mansion with a quartet of hormone-driven teenagers when the X-Men were suddenly sent on their first mission as a team to take on the mutant supervillain known as Magneto. In retrospect, it really was awfully irresponsible of Xavier to send them into action on Jean's first day as a member of the team. Later in the issue, after the X-Men successfully defeated Magneto, Xavier even specifically noted that their victory justified all their long hours of training together—Jean had just met them that day!

In the early days of the X-Men, they spent a lot of their time investigating new mutants rather than actively seeking out trouble. Their battles were often reactive ones, like responding whenever Magneto (and later, his Brotherhood of Evil Mutants) did something evil. Very often, they relied upon Professor X to miraculously save the day through the use of his astounding telepathic powers.

With Xavier holding such a powerful control over the team, the natural inclination of most writers on the series was to write Xavier out whenever they could (less than a year in, Cyclops had to temporarily take over as the head of the team when it seemed like Xavier was out of action). When Roy Thomas took over, he went one step further and even killed Xavier off (don't worry, he got better). Around this time, the X-Men finally graduated from school and, as a result of their graduation, added personalized costumes to replace their team uniforms.

Over the years, the original five X-Men gained a few new members. The first one, Mimic, did not even appear to be a mutant (although years later he found out that he was, in fact, a mutant). Mimic could mimic the abilities of the mutants around him. His stint on the team was a brief one. Lorna Dane had a longer stay on the team. Introduced as the green-haired daughter of Magneto, she had powers like her father. The X-Men then met the long-lost brother of Cyclops, Alex Summers, who took on the name of Havok.

As the 1960s ended, though, and the 1970s were getting ready to start, it was clear that the X-Men were just no longer working as a series. The book was canceled in early 1970. Luckily, the title had a quick reprieve from total cancellation a few months later. Back in the '60s and early '70s, there really was no such thing as a "back issue," so both Marvel and DC routinely reprinted older comic book stories. Marvel had a whole line of comic books that reprinted older comic books, while at the same time, they would also keep a few lower-selling titles going by turning them into reprint-only books. That was what happened to *Nick Fury, Agent of S.H.I.E.L.D.* at the turn of the 1970s and the same thing happened to *X-Men*. The book went reprint-only until 1975, when the All-New, All-Different X-Men changed everything.

This doesn't mean that the X-Men disappeared during this time. Beast went off and got his own short-lived starring feature in *Amazing Adventures,* while the rest of the team made sporadic guest appearances (sometimes with Professor X and sometimes by themselves) throughout the early '70s. This even included a memorable stint working alongside Captain America to stop the evil organization known as the Secret Empire, who had taken control of the United States government and had turned the country against Captain America and mutants, leading to a natural team-up between Cap and the X-Men.

5 Stan Lee

When the 1960s began, Stan Lee had been working in comic books for more than 20 years. He was only 17 years old when he first got a gig at Martin Goodman's Timely Comics in 1939 (Goodman was married to Lee's cousin, Jean), working as an assistant and eventually writing text pieces for the comic books (back in the old days, comic books needed to include two pages of text to qualify for the cheaper magazine shipping rate). He was still less than 20 years old when Goodman suddenly made Lee the interim editor-in-chief of the company in 1941, when Goodman's star creators, Joe Simon and Jack Kirby, left the company in a financial dispute with Goodman over their hit comic book series, *Captain America Comics*. Intended as a fill-in, Lee excelled so much at the job that Goodman gave it to him full-time, even keeping the job waiting for him while Lee served during World War II.

By the end of the 1940s, superhero comics were on the way out and Lee spent the 1950s writing western and monster comic books. The company went through a few different names during the period, most notably Atlas Comics (Goodman didn't really need a steady name for the comic division of his publishing company), but sales were just barely good enough to keep the lights on. Goodman made a mistake in the late 1950s when he decided to stop distributing his own comic books and joined a large distributor, which then promptly went out of business. Atlas nearly went out of business but was saved by Goodman cutting a deal with International Distributors, which was owned by National Comics (now known as DC Comics), the largest comic book company in the industry at the time. The deal allowed Marvel to continue publishing comics, but only a reduced amount of titles (roughly eight comic books a month). A lot of artists had to be let go, but by the start of the 1960s, sales had picked up to the point where most of the fired artists had been hired back by Atlas.

When Goodman saw the success that National was having with their revived superhero series, including the Flash, Green Lantern, and the newly launched Justice League of America, he told Lee to make a superhero team comic as well. Lee and Jack Kirby then launched the Fantastic Four, which was a major hit and led to the Marvel Age of Comics (as the company took on the name Marvel Comics). Slowly but surely, superhero comics began to take the

Top Five Greatest X-Men Writers

5. **Scott Lobdell**
   Paired with Fabian Nicieza for years as the two main X-Men writers from 1992 to 1996, Scott Lobdell deftly mixed humor with touching heartfelt moments, like the deaths of Illyana and Piotr Rasputin.

4. **Roy Thomas**
   Thomas took the X-Men out of the classroom and into the world, plus set the groundwork for a whole lot of future stories, especially the Sentinels story arc.

3. **John Byrne**
   Originally just the artist on X-Men, John Byrne began cowriting the book with Chris Claremont, and soon Byrne was doing the lion's share of the plotting. Some of the most famous stories in X-Men history originated in Byrne's mind.

2. **Grant Morrison**
   Comic book properties tend to get stale over the decades, but Morrison fixed that by dramatically invigorating the X-Men over a period of four years at the start of the 21st century.

1. **Chris Claremont**
   The greatest X-Men writer of all time, pretty much everything we think of when we think of the X-Men originated either by Claremont or in stories cowritten by Claremont.

place of the western, sci-fi, and romance comic books that Marvel had been publishing.

In 1963, Goodman asked Lee to launch two new series—a Spider-Man-esque series and a Fantastic Four–esque series. The Spider-Man-like series turned out to be Daredevil (whose first issue was so delayed that it did not come out until 1964) and the Fantastic Four-like series was the X-Men. Lee had noted that it was getting tiresome coming up with new origins for superheroes, so he thought it might be interesting if they all had the same origin, hence the idea of them all being mutants. Lee originally wanted to call the book *The Mutants*, but Goodman objected and Lee ultimately came up with the name *The X-Men*.

Lee wrote the series for the first 19 issues. It was clear that the X-Men did not hold the same interest for Lee as some of the other series that he had written, like the Fantastic Four or Amazing Spider-Man. Characters' personalities changed seemingly overnight as Lee routinely tried out new ideas (including the infamous bit in *X-Men #3* where Professor X pines for Jean Grey, but admits that she would never go for him…not because of his age or the fact that he was her teacher, but because he was in a wheelchair).

It was during Lee's time on the series that we saw the first hints of the anti-mutant prejudice that would play such a major role during Chris Claremont's tenure on the book. In *X-Men #14*, Lee cleverly evoked an old article in *Mechanix Illustrated* that Golden Age comic book writer Otto Binder had written about the possible menaces that could be caused by radiation leading to mutations in people and showed how the people of Earth were in constant fear of mutants walking among them (back then, though, Lee was evoking the "Red Menace" era much more than the "Civil Rights" era with his metaphors). This led to the creation of the mutant-hunting robots known as the Sentinels. While Lee never returned to the X-Men, he did lay the groundwork for generations to come.

6 Jack Kirby

In June 1958, a tragic accident changed the history of Marvel Comics forever. Atlas Comics' freelance artist Joe Maneely was killed when he fell between the cars on the commuter train from New York City back to his home in New Jersey (a home he had only recently purchased). The reason that death was so important was because Maneely had been Atlas' star artist during the 1950s. Whenever Stan Lee launched a major project, Maneely was his guy. He was a very talented artist and he was also quite fast. Stan Lee once said of Maneely, "Joe Maneely to me would have been the next Jack Kirby. He also could draw anything, make anything look exciting, and I actually think he was even faster than Jack." You will note, of course, that Lee said "the next Jack Kirby," which was because Kirby was not working for Atlas during the 1950s, as he was one of the most popular artists in the industry and had plenty of work to keep himself busy.

Later in the decade, though, Kirby began to do some side work for Atlas, while primarily working for National Comics (now DC Comics), and when Kirby and National ran into some conflicts, Kirby ended up working for Atlas full-time in 1958. Ever since Kirby launched *Captain America Comics* for Timely Comics in 1940, he and his collaborator, Joe Simon, were two of the biggest names in comic books. They went to work for National Comics after Timely's Martin Goodman reneged on some financial promises regarding Captain America. They became stars at National Comics but had to abruptly stop their work to serve in the military during World War II.

After the war, they went into business for themselves, producing finished comic books for a variety of comic book publishers. By

The cover of 1963's X-Men #1, *written by Stan Le and illustrated by Jack Kirby.* (Cover art by Jack Kirby and Sol Brodsky)

the mid-50s, overall comic book sales had decreased enough that Simon and Kirby couldn't support themselves as a team and had to go their separate ways. Kirby ended up at National for a second stint with the company, until he left in 1958. So when Kirby then went to work for Stan Lee and Atlas Comics, it was a huge deal for Lee. Kirby was their star artist and he would have been even if Joe Maneely had lived.

However, as Atlas became Marvel in the early 1960s and their superhero titles began to flourish, it became clear that there was going to be too many superhero titles for Jack Kirby to draw them all. Another one of Atlas' regular artists, Steve Ditko, launched

Spider-Man and the Doctor Strange feature in *Strange Tales*, but Lee needed more than just Kirby and Ditko. In general, Kirby would launch new features and new titles and eventually give way to other artists on the series (except for the series that Kirby took a particular interest in, in which case he would remain on the book). Had Maneely been alive, it's clear that he would have taken some of the stress off of Kirby and Kirby would not have had to launch so many series. It is possible that X-Men would have been one of those books.

We mention X-Men, in particular, because Kirby left the series less than a year in (as Marvel would typically do when Kirby left, Kirby would provide layouts for the artists who followed him so that the transition would be a smooth one). In addition, it is not a series that Kirby spoke much about over the years. Even during the late 1980s, when Kirby was in a major dispute with Marvel over their failure to return his original artwork and he was routinely giving interviews where he claimed to have invented every major Marvel hero of the 1960s by himself, he barely took credit for the X-Men.

This is not to say that Kirby did not still do a wonderful job on the X-Men, as obviously he did. The man was a master and even something as seemingly simple as the X-Men's team uniforms were a master class in design. Kirby's uniforms were used years later when the New Mutants debuted and Jim Lee used a variation of them in the early 1990s when the X-Men briefly went back to team uniforms. His designs for Magneto, Scarlet Witch, Quicksilver, Juggernaut, and the Sentinels all really stood out. Interestingly enough, a panel of Magneto by Kirby from *X-Men #1* was later used by Roy Lichtenstein for one of his famous pop art paintings, where Lichtenstein would take a comic book panel and redraw it as a large painting.

7 All-New, All-Different X-Men

After being strictly a reprint series for over five years, the X-Men had their triumphant return to the world of comic books with the release of *Giant-Size X-Men #1* in 1975. Written by Len Wein and drawn by Dave Cockrum, with a cover by comic book legend Gil Kane, the comic book introduced a brand-new team of X-Men. The concept behind the issue was that Professor X discovered one of the most powerful new mutants on Earth and sent the X-Men to investigate this new mutant, who was living on a mysterious island. The roster of the X-Men at the time was Cyclops, Marvel Girl, Angel, Iceman, Polaris, and Havok (basically everyone except Beast, who had left the team during their hiatus). However, something went terribly wrong on the island and Cyclops was the only member of the team to escape.

With the rest of the team trapped on the island, Professor X quickly put together an international team of X-Men to rescue his original students. He first went to two mutants that he was already familiar with: the Irish mutant, Banshee, and the Japanese mutant, Sunfire. He then recruited the Canadian mutant, Wolverine; the African mutant, Storm; the German mutant, Nightcrawler; the Russian mutant, Colossus; and the Native American mutant, Thunderbird.

Led by Cyclops, this new team headed back to the mysterious island to rescue Cyclops' friends. When they discovered the other X-Men, they were being drained, like batteries. Cyclops was then shocked to learn that this was all a trap! The mutant who had captured the X-Men had intentionally let Cyclops go so that he could bring more mutants to serve as energy sources. In addition, he realized that the strange island was the mutant! The island was called Krakoa and it wanted to kill them all. After a pitched battle against the combined forces of the two teams, Krakoa was sent into outer space. Flying back home in their cramped ship, the X-Men had to ask themselves, "What are we going to do with thirteen X-Men?"

The answer, of course, was clear (after all, when they took over the X-Men ongoing series with #94 for the first new stories in that series since X-Men #66, the cover of the comic proudly boasted that these were the "All-New, All-Different X-Men"). The original members of the team all left, except for Cyclops, who remained to lead the new recruits (Banshee, Wolverine, Storm, Nightcrawler, Colossus, and Thunderbird) under Professor X's overall guidance. Sunfire also left, as he had always told them that he was only committed to the one mission. A tragedy led to Thunderbird dying on their first mission together as a new team. That was right when Chris Claremont officially took over as the writer on the series (artist Dave Cockrum continued on the book, working with a variety of inkers, with veteran inker Sam Grainger being his most common collaborator).

Jean Grey soon returned to the team, only no longer as Marvel Girl, but now as the much more powerful Phoenix. Claremont and Cockrum balanced out the series beautifully between character moments among the teammates, who were just getting to know each other, and clever action setups, like when the X-Men suddenly discovered that they were the only thing standing in the way of the universe being destroyed by the mad emperor of the alien race known as the Shi'ar Empire.

When John Byrne replaced Dave Cockrum (and Terry Austin took over as the inker on the series), things got even more interesting. The X-Men faced off against their old foe, Magneto, and in the process, Cyclops and the new team members were thought to

Giant-Size X-Men #1, *the debut of the All-New, All-Different X-Men.* (Cover art by Gil Kane, Dave Cockrum, and Danny Crespi)

be killed. Instead, they went off on an adventure across the world while trying to find their way back home. It was during this period that Wolverine became more of a prominent member of the team.

Soon, the All-New, All-Different X-Men were no more. Not because they were replaced (well, Banshee did lose his powers during their international journey home and left the team when they finally got back to the X-Mansion), but because they were simply the X-Men now. In fact, after a few years, with Byrne, Claremont, and Austin working together in full force, they decided to mix things up by both bringing Angel back to the team (it did not last long) and also introducing a brand-new team member—a young teen named Kitty Pryde, who served as the new reader "point of view" character for the series. It was time for someone else to be "all-new and all-different."

8 Dave Cockrum

Even before he ever started work on the X-Men, Dave Cockrum was already known as one of the best costume designers in the comic book industry. After returning to the United States after serving in the Vietnam War, Cockrum got a gig in 1972 as the artist on the DC Comics' superhero series *Superboy and the Legion of Super-Heroes*, about a group of teen superheroes in the future. Despite living in the future, their costumes had stayed mostly stagnant since they were introduced in the late 1950s. Cockrum redesigned most of the team, giving them costumes that would last for decades in some instances. After working on the series for a few years, Cockrum moved to Marvel in 1974 over a dispute with DC Comics over his original art (namely that DC wouldn't return it to him, which they did not do at that point in time).

While at DC, Cockrum developed some new characters that he wanted to introduce in the Legion of Super-Heroes as a new team (and if they proved popular, they would get their own spinoff series). When he left DC and got the chance to work on the All-New, All-Different X-Men, Cockrum worked with writer Len Wein to adapt a number of these characters to make them new characters for the X-Men. Nightcrawler and Storm were the two most notable characters to be adapted from Cockrum's Legion pitch, with Colossus also being from those original pitches, in a more roundabout fashion. Cockrum's costumes for Nightcrawler, Colossus, and Storm were classics of the genre. In a world where superheroes get new costumes every other year, Nightcrawler and Colossus effectively still wear the same costumes today that Cockrum designed for them in 1975.

After launching the All-New, All-Different X-Men with Len Wein, Cockrum remained on the ongoing X-Men series while Wein left the book. Incoming writer Chris Claremont collaborated with Cockrum in the truest sense on the title, as the two men went over ideas for the series. Cockrum was particularly a fan of Nightcrawler, and so Claremont made a point to write more Nightcrawler into the series. Cockrum designed another great costume when he and Claremont revamped Marvel Girl, Jean Grey, into the powerful Phoenix.

Cockrum's art helped the X-Men to stand out visually, but Cockrum had troubles meeting his deadlines on the series. The book was becoming more popular and Marvel was hoping to make it a monthly and since Cockrum couldn't handle a bimonthly schedule, he left the book with *X-Men #107* and John Byrne took over. Cockrum's last story arc introduced the space pirates known as the Starjammers (who Cockrum initially intended for their own series) and the Shi'ar Empire's special superhero group, the Imperial Guard (who Cockrum cleverly based on the members of his former series, the Legion of Super-Heroes, with Gladiator of the Imperial Guard being Superboy and so on and so forth). Cockrum also tried to give Wolverine a new costume in his last issue, but John Byrne successfully convinced Marvel to let him return Wolverine to his original costume.

After X-Men became an even bigger hit with Byrne than it was with Cockrum, Cockrum naturally felt somewhat like he had missed the boat a bit. Therefore, when Byrne announced that he was leaving the series, Cockrum quickly jumped in and returned to the title with *X-Men #145* (to help with deadlines on this second go-around, Cockrum did loose blue pencils and artist Joe Rubinstein would finish Cockrum's pencils and then ink them).

Things had changed, though, in the time that Cockrum had been away. There was a burgeoning independent comic book market in the early 1980s and these creators owned their creations themselves, unlike Cockrum, who helped create some of Marvel's biggest characters but had no financial investment in any of them. Cockrum began developing his own new characters and in 1983, he left *Uncanny X-Men* after #164 to work on them. They debuted as the Futurians in a *Marvel Graphic Novel*. However, Cockrum then received an impressive offer from a new, independent comic book company to launch the characters in their own series. He took it and left Marvel. The new series promptly flopped. In the meantime, sales on *Uncanny X-Men* (which had been going up during Cockrum's run) kept going up under his successors and Cockrum missed out on the subsequent royalties that Marvel paid out to the creators on their best-selling titles.

Cockrum passed away in 2006, sadly never having quite the same success in his later years as he previously had on *Legion of Super-Heroes* and *X-Men*.

9 Len Wein

Len Wein was one of the very first of a new generation of comic book writers, namely comic book writers who grew up as fans of comic books. The original comic book writers, naturally, could not be fans of comic books because they were too busy inventing the genre. Then, for the most part, the comic book companies kept employing those same stable of writers for the next two decades. It was not until the 1960s that the next generation of writers began to break into the comic book industry. Wein and his childhood friend, Marv Wolfman, were two of the earliest ones to do so, as they both became professional comic book writers for DC Comics while only in their early twenties.

While at DC Comics, Wein and artist Bernie Wrightson invented Swamp Thing in the pages of *House of Secrets #92*. Wein became a prolific writer for DC, while still doing an occasional story for Marvel. Eventually, though, Wein migrated over to Marvel as a regular writer. In 1974, he and Wolfman actually became the new editors-in-chief of Marvel Comics, with Wein being in charge of the color comic book line while Wolfman was tasked with the black-and-white magazine line.

Before Wein was given the editor-in-chief job, though, he was tasked by former editor-in-chief Roy Thomas with introducing a new Canadian superhero in the pages of a series Wein had just taken over writing, *Incredible Hulk* (a book Wein had wanted to write for years). Thomas told him to name the character either Badger or Wolverine and after Wein read about wolverines, he knew that they were the perfect animal to adapt into a superhero. Wein noted that wolverines were small animals, but they were so feisty that they were able to take down much larger animals when they fought. Thus, Wein (working with Marvel art director John Romita) developed Wolverine, a short Canadian superhero who was so feisty that he was able to use his claws and never-give-up attitude to take on the Hulk!

Wein was then assigned a reboot of the X-Men, using international characters. Naturally, he used his own creation, Wolverine, and then he and artist Dave Cockrum worked together to create four more new mutant heroes—Storm, Nightcrawler, Colossus, and Thunderbird. The All-New, All-Different X-Men debuted in *Giant-Size X-Men #1*. The characters were set to continue as part of a quarterly *Giant-Size X-Men* series by Wein and Cockrum (this would give Cockrum a chance to draw each issue on time). However, Marvel decided to instead bring the characters back to the X-Men ongoing series (which had been in reprints since 1970's *X-Men #67*). Between being assigned the X-Men gig and actually releasing *Giant-Size X-Men #1*, Wein had been named the editor-in-chief of Marvel and he just did not have time to write more than one ongoing series. He had already been writing *Incredible Hulk*, which was a favorite character of his, so he decided to drop *X-Men*. He had Chris Claremont script over his plots for *Giant-Size X-Men #2* (which then became *X-Men #94* and *#95*) and then Claremont took over the series full-time.

Ironically enough, Wein would then soon give up the editor-in-chief gig to concentrate on writing full-time (Wolfman took over the full editor-in-chief gig, although he then left the job himself soon after). Wein never had a chance to implement some of the ideas that he had for some of the characters, some of which were much different than what Cockrum and Claremont ended up doing. In Wein's mind, Wolverine (who we had never seen without his mask) was a young man and the claws on his hands were part of a glove. Cockrum and Claremont later temporarily had the idea of making Wolverine a literal mutated wolverine, but Wein had nothing to do with that idea.

Wein had long runs on a number of major Marvel Comics throughout the 1970s. For four years, he was the regular writer on *Amazing Spider-Man, Incredible Hulk, Fantastic Four,* and *Thor.* He was eventually lured to DC Comics in 1978 to become the new writer on *Batman.* While there, he introduced Bruce Wayne's top business advisor, Lucius Fox. Due to DC Comics introducing a new royalty paid to creators if their creations were used in outside media, Wein amazingly made more money from Lucius Fox's appearances in the Christopher Nolan Dark Knight films than he ever made from Wolverine's multiple hit films. Wein sadly passed away in September 2017.

10 John Byrne

What's really amazing when you look back on their history together is that by the time that John Byrne came to X-Men to work with writer Chris Claremont, the two men had already worked together on a remarkable *three* different series. Claremont had seen Byrne's artwork in some books by the small comic book company Charlton, and had asked to work with him. When the artist Claremont had been working with on the Iron Fist feature in *Marvel Premiere* missed a deadline, Byrne was hired and Iron Fist soon graduated into his own ongoing series by Claremont and Byrne. Byrne quickly started getting more gigs from Marvel, including the Spider-Man team-up series, *Marvel Team-Up,* where he worked with Claremont on a number of issues. He, Claremont, and inker Terry Austin also worked together on a revamped version of the Star-Lord character in the black-and-white magazine *Marvel Preview*.

When Dave Cockrum left *X-Men*, Byrne was the clear choice as his successor. In fact, the X-Men even guest starred in an issue of Iron Fist as a specific sort of "test" for Byrne (and then, bizarrely enough, Marvel had Cockrum redraw the faces of all of the X-Men, thus defeating the entire purpose of the test). Byrne's first issue was *X-Men #108*, which finished up a Claremont/Cockrum arc involving the alien Shi'ar Empire. Byrne was Canadian and thus he was interested in the Canadian member of the X-Men, Wolverine. So in his next issue, he and Claremont introduced the Vindicator, a

Top Five Greatest X-Men Artists

5. Dave Cockrum
The cocreator of most of the major members of the All-New, All-Different X-Men (and one of the best costume designers of all time), Cockrum put his stamp on the book in a relatively short run overall.

4. Paul Smith
An unknown artist coming in to *Uncanny X-Men*, Smith became a superstar as *Uncanny X-Men* hit number one. His action sequences were stunning.

3. Neal Adams
One of the greatest comic book artists of all time, Neal Adams only had a short run on *X-Men*, but it was an amazing stint that showed why he changed the way comic books looked for decades to follow.

2. Jim Lee
The dynamic and sharp lines of Jim Lee practically leaped off of the page, as he became the top artist in comics, so popular that *X-Men #1* was the highest-selling comic book issue ever.

1. John Byrne
The perfect mixture of brilliant storytelling, action-packed sequences, and character-rich expressions, Byrne was paired with inker Terry Austin in a master class of comic book art.

Captain America–like hero with a Canadian flag–themed costume designed by Byrne that was Wolverine's old boss at Department H (the Canadian government group that Professor X recruited Wolverine from back in *Giant-Size X-Men #1*). Byrne pushed Claremont to spotlight Wolverine more and the feral mutant began to take a more prominent role in the series.

Byrne was paired with inker Terry Austin and they combined for crisp lines, sharp designs, and a dynamic sense of action. Byrne was quickly becoming one of the most popular new artists working at Marvel Comics in the late 1970s (along with George Perez, who was drawing *Fantastic Four* and the *Avengers*). Claremont famously was open to collaborating on plots with his artists and soon he and Byrne began to work together on the plots of the series (with Byrne beginning to get coplotter credit as soon as *X-Men #113*).

Over time, Byrne began to become the dominant voice between the two creators during the plotting stages. They were still collaborating on the plots, but where Claremont was originally the driving force of the stories, Byrne was now taking control a bit. This period resulted in two of the most popular story arcs of Byrne and Claremont's run.

The first arc was the "Dark Phoenix Saga," where the X-Men gained a new member (Kitty Pryde, named after a girl that Byrne knew back in art school in Canada) while having to face off against one of their original members, as Jean Grey had become mad with power (turning from the Phoenix into the Dark Phoenix). The second was "Days of Future Past," a clever two-part time travel story where an adult Kate Pryde leaps into her younger self to help the X-Men avoid the murder of an anti-mutant U.S. Senator whose death would turn him into a martyr and lead to a future where mutants were hunted down and forced into concentration camps.

However, when you have two strong creative forces working together on a series like this, you're bound to have some conflicts, and that was certainly the case with Byrne and Claremont. The problem for Byrne was that while he had become the dominant force in the plotting stages, since Claremont was scripting the comic books, he was still the last one of the two men to work on the comic book. Therefore, Byrne could plot the comic book a certain way, but since Claremont had the book last, he could change things in the dialogue and the caption boxes. Byrne would complain to the editors, but by this point, the changes would already be in the final book.

After a few years of this, Byrne realized that while he had his own views on how the X-Men should be, Claremont obviously had his own and since Claremont's was the one that was actually seeing print, that was the "real" X-Men to everyone, so Byrne decided to leave to go take over a title that he could write on his own. Byrne landed on the *Fantastic Four*, which was a hit series during Byrne's time on the book.

Byrne returned to Wolverine to draw an arc of the *Wolverine* ongoing series as a favor to writer Archie Goodwin (one of the most beloved men in comics) and in the early 1990s, Byrne was briefly the scripter on *X-Men* and *Uncanny X-Men* when Jim Lee and Whilce Portacio took over the plotting duties on both books. Lee and Portacio were so late with their pages, though, that Byrne never had enough time to script them and Marvel abruptly fired him to get someone closer to Marvel's offices who could script them as Marvel received them from Lee and Portacio.

Byrne's last stint with the X-Men was with an ongoing series called *X-Men: The Hidden Years*, where Byrne would create new stories showing what happened to the X-Men between *X-Men #66* and *X-Men #94*. The series was canceled when Joe Quesada took over as Marvel editor-in-chief in 2000 and drastically revamped Marvel's X-Line of comics. Byrne has not worked for Marvel since.

11 Must Read: "The Dark Phoenix Saga"

Throughout this book, we'll let you know about the X-Men story arcs that every X-Men fan should really get around to reading during their life. We start with what is most likely the most famous X-Men story arc of all-time, "The Dark Phoenix Saga" by Chris Claremont, John Byrne, and Terry Austin, which ran from *X-Men #129–137*.

After being separated for over a year's worth of stories (during which time Professor X and Phoenix believed them to be dead), Cyclops, Wolverine, Nightcrawler, Storm, Banshee, and Colossus had finally reunited with their family and friends in a story line from *X-Men #125–128* that saw them travel to Muir Isle in the United Kingdom, where they were pitted against Proteus, the super-powerful mutant son of longtime X-Men ally, geneticist Moira MacTaggert. The X-Men succeeded in defeating Proteus and headed back to the X-Mansion (Banshee stayed behind with Moira, who he had recently started dating).

Now that the team was reunited in the United States, Professor X believed that it was time to start recruiting new mutants for the team. He split the team up into two teams. One investigated a young mutant in Chicago named Kitty Pryde, while the others met a mutant singer known as Dazzler. The problem for the X-Men was that there was a new player in town—the society club for rich mutants known as the Hellfire Club, and the Club was recruiting mutants itself for its own nefarious purposes. Emma Frost, the White Queen of the Hellfire Club, personally convinced Kitty's parents to let Kitty attend Frost's Massachusetts Academy (her version of Xavier's School for Gifted Youngsters). The Hellfire

Club clashed with the X-Men and captured them. Luckily, with help from Kitty and Dazzler, the other group saved their captured friends and Xavier used his powers to get Kitty's parents to let her join Xavier's instead.

As it turned out, one of the original X-Men, the high-flying Angel, was actually a member of the Hellfire Club. He helped the X-Men confront the heads of the Hellfire Club. The problem was that for the last few months (while the X-Men were separated from Phoenix), the former X-Men foe known as Mastermind, who could mess with people's minds, had been working on breaking Jean and using her to gain a place in the Hellfire Club. His plans seemed to work when he had Jean turn on her teammates in the confrontation between the X-Men and the Hellfire Club in *X-Men #132*. During the fight, Wolverine had been punched through the Hellfire Club's headquarters and seemingly killed. Jean used her powers to capture the rest of the team and seemingly took her place as the new Black Queen of the Hellfire Club.

Wolverine, though, famously popped out of the sewers still alive, vowing vengeance. In the next issue, he cut through the Hellfire Club's guards on his way to free his teammates. He did so, but they were still stuck against the mind-controlled Jean Grey. Cyclops eventually connected with Jean and she broke free of Mastermind's control, but the experience had snapped something inside of her. She drove Mastermind insane and transformed into the Dark Phoenix! Her teammates tried to restrain her and she effortlessly defeated them and headed into outer space. While in space, just to amuse herself, she destroyed an entire star system, killing a planet of billions.

When she returned to Earth, it took all of Professor X's tremendous mental abilities to restrain Dark Phoenix's powers and bring the Phoenix back. The X-Men were thrilled to have their friend back, but then the Shi'ar showed up. It seemed as though they were

The cover of Uncanny X-Men #135, *part of "The Dark Phoenix Saga."* (Cover art by John Byrne, Terry Austin, and Jim Novak)

here to arrest Jean for the destruction of the star system (which also destroyed a Shi'ar spacecraft). They were going to kill her. Since Professor X was dating Lilandra, the Empress of the Shi'ar Empire, he knew enough of their customs to force them to accept a trial by combat. The X-Men would fight the Shi'ar Imperial Guard for the life of Jean Grey.

When the actual fight took place, however, the Imperial Guard were just too much for the X-Men to handle. One by one, they were picked off (even after adding Angel and former X-Men Beast to their numbers, as Beast had seen their fight against Dark Phoenix while on monitor duty for the Avengers). Soon, it was just Jean and Cyclops alone against the entire Imperial Guard. Jean found herself transforming back into Dark Phoenix and decided that the only way out was for her to sacrifice herself to protect the galaxy from Dark Phoenix. So she stepped in front of a laser and killed herself.

Claremont, Byrne, and Austin were doing things that were unheard of at the time in superhero comics, with the death of Jean Grey being one of the biggest shockers in comic book history. Sales on the series saw a dramatic rise during this arc, with the final part of the story (1980's *X-Men #137*) becoming the highest-selling Marvel Comic of the month (sales settled back down after *#137* before slowly creeping up throughout 1982 and 1983). This changed the way that people would view the X-Men forever.

12 Roy Thomas

In 1897, Roger Connor retired from professional baseball with 138 home runs in his career. That was the most home runs anyone had ever hit over their career. That record lasted a remarkable 24 years, before Babe Ruth passed Connor in 1921. By the time Ruth retired in 1935, the record was 714. We bring this up to celebrate Roy Thomas, who for a number of years had the most acclaimed stint on X-Men by any writer, but soon saw his run dwarfed by Chris Claremont's 17-year stint on the series. So much so that people now fail to respect just how important Thomas' run was at the time, not to mention the major role Thomas played in the 1970s revitalization of the X-Men.

After a brief stint at DC Comics, Roy Thomas joined Marvel Comics in 1965 as essentially the company's second "main" writer. At this point, Stan Lee was handling much of the writing work for Marvel Comics. Other writers often scripted comics over Lee plots (including Lee's younger brother, Larry Lieber) but no one really stood out as someone that Lee could confidently just pass off an entire series to handle by themselves, which was something that Lee very much wanted to do at that point in time. Thomas stood out and by 1966, Thomas had taken over writing studies on *Sgt. Fury and the Howling Commandos*. Later in the year, he took over both *X-Men* and *The Avengers*.

Thomas wrote *X-Men #20–44*, in which time he had the X-Men graduate from Professor Xavier's School for Mutants and gain their own unique superhero costumes (he also introduced the Irish mutant known as Banshee). In *X-Men #42*, he also killed off Professor X and had the X-Men take control of the series themselves. After brief stints by Gary Friedrich and Arnold Drake, Thomas returned on *X-Men #55*.

The following issue, he began a legendary stint with artist Neal Adams where they delivered a series of classic stories, including a brilliant arc about the X-Men facing off against the mutant-hunting Sentinels, followed by a trip to the Savage Land, where they encountered their old foe, Magneto. After Adams left the book, Thomas then introduced the Japanese mutant hero, Sunfire, and revealed that Professor X had faked his death. After *X-Men #66*, X-Men was briefly canceled before returning with reprints of old Lee and Kirby issues.

In 1972, Stan Lee was promoted to publisher of Marvel Comics and Lee chose Thomas as his successor as Marvel's new editor-in-chief. It was not a role that Thomas particularly enjoyed and he quit the job in 1974 (he continued to work for Marvel as a writer and editor for the rest of the decade). While he was still editor-in-chief, however, Thomas made two major decisions that would change X-Men history forever.

First, he told *Incredible Hulk* writer Len Wein to introduce a new Canadian superhero who would fight the Hulk in an upcoming issue. Thomas told him to name the character either Badger or Wolverine and base the character on whichever animal that Wein chose. Wein, of course, picked Wolverine and the Canadian superhero debuted in *Incredible Hulk #181*.

Secondly, Thomas had been planning a revival of the X-Men for a while and thought that an international team of heroes might make for a good book, much like the classic World War II fighter pilot series, *Blackhawks*, which was made up of pilots from many different countries. Al Landau, the president of Marvel Comics at the time, owned a company that repackaged American comics for the international market. Landau really liked the idea of having a series that featured heroes from different countries, as that would make it easy to sell the series to those countries.

Thomas saw Cyclops leading a group of X-Men around the world, recruiting new X-Men in all sorts of different countries. The reboot stalled for a bit (Thomas originally planned on Mike Friedrich to write the series along with artst Dave Cockrum) and when *Giant-Size X-Men #1* finally debuted in 1975 by Len Wein and Dave Cockrum, Thomas was no longer editor-in-chief (Thomas was succeeded by Wein, who also quit the job soon after he accepted it). The new team of X-Men was notably made up of heroes from all different countries, including two characters created by Thomas (the Irish Banshee and the Japanese Sunfire) and one character created at Thomas' direction (the Canadian Wolverine).

So despite Thomas' run on X-Men not being as well remembered as the stories that came after, his impact on the history of the X-Men was still quite uncanny.

13 Professor X

One of the best examples that we have in the change of societal views on authoritarian figures is the way that Professor Charles Xavier has been depicted in the last few decades versus how he was depicted when the X-Men first debuted in 1963. Originally, Xavier was not just the voice of authority, he was the voice of authority that the comic book makes clear is right and should be followed no matter what. Even when he pulled plenty of stunts on the X-Men in the early years that bordered on outright cruelty (early on, he was repeatedly "testing" his students by pretending to lose his powers or things like that), it is clear within the comic that he means well and the X-Men understand that he is just trying to help them. Even later on, when he fakes his own death (so that he can prepare to stop an incoming alien invasion of Earth), the X-Men gladly accept his flimsy reasoning for having to pretend to be dead.

As time has gone by, however, modern writers are not willing to buy into the conceit that authority should be followed blindly and as a result, not only have the X-Men questioned Xavier more and more over the years, but in the process, his methods have become crueler and crueler. For a while there, it seemed as though every other story arc would reveal a shocking secret from Professor X's past that would possibly change your view on the Professor forever!

The most shocking one came in the miniseries event, "Deadly Genesis" (by Ed Brubaker, Trevor Hairsine, and Scott Hanna) that revealed that after the original X-Men had been captured back in *Giant-Size X-Men #1*, the All-New, All-Different X-Men were actually the second new group of X-Men that Xavier put together. The first time was an American-based squad that also happened to include Cyclops and Havok's long-lost brother, Vulcan. When this new team was then wiped out in battle on the mutant island of Krakoa, with only Cyclops surviving, Xavier felt that it was better to erase Cyclops' memory of their deaths and just let him go recruit another new team of X-Men (and then never tell anyone about the ill-fated second X-Men team until years later when Vulcan turned out to have survived and sought out his revenge on Xavier and the X-Men). So yes, Xavier saw a new team of X-Men get slaughtered and his next idea was, "Let's try that again! And be sure not to let the third team know that this is probably a suicide mission. You can't bake a cake without breaking some eggs!"

Another shocking revelation was that the X-Men's training facility, the famous Danger Room, was actually sentient and Xavier kept it a secret because he didn't know how to help it, so he figured better to just keep quiet than try to do anything about it. Later, we also learned that before Xavier recruited Wolverine to join the X-Men, Wolverine had actually tried to kill Xavier (due to programming put into Wolverine's brain by a mysterious villain known as Romulus) and Xavier broke that programming but then put in some of his own so that Wolverine would agree to join the X-Men (who, as we just noted, were replacements for a new X-Men team that Xavier just watched get killed right before recruiting Wolverine and the other All-New, All-Different X-Men).

Despite all of his many, many lies to the X-Men over the years (it makes you wonder whether he was lying when he told the X-Men that their team name came from their "x-tra powers" that they had due to their mutant abilities and not that he simply named the team after himself egocentrically), Xavier's overall message really is a strong one. As the years went by, Xavier was often compared to Martin Luther King Jr. in how Xavier wanted mutants and humans to live together in harmony, while his old friend, Magneto, was cast in the Malcolm X role as the person who did not believe that mutants and humans could peacefully coexist and would therefore do whatever it takes to protect the mutant race, even if it means conflict with humanity. That truly became an important part of Xavier's character, that he was the guy who wanted harmony more than anything else.

Sadly, during the crossover event "Avengers vs. X-Men," a Phoenix-possessed Cyclops seemingly killed Professor X. Even worse, his brain (and his mutant powers) was co-opted by the evil Red Skull. More recently, though, it appears as though Xavier might have found a way to survive in the astral plane, the place where thoughts live and where a telepath like Professor X is a powerful figure, perhaps powerful enough to continue to live after his "death."

14 Magneto

Few characters in comic book history have gone through quite as dramatic of a transformation as Magneto, originally the explicitly evil nemesis of the X-Men, then a noble villain with a tragic back story, and finally an outright hero and leader of the X-Men.

Even in his earliest days, Magneto was the standout character of Stan Lee and Jack Kirby's X-Men run. His cool power set (he was the master of magnetism) and his striking Kirby-designed costume made him a lot more memorable than any of the heroes within the series. And when the X-Men series was more or less canceled in 1970, Magneto continued to appear as a villain in other series. The big difference between Magneto then and Magneto now is that old-school Magneto was just a flat-out villain.

What is interesting is that in recent years, Stan Lee has attempted to take credit for the more nuanced version of the character. For instance, Lee has said, "I did not think of Magneto as a bad guy. He was just trying to strike back at the people who were so bigoted and racist. He was trying to defend mutants, and because society was not treating them fairly, he decided to teach society a lesson. He was a danger, of course, but I never thought of him as a villain." In Magneto's second appearance, he tries to nuke a country just because he is pissed that the X-Men defeated him. He was clearly an outright villain in those early years. The guy had a team that was literally called the Brotherhood of Evil Mutants.

No, it would not be until Chris Claremont had been writing the X-Men for a number of years before Magneto began to see some redemption. In an early story arc after John Byrne joined the creative team on *X-Men*, Magneto captured the X-Men and he began to spout some of his "I'm just responding to humanity's hatred of mutants" rhetoric. But it was not until Byrne left the series that Claremont was able to take the next step in Magneto's character transformation (Byrne preferred the original Lee/Kirby version of Magneto).

In *Uncanny X-Men #150* (by Claremont, Dave Cockrum, and Joe Rubinstein), Claremont revealed for the first time that Magneto was a Holocaust survivor. This tragic backstory suddenly placed the character in a whole new light for readers (even though in that same issue he also sinks a Russian submarine, killing all of the sailors aboard). In a later story, Claremont revealed that Magneto and Professor X were actually friends when they were young men. Magneto fought alongside Xavier against the evil Nazi villain Baron Von Strucker before the two men split over their differing philosophies over how mutants should go about dealing with humanity's anti-mutant hysteria. Being a victim of an extreme example of what happened when you treat groups of people as "other," Magneto

The two Professor Xs—Patrick Stewart and James McAvoy—and the two Magnetos—Sir Ian McKellen, and Michael Fassbender—attend the UK Premiere of X-Men: Days Of Future Past *in London in May of 2014.*
(Photo by Paul Treadway/Retna/Photoshot/Newscom)

naturally wanted to respond to prejudice with force, while Xavier tried to maintain peace between humans and mutants.

In the acclaimed graphic novel, "God Loves, Man Kills," Claremont implicitly presents Magneto and Xavier as noble men who just have different approaches for the same basic goal—equal rights for mutants. It was during this time that the famed analogy of Magneto and Xavier to Malcolm X and Martin Luther King Jr. became a prevalent one among comic book readers.

Soon, Claremont went one step further and wrote Xavier out of *Uncanny X-Men* due to an injury and had Xavier ask his old friend (who had just been cleared of any crimes by a world tribunal) to take over as the new headmaster of Xavier's school. Magneto agreed, becoming an official superhero for the first time. However, there were other people at Marvel Comics in the era who hated the idea of Magneto becoming a superhero, including Byrne and former X-Men editor Roger Stern. By the end of the 1980s, Magneto was back to being an enemy of the X-Men.

In the 1990s, Marvel even more explicitly turned Magneto into an outright villain again (while, at the same time, temporarily trying to claim that Magneto was not in a concentration camp because he was Jewish but because he was Romani. That was quickly written out and Magneto has been Jewish ever since). It was during this period that he used his power to literally tear the adamantium off of Wolverine's skeleton (Professor X responded to that move by temporarily wiping Magneto's mind entirely).

After regaining his mind, Magneto has turned to the side of good once more in recent years, serving alongside the X-Men in a number of different incarnations of the team (including a *proactive* version of the X-Men—mostly made up of other former villains— that he formed to eliminate threats to mutantkind). He is currently the teacher and leader of the time-displaced original X-Men, establishing a strange new status quo for the young heroes who only knew Magneto as the horrible villain that he was in their time.

The Original X-Men Film Trilogy

It is difficult to describe just how bleak the scene was for super-hero movies in 2000. New Line Cinema had just had a major hit with Marvel's *Blade* in 1998, but with 1997's *Batman and Robin* seemingly ruining the Batman film franchise, things were looking bleak for the future of superhero movies. It did not help that in the history of Marvel Comics, Blade was only the third Marvel character to receive a theatrical film, following the 1944 Captain America film serial and 1986's *Howard the Duck* (*Punisher* had a very limited theatrical release in 1989 but was essentially a direct-to-video film, just like 1990's *Captain America*. A Fantastic Four film in 1994 was so bad that it was pulled from being released).

Therefore, when Fox's *X-Men* (directed by Bryan Singer) was released in May 2000, the whole world of superhero films sort of rested on its shoulders. Luckily, it was a monster hit, thereby showing everyone that you could do a big-budget superhero movie and have it be a success (two years later, Sam Raimi's *Spider-Man* came out and made that lesson painfully obvious by becoming the highest grossing film of 2002, and there was both a *Lord of the Rings* movie and a *Star Wars* movie released that year). The big change from the X-Men comics to the film was that they no longer wore traditional costumes, but instead all dressed in black leather outfits. This was one of the concessions to a world that was unsure if audiences would ever buy a colorfully garbed superhero again (again, Spider-Man answered that concern nicely in 2002).

Otherwise, *X-Men* was true to the comics, with Patrick Stewart's Professor X leading the X-Men against Ian McKellan's Magneto and his evil Brotherhood. Hugh Jackman played Wolverine, a new addition to the team (along with a young mutant named Rogue, played by Anna Paquin) who was searching for answers about what happened to him during his past. The X-Men have to stop Magneto from using a new weapon that would "mutate" the leaders of the world (likely killing them in the process). The X-Men succeeded, of course, and the movie ends with Wolverine following up on a clue to his past provided by Professor X, while Professor X visits Magneto in prison.

The script for the film was a group affair, with half a dozen writers working on the story, although David Hayter got the sole writing credit in the end. Joss Whedon famously added a few lines of dialogue, including the well-received "You're a dick" line by Wolverine to Cyclops when Cyclops was trying to prove that Wolverine was not an impostor, as well as the much less well-received "Do you know what happens to a toad when it is struck by lightning? The same thing that happens to everything else!" line when Storm blasted Toad with electricity (Whedon later said that the line was meant to be delivered matter-of-factly like a joke, while Storm actress Halle Berry instead gave the line a dramatic reading).

The sequel, *X2*, came out in 2003 and was an even bigger hit than the first film. Once again working with multiple writers (Hayter teamed up with Zak Penn to write the screenplay, but by the time the film was released, a half dozen people got a writing credit on the movie), director Bryan Singer (who also got a story credit for this film) saw Wolverine discover the Weapon X project that he had come from, headed up by the evil General William Stryker, who was setting out to find a way to detect all the mutants of the world so that he could wipe them all out at once (Stryker's rage stemmed from the fact that his own son was a mutant). In the end, Jean Grey seemingly sacrificed herself to save everyone, setting up a return as Phoenix in the third film.

Hugh Jackman, James Marsden, Patrick Stewart, and Halle Berry in 2000's X-Men. (Photofest)

That is what ultimately happened, but Bryan Singer was no longer part of the process. His success with the first two films allowed him to relaunch the Superman film franchise with 2005's *Superman Returns*. Initially replacing him on 2006's *X-Men: The Last Stand* was Matthew Vaughn, but when Fox dictated a very short turnaround on the film production, Vaughn backed out and Brett Ratner stepped in to direct the film. Zak Penn returned to write this new film, working with writer Simon Kinberg (who would remain a part of the X-Men franchise for years to come).

In the final film in the trilogy, the X-Men deal with news of a possible "cure" for being a mutant. They also have to deal with the return of their seemingly dead teammate, Jean Grey, whose mental powers had become so powerful that she became a separate being known as Phoenix. She couldn't control her new powers and soon became Dark Phoenix, killing Cyclops and Professor X. Jean managed to control the Phoenix long enough to let Wolverine get close to her. She begged him to kill her and he obliged. It was a bleak ending to the X-Men trilogy. It technically made the most money of the three films, but its budget was twice as large as *X2* and only made eight percent more money. This led to Fox making this film the final one in this series (not counting a 2009 solo Wolverine film, *X-Men Origins: Wolverine*).

Top Five Greatest X-Men Romances

5. Havok and Polaris

In the history of the X-Men, very rarely had any couple had as normal of a relationship as Havok and Polaris after the original X-Men broke up. In the years since, circumstances kept pulling them apart but they kept ending up back together.

4. Psylocke and Archangel

Originally paired together mostly through shared interests (they were both from old money), Archangel and Psylocke eventually had a strong romance, spotlighted when he became possessed by Apocalypse and she used her telepathy to let him experience a whole life together before she then killed him.

3. Kitty Pryde and Colossus

Their original relationship was a bit strange, seeing as how she was 13 and he was 18 when they met, but when they reunited in Joss Whedon and John Cassaday's "Astonishing X-Men" (when Kitty was now a young adult), their chemistry was impressive.

2. Jean Grey and Cyclops

There is an argument to be made that Jean and Scott never had the most passionate relationship, but were more like friends who just stuck with each other over the years, but the end result was that they had a long and healthy relationship (generally).

1. Gambit and Rogue

In the world of "will they or won't they?" Gambit and Rogue had one of the most reasonable explanations for the uncertainty, since she couldn't actually touch him without absorbing his powers and personality. They more than made up for it in the rare times that they have both been powerless.

16 Mutants as a Metaphor for Prejudice

As noted in our earlier spotlight on Stan Lee, when Lee was first writing the X-Men, while he clearly established that mutants were distinct from the rest of the human race (as they were "Homo superior"), he did not explore the prejudice angle all that much. The notable exception was when he introduced the mutant-hunting Sentinels in *X-Men #14*. Years later, Roy Thomas and Neal Adams further explored the foolishness of treating mutants as "other" during a classic three-part story where Larry Trask, son of Bolivar Trask (who created the Sentinels), sent Sentinels to eradicate all mutants in the world. What Trask did not realize, however, is that he, himself, was a mutant (thus showing how ridiculous it was to view people who were "different" as being "less than")! For the most part, though, the only difference between the X-Men and the other Marvel superheroes was that the X-Men got their powers from their own genes (due to their parents being exposed to radiation before they were born).

That changed during Chris Claremont's *X-Men* run, where he began to explore the idea that mutants were treated in the Marvel Universe as minorities akin to African Americans in actual society. Only in the Marvel Universe, the minority group also had super powers! That only made the majority hate and fear mutants even more. The fact that mutants were treated so poorly by the rest of the world made it easier for Claremont to redeem Magneto, as Magneto's separatist views from the original Stan Lee and Jack Kirby era did not seem so absurd when placed in the context of a world that seemed to constantly want to eradicate mutants (in "Days of Future Past," the X-Men even learned of a possible future where that's explicitly what happened). As time went by, Claremont more explicitly linked "mutant rights" with real life civil rights. The term "mutie" became an ethnic slur on par with some of the worst slurs around. After a mutant teen kills himself after his schoolmates discovered that he was a mutant, Kitty Pryde gave an eloquent speech talking about how the world will always try to define people by easy-to-understand terms. It is up to us to relate to each other as just people.

After decades of exploring mutants in terms of the Civil Rights Movement, though, the X-Men films took the prejudice metaphor in a whole other direction in the 21st century. Bryan Singer, the first *X-Men* director, adapted the metaphor to apply more specifically to the LGBT rights movement. The world of the X-Men is one where very often, you can't tell who is a mutant or not. You often have to actively choose to "come out" as a mutant. In a way, being a mutant is more comparable to minorities who can "assimilate" (like Jewish people or gay people) than it is to minorities like African Americans who cannot hide who they are (of course, there are plenty of mutants, like Nightcrawler and Beast, who cannot hide their mutation so easily).

Singer specifically tapped into the parallels between mutants and the gay rights movement when he tried to convince Sir Ian McKellen, the openly gay Shakespearean actor who had starred in Singer's first studio film, the 1998 adaptation of Stephen King's *Apt Pupil*, to sign on to play Magneto in *X-Men*. McKellen later recalled, "I was sold it by Bryan who said, 'Mutants are like gays. They're cast out by society for no good reason.' And, as in all civil rights movements, they have to decide: Are they going to take the Xavier line, which is to somehow assimilate and stand up for yourself and be proud of what you are, but get on with everybody, or are you going to take the alternative view, which is, if necessary, use violence to stand up for your own rights? And that's true. I've come across that division within the gay rights movement."

The most explicit reference in the X-Men films to the parallels between being a mutant and being born gay was in the second X-Men film, *X2*, where Rogue helps her friend and fellow student Bobby Drake (Iceman) reveal the fact that he is a mutant to his parents (note, too, that people's mutant abilities manifest themselves at puberty, which is also often when sexual desires start to become explicit in people, gay or straight). The sequence very much reads like a typical gay coming-out story. There is even a line where Bobby's mother Madeline asks him, "Have you tried...not being a mutant?"

In the comics, the X-Men continue to deal with anti-mutant prejudice in both *X-Men: Gold* and *X-Men: Blue*, where even the people that they save treat them poorly. It sadly does not seem as though the multiple times that the X-Men have saved the world in the past 50 years has been enough to get the world to accept mutants as much as they accept good ol' fashioned superheroes like Spider-Man and the Fantastic Four that got their radiation-based powers after birth.

17 Hugh Jackman

Due to the very nature of film casting, there is always going to be those great "What If?" scenarios, where people will debate over what would have happened had Person X been cast in a famous role instead of Person Y. One of the most famous examples is when Tom Selleck had to give up the role of Indiana Jones in *Raiders of the Lost Ark* due to a scheduling conflict with his then-new TV series, *Magnum P.I.* In the world of superhero films, though, there is no "What If?" casting story greater than how

Hugh Jackman got the role of Wolverine in the first X-Men film over Dougray Scott.

Dougray Scott was an up-and-coming actor in the late 1990s. He had a standout performance as the prince in the hit film, *Ever After*, opposite Drew Barrymore. He was cast as the lead villain in the next Mission Impossible film opposite Tom Cruise and he was constantly being referenced as a possible James Bond for whenever the Bond franchise finally moved on from Pierce Brosnan, who was 45 when his third James Bond film, *The World Is Not Enough*, was released in 1999. Right off of his role in *Mission Impossible II*, Scott was set to take on perhaps his biggest role to date, that of Wolverine in *X-Men*.

There is a legend surrounding Scott not being able to do the role. Hugh Jackman once said, "Yes, the director, Bryan Singer, originally wanted Dougray Scott, but he got injured and Bryan couldn't delay forever. I had auditioned for the role. When Bryan called me, they were already shooting. So I did another test and was hired on the spot." That is not true. It is true that Singer had to move on because he could not wait for Scott, but it was not due to an injury. Scott had been injured while filming *Mission Impossible II*, but it was a minor injury that did not delay shooting. No, the issue was that the filming on *Mission Impossible II* just took far longer than originally intended, causing Scott to be unable to star in *X-Men* (why the filming took longer is still a mystery: some say they had poor weather, some say director John Woo was too slow, and some say that Tom Cruise delayed filming to improve the film's script).

Singer turned to Jackman, who had been in the running for the role, to take over. Jackman's biggest credit at the time (outside of his native Australia) was as the lead in a West End production of the Rodgers and Hammerstein musical, *Oklahoma!*, which netted Jackman an Olivier Award nomination (the British equivalent of the Tony Award) for Best Actor in a Musical. Amusingly enough, while Jackman today is well known for how physically fit he is in the X-Men and Wolverine films, when he first showed up he was not nearly as well built as he would soon become. Singer specifically used camera tricks to hide Wolverine's body through much of the filming, while Jackman worked out like crazy—so much so that when it came time to film the earliest scenes in the movie, which spotlight Wolverine's body, Jackman insisted that he shoot the scenes without a shirt.

X-Men was a huge hit and Jackman became a superstar. He also became the face of the X-Men film franchise, starring in the first three X-Men movies, one of the reboot films (plus a cameo in a second), and three solo Wolverine films. As Jackman continued in the role, he took on more of a role in the shaping of Wolverine's future. Singer famously banned comic books on the sets of his films, but Jackman still managed to read some, and reading the classic Chris Claremont, Paul Smith, and Bob Wiacek story line set in Japan (at Wolverine's ill-fated wedding), Jackman became insistent that the story would make for a great movie and that directly led to 2013's *The Wolverine* by director James Mangold.

It was Jackman, as well, who pushed for his final performance as Wolverine (for now—you never know when someone might be wooed back to do a role that he or she claimed that she was through with), 2017's *Logan* (also with James Mangold), to be an R-rated film. In fact, he went so far as to accept a pay reduction in exchange for Fox being willing to release the movie as an R rather than PG-13, like all of the previous Wolverine and X-Men films. Jackman's bet was a good one, as the film was a blockbuster and became the most critically acclaimed Wolverine film to date. For a large segment of the population, when they think of Wolverine, they don't think of a 5'3" hairy runt like in the comics, but rather they think of a tall Australian musical-theater star.

18 Bob Harras

When the X-Men debuted in 1963, Marvel's editorial staff was basically just Stan Lee and Sol Brodsky (Marvel's production manager). Even when the All-New, All-Different X-Men got their own ongoing series in 1975, Marvel still generally worked under a loosely affiliated group of editors under the direction of the editor-in-chief (Len Wein was the editor-in-chief when *X-Men #94* came out, but Marv Wolfman soon followed). It was not until Jim Shooter took over as Marvel's editor-in-chief in early 1978 that he decided that he was going to change the way things were done editorially at the company. He hired a bunch of editors and from that point on, every title would have an editor and an assistant editor.

The original dedicated editor on *X-Men* in 1978 was Roger Stern, with Jim Salicrup as his assistant editor. Stern was a good friend of X-Men artist John Byrne and the two men shared a lot of similar views on things, so when Byrne would have a dispute with writer Chris Claremont (who plotted the series with Byrne), then Stern tended to side with Byrne a bit more than Claremont.

Stern, though, became a full-time freelance writer after working on the series for roughly a year and a half. Salicrup was promoted to the main editor and Bob Budiansky became Salicrup's assistant editor. Salicrup took over the book right as the famed "Dark Phoenix Saga" was in full swing, and it was Salicrup who had to deal with the fallout over Jim Shooter having a problem with the original ending of the story (where Jean is "telepathically lobotomized," losing her powers but living). Salicrup left the book with the end of the story and Louise Jones took over as the editor of the series (Budiansky stayed with Salicrup as they left to take over

Fantastic Four. Salicrup soon brought Byrne to that series as the writer and artist).

Jones remained on the series for four years. She developed a very close working relationship with Claremont (Byrne left the series after Jones' first solo issue of *X-Men*, feeling—rightly or wrongly—that his problems with Claremont were only going to get worse now that Jones was the editor on the series). Jones went through three different assistant editors—Danny Fingeroth, Elliot Brown, and Ann Nocenti. When Jones left the book to concentrate on freelance writing (which she did under her married name, Louise Simonson), Nocenti took over the book. Louise Simonson ended up writing *X-Factor* and then took over *New Mutants* from Chris Claremont. She continued to work very closely with Claremont during their period as basically the two main writers on the X-Men franchise.

Nocenti and Claremont also worked closely together over the next four years, before Nocenti, too, left the book to concentrate on her own burgeoning freelance writing career (during her time as the editor of *X-Men*, she introduced a new character, Longshot, in a miniseries with artist Arthur Adams, and Claremont liked the series enough that he quickly had Longshot join the X-Men). Nocenti was followed by Bob Harras, who had been Ralph Macchio's assistant editor for a few years before the promotion.

Harras was the editor on the series when the speculator's market of the late 1980s/early 1990s saw comic book sales rise tremendously in a short period of time. Meanwhile, Marvel had recently been sold and the new owners wanted editorial to cash in on the speculator's boom as much as possible, so Harras oversaw a ramped-up production schedule on both *Uncanny X-Men* and *Wolverine* (at one point, *Uncanny X-Men* released three issues in a single month) and saw an increase of spinoff titles. Soon, Harras was practically editing his own line of comics!

However, Harras also saw that much of the increased sales was a result of a new breed of superstar artists, like Marc Silvestri, Rob Liefeld, and Jim Lee. Lee became the regular artist on *Uncanny X-Men* in mid-1990 and sales went through the roof. Lee began plotting the series with Claremont, but soon Lee and Claremont had some conflicts. Not big arguments or anything like that, but simple disagreements over how the series should proceed. Harras began to side with his new star artist and eventually, when Marvel editorial decided to launch a second X-Men ongoing series, Harras put Lee in charge of it over Claremont. Claremont left *X-Men* after a 17-year run on the book.

Trouble struck, however, when Lee then left the series after less than a year and Harras had to quickly put together replacement creative teams for pretty much all of his most popular titles as the creators left to join Image Comics with Lee. Flying by the seat of his pants, Harras managed to keep the line together and it all went over great in the sales department, as the X-Men books continued to sell like crazy throughout the early 1990s, even when other books started to see sales drop offs when the speculator bubble burst (by the way, during all of this, Harras also had a side gig as the regular writer on *The Avengers*).

In 1994, Marvel replaced Tom DeFalco as editor-in-chief by splitting the job between five "groups," with Harras continuing to be in charge of the burgeoning X-Men group. When the whole "five editors-in-chief" idea did not work out, Harras was put in charge by himself in 1995. He remained Marvel's editor-in-chief through 2000. No single X-Men editor ever left their mark on the series quite like Bob Harras.

19 Jim Lee

In 1989, Chris Claremont started a new story line in the pages of *Uncanny X-Men*. His plan was to break the X-Men up and scatter the team members around the globe and then follow the adventures of the individual team members as they slowly re-formed the X-Men. After Rogue was temporarily written out of the series in *Uncanny X-Men #247* when she pushed the deadly killer robot known as Master Mold through the mystical portal known as the Siege Perilous, the following issue also saw both Longshot and Storm leave the team, with Storm being captured by a bizarre villain known as Nanny, who would kidnap young mutants so that she could "protect" them. She de-aged Storm as part of her kidnapping plan. The X-Men tried to shoot down Nanny's ship, but Havok appeared to accidentally blow the ship up instead, seemingly killing Storm.

While the issue certainly furthered Claremont's story line along (Longshot leaves in a dream sequence in the issue), the more important thing was who drew the issue. As a fill-in for regular artist Marc Silvestri, a young artist named Jim Lee drew the book. Lee had gotten his start at Marvel when editor Carl Potts hired him as the artist for *Alpha Flight* in 1988. Potts, though, then brought Lee to a newly launched Punisher spinoff series, *Punisher War Journal*, which was a very high-profile assignment for the young artist. On *Punisher War Journal*, Potts would do layouts for the issues and then Lee would finish and ink the work, therefore giving him on-the-job training on how to lay out a comic book. All throughout Marvel, people were raving about Lee, so it was not long before he got his chance to do a fill-in issue of Marvel's No. 1 book, *Uncanny X-Men*.

After his first issue was well received, Lee returned to draw an arc later in 1989 for *Uncanny X-Men*'s tie-in with the "Acts of Vengeance" crossover, where Marvel's villains all attacked heroes they had never fought before. Iron Man–villain Mandarin attacked the X-Men, working with a new female Mandarin, who turned out to be former X-Men member Psylocke, who was now in the body of an Asian woman! Lee designed Psylocke's new look. When Silvestri left *Uncanny X-Men* in 1990 to take over *Wolverine*, Lee became the full-time artist on the book. At the same time Lee was joining the book, sales on comic books were skyrocketing as news about how good of an "investment" comic books were led to a big speculator's market. With sales increasing, Marvel saw that their most popular artists (like Lee, Todd McFarlane, and Rob Liefeld) were raising sales exponentially on the books that they drew.

Chris Claremont, like everyone else in the world, was also big fan of Jim Lee's work and he began to involve Lee in the plotting of the series, essentially letting Lee tell him what he wanted to draw and Claremont would try to work it into the story. That was a bit of a problem with the two, as Claremont had been on the series for 16 years, so he wanted to try new stories, while Lee, who was just joining the book, wanted to revisit some of the X-Men's classic villains. Like where Claremont wanted to use Loki in a story, Lee wanted to use Magneto. With sales booming in great part due to Lee's artwork, X-Men editor Bob Harras tended to side with Lee on these debates.

As 1991 came along, Lee was somehow becoming even more popular than ever. He was firmly established as the single most popular artist working in comics. He did a best-selling X-Men trading card series where he drew each card. Finally, Lee was given control of the entire X-Men franchise when Marvel launched a second X-Men series, titled simply *X-Men*. Drawn and plotted by Lee, the first three issues would be Claremont's final issues of

One of five variant covers for 1991's X-Men (Vol. 2) #1, *the highest selling comic book of all time.* (Cover art by Jim Lee)

his 17-year run on X-Men. Lee plotted both *Uncanny X-Men* and *X-Men* (with Whilce Portacio) and penciled *X-Men*. Marvel had put all of their eggs into the Jim Lee basket. The problem was, of course, that Jim Lee suddenly wanted more than what Marvel could give him.

When a group of Marvel's hottest artists decided that they would launch their own comic book company where they would own all of the rights to their properties, they pushed hard to include Lee in their new venture, since he was the undisputed top artist at the time (Lee's *X-Men #1*, which shipped with multiple covers that could form one large combined image, was the best-selling single issue in the history of comics). Lee ultimately agreed and cofounded Image Comics. Image was built out of an affiliation of independent studios. Lee's studio was ultimately called Wildstorm and Lee launched the best-selling series, *WildC.A.T.s*, in 1992. After less than a decade on his own, Lee then sold Wildstorm to DC Comics in 1998 so he could spend more time with his family. Lee worked his way up the ranks at DC Comics and has been their copublisher (with Dan DiDio) since 2010.

20 The X-Men Animated Series

In 1989, Marvel Productions, the high-quality animation studio that had produced some of the most iconic cartoons of the 1980s (*Spider-Man and His Amazing Friends, G.I. Joe: A Real American Hero, Transformers, My Little Pony, Dungeons and Dragons, Muppet Babies*, and *Robocop*, just to name a few), stopped producing new content outside of finishing out their run on *Muppet Babies* (they started doing more new content a year later and continued producing cartoons until 1993). As a result, the pilot that they had created for a proposed X-Men animated series ended up being the only episode released.

Dubbed "Pryde of the X-Men," the episode was released as a standalone TV special in 1989 and would repeat a few times in syndication. It was an impressive attempt at adapting the X-Men (specifically the X-Men of Chris Claremont and John Byrne's era) outside of Wolverine being Australian for some bizarre reason.

Some of the familiar faces of X-Men: The Animated Series—*Cyclops, Jubilee, Rogue, and Storm.* (FOX Kids/Photofest)

"Pryde of the X-Men" became a bit of a cult classic, and luckily, one of the fans of the special was Margaret Loesch, the president and chief executive officer of Marvel Productions.

Loesch was put in charge of Fox Childrens Network in 1990 and she remembered how good "Pryde of the X-Men" was, so when Fox expanded their children's programming in 1991 (also re-branding it as Fox Kids Network), she felt that an X-Men cartoon would be a great addition to the network. Saban Entertainment was hired, but they farmed out much of the work to a smaller studio, Graz Entertainment. It was originally meant to air in September 1992, when the fall TV season began (the children's programming market usually starts a bit earlier than the primetime lineups, as new kids shows usually roll out in the beginning of the month), but the show was delayed well over a month. People were working on the shows to the very last minute. In fact, when *X-Men* finally premiered on Halloween 1992, the episodes literally were not finished. They released the episodes with incomplete backgrounds that were fixed for later airings.

The series was notable in just how well it followed the comic book adventures of the X-Men. Typically, animated adaptations played it fast and loose with their source material (as a notable example, *Spider-Man and His Amazing Friends* showing Spidey being in a superhero team with Iceman and Firestar, who wasn't even a comic book character), but *X-Men* adapted the early 1990s X-Men stories very well. The character designs were all based on

Top Five Most Iconic X-Men Panels

5. *X-Men #134*
   Dark Phoenix reveals herself for the first time to the shock of the X-Men!
4. *X-Men #137*
   Phoenix sacrifices herself to save the universe in one of the most memorable deaths in Marvel Comics history.
3. *Uncanny X-Men #142*
   Wolverine pushes his luck a bit too far when he is killed by a Sentinel in the future, in a panel that was adapted into one of the most iconic X-Men covers.
2. *X-Men #101*
   Phoenix makes her first appearance in a powerful moment as she emerges from the waters of a bay outside of New York after the X-Men's spaceship miraculously survived reentry.
1. *X-Men #132*
   Counted out for dead, Wolverine surprised the reader by bursting out of the sewers to let everyone know that he might be done, but he is not out, in this gorgeously framed panel.

Jim Lee's iconic costume redesigns for 1991's *X-Men #1*. Graz paid close attention to the character interactions from the comic books and translated them beautifully.

The series was a huge hit. It was one of the highest-rated cartoon series in history. Along with *Batman: The Animated Series*, which debuted the same year (but on time, so it was on the air for nearly two months before *X-Men* came out), it led to a deluge of comic book–related animated programming throughout the 1990s and beyond. The series was so big that Pizza Hut used to sell video tapes with a pair of episodes on them (an early X-Men tie-in comic book for Pizza Hut was drawn by a young Joe Madureira).

The show did literal adaptations of famous X-Men comic book stories in every season (the show ran for 76 episodes over five seasons), with a particularly famous adaptation being the long-form translation of the entire Phoenix and Dark Phoenix Saga, which the show spread out over a remarkable nine episodes, showing an impressive commitment to translating the story well.

One of the areas where the show especially excelled was in tackling serious issues. The moral lessons taught during the series were powerful ones, especially the ones about prejudice (couched in terms of anti-mutant prejudice). Jubilee, the youngest of the X-Men, once asked why the X-Men even bother to protect humanity if humans are just going to hate them anyway. Storm explained, "It is an evil in men's hearts that must be fought! If we stand up to the troublemakers, they will give up their cruel designs. If we fail, their intolerance will grow and many could perish!"

For more than one generation of fans, their first and most notable exposure to the X-Men came through the animated show, which replayed for years after they stopped producing new episodes (when the X-Men movies came out, they began airing more frequently again).

21 Jean Grey/The Phoenix

During the early years of the Marvel Universe, being a female member of a superhero team was a thankless task. Every guy on the team not related to you would pine over you, you got taken hostage constantly (Invisible Girl was literally taken hostage 13 times in the first 50 issues of *Fantastic Four*), and your powers were often not as good as your teammates. Jean Grey, Marvel Girl, certainly fit into most of those categories. She was the object of affection for most of her X-Men classmates (and, in one bizarre issue, even Professor X lusted after her) and her telekinetic powers were unimpressive (even when she added telepathy later, it was low level). When the original X-Men were replaced by the All-New, All-Different X-Men, Marvel Girl was an easy choice to remove from the team.

However, she was still dating Cyclops, so she was still a part of the book. So Dave Cockrum and Chris Claremont decided that they would quickly bring Jean back to the team, only now with a major power upgrade. In *X-Men #98*, the X-Men were celebrating Christmas Eve when they were attacked by Sentinels. Jean, Wolverine, and Banshee were each captured and taken to a space station. Their teammates got a hold of a spaceship and traveled to rescue them. When they were all ready to go home in *X-Men #100*, they ran into an issue—the shields in the cockpit of the space ship were damaged and they were in the midst of some major solar flares. Whoever flew the ship was almost certainly going to die from the radiation exposure. Jean stepped up and used her powers to absorb the knowledge on how to fly the ship from the pilot and then knocked Cyclops out so that he couldn't stop her. She sent her teammates to the back of the ship where the shields still worked and she landed the space plane, even as she was seemingly dying from the radiation.

The next issue, however, showed the space plane making a water landing in a bay off the coast of New York City and Jean then suddenly erupted from the water wearing a brand-new costume! She had been transformed by the radiation into the Phoenix! Her powers had all been dramatically increased. She was now by far the most powerful member of the team. Soon, she was battling against Firelord, a former herald of Galactus (and thus someone who had the Power Cosmic), and more than holding her own!

Jean had grown so powerful that Chris Claremont and new X-Men artist John Byrne decided to split her from the rest of the team by making Jean believe that the X-Men were killed after a battle with Magneto in Antarctica. The rest of the team, meanwhile, believed that she was dead as well. The X-Men took a year (of real time) to return to the United States and in that time, Jean was finding herself, but was actually being manipulated by a former X-Men foe known as Mastermind. When the X-Men reunited with Jean, they fought the Hellfire Club and Mastermind's plan went into effect and he showed that he had brainwashed Jean into being a servant of the Hellfire Club. Cyclops managed to snap her out of it, but then her brain couldn't take it and created an alternate personality known as the Dark Phoenix. She flew off into outer space and, just to amuse herself, she destroyed a star system and a Shi'ar Empire warship!

The Shi'ar Empire determined that she needed to pay for her crimes and captured her with the intent to kill her. The X-Men, though, challenged the Shi'ar Imperial Guard to a trial by combat. Jean was so touched to see her X-Men friends willing to fight to protect her. In the end, though, as the Imperial Guard was slowly but surely whittling down the remaining X-Men until it was just Cyclops and Jean, Jean felt herself turning back into Dark Phoenix, so she decided to just kill herself to protect the universe. She stepped in front of a laser and was disintegrated.

It was one of the most shocking moments in comic book history! One of the original X-Men was dead? Superheroes did not really die back in the early 1980s, especially not famous ones like Jean Grey!

After being dead for five years, Jean suddenly showed up alive in a cocoon at the bottom of the bay where Phoenix debuted. As it turned out, Jean had never become the Phoenix, but rather, while she was dying back on the ship, a cosmic entity known as the Phoenix Force came to her and offered to save her life (and the lives of her friends) if Jean let the force take over Jean's life. So it was the Phoenix who died, not Jean. That shows you how heroic Jean was, that a copy of her was noble enough to sacrifice itself for the good of the universe.

The newly resurrected Jean reunited with her friends in the original X-Men and they formed their own mutant team, X-Factor. Eventually, they all rejoined the X-Men and Jean married Cyclops. Over time, though, it turned out that Jean had a special affinity for the Phoenix Force (which is why it chose her in the first place), so she began to exhibit the Phoenix powers, even choosing to take the code name Phoenix. She died again (for the first time) in battle with Magneto. After remaining dead for 14 years (nearly three times as long as her original "death"), Jean returned to life in the comics in December 2017.

22 Cyclops

In the first X-Men film in 2000, the X-Men were fighting against Magneto's Brotherhood of Evil Mutants, which included the shape-shifting Mystique. When Cyclops and Jean Grey ran into Wolverine, they were unsure if he was the real deal. They asked him to prove his identity and he said to Cyclops, "You're a dick," at which point Cyclops realized it's the real Wolverine. That one line really symbolizes how X-Men comic books have treated Cyclops for the past 30 years, which is fascinating, considering how much of a centerpiece for the book that he had been for the previous two decades.

When the series began, Cyclops was Professor X's prized pupil and the leader of the team. Plus, his struggle with his mutant power (he had the ability to shoot powerful optic beams out of his eyes, but he could not control the beams; only special ruby quartz lenses could prevent the beams from destroying everything around him) and his burgeoning love for his teammate Jean Grey (then calling herself Marvel Girl) were the emotional center of the series. After the original X-Men departed, Cyclops was the only one to stay behind to lead the new group of recruits. His love for Jean Grey grew, even as her powers increased and she became known as the Phoenix (we know that they were in love because Chris Claremont kept having Jean and Scott tell each other that they loved each other "...with all my heart"). Therefore, it was devastating for Cyclops when Jean Grey killed herself to keep from turning into Dark Phoenix and possibly destroying the universe.

This is when things really came off the rails for Cyclops. After taking a break from the X-Men, he eventually met a beautiful pilot by the name of Madelyne Pryor while visiting his grandparents in Alaska. Pryor looked exactly like Jean Grey and she had been involved in a plane crash at the exact time Jean died. Instead of sending Scott running the other way, he decided to marry Madelyne and they soon welcomed a son to their family. However, right when this was happening, Jean Grey turned out to *not* actually be dead. As it turned out, a cosmic force called the Phoenix Force had taken Jean's place for a few years and it was this cosmic force that died, not the real Jean. Once the real Jean came back, Scott quickly ditched his wife and infant son in Alaska to go be with Jean in New York City. They even formed a new superhero team called X-Factor.

In an attempt by the writers to absolve Scott of his behavior, Madelyne was revealed to be a clone of Jean and was part of an evil plot by Mister Sinister to create a baby with the shared DNA of Scott and Jean. Madelyne then was killed in battle. A couple of years later, Scott's son was infected by a "techno-organic virus" and had to be sent to the future to survive. Now with his life a clean slate again, he was free to marry Jean Grey. He and Jean continued to be X-Men after getting married and they remained major team leaders.

This being Cyclops, though, he had to screw things up, so it turned out that he had grown bored of his marriage to Jean and began to carry out a psychic love affair with his teammate, Emma Frost. After Jean died for her second time, Scott and Emma started dating and became the coheadmasters of Xavier's School for Mutants. After a Marvel crossover, "House of M," ended up with the mutant population decimated to less than a thousand mutants on Earth, Scott had all the mutants he could find move to an island sanctuary off of the coast of California called Utopia.

Following a dispute with Wolverine over the training of the young mutants on Utopia (Cyclops had been trained by Professor X to basically be a soldier since he was a young teen, so he had no problem asking teenagers the same that was asked of him, even if that meant killing), the X-Men split, with roughly half going back to the school (which Wolverine renamed the Jean Grey School for Mutants) and the other half staying with Cyclops. Soon afterward, though, the Phoenix Force returned to Earth and Cyclops believed that it was a sign that the mutant race was going to be restarted. The Avengers tried to destroy the Phoenix Force and it instead ended up possessing five members of the X-Men, including Cyclops. While possessed by Phoenix, Cyclops went power mad and actually killed Professor X in battle.

After being arrested following the Avengers/X-Men war (which, by the way, did end up exactly how Cyclops believed it would, as the mutant race was revived by the Phoenix Force), Cyclops broke free and formed a rogue team of X-Men. He eventually reconciled with the rest of the X-Men, but sadly then died due to exposure to the Inhumans' Terrigen Mists (which proved fatal for mutants). A younger version of Cyclops, though, had traveled from the past and remains in the future as part of the X-Men, hoping to avoid the mistakes his older self made.

Fabian Nicieza/ Scott Lobdell

In 1991, X-Men editor Bob Harras essentially gave the keys to the kingdom to Jim Lee, as Lee and his fellow artist Whilce Portacio were now in charge of the direction of the two main X-Men titles, *Uncanny X-Men* and *X-Men* (Portacio drew *Uncanny X-Men* while Lee drew *X-Men*). The two artists served as the plotters for both books, but they were not yet adept at writing dialogue, so they needed a scripter. Legendary former X-Men plotter and artist John

Byrne returned to script the comics. The problem, though, was that Lee and Portacio were very late with their pages. Byrne would have very little time to receive them in the mail, script them, and then return them to Marvel. Harras realized that he really needed to have someone in Marvel's New York offices that could script the pages as they came in. As luck would have it, freelance writer Scott Lobdell happened to walk into Harras' office right when he thought about how much he needed someone then and there who could script the books. Lobdell, who had recently finished a run on *Alpha Flight*, became the scripter on both *Uncanny X-Men* and *X-Men*.

Then Bob Harras' worst nightmare occurred—both Lee and Portacio decided to leave Marvel to cofound the independent comic book company Image Comics, where they could own their own properties. Suddenly, Harras had no writers in charge of Marvel's most popular line of titles (with Chris Claremont having been pushed out a year earlier). So since he was already scripting both *Uncanny X-Men* and *X-Men*, Lobdell was given the chance to become the regular writer on *Uncanny X-Men*.

On *X-Men*, Marvel turned to a writer who was already quite familiar with mutants. Former Marvel editor Fabian Nicieza had been picked by Rob Liefeld to be his scripter for the last few issues of *New Mutants* and then the 1991 launch of *X-Force*. When Liefeld left *X-Force* (he left Marvel before Lee and Portacio left), Nicieza became the regular writer on *X-Force*. So since he was already writing one of their more popular mutant titles, Nicieza was a logical pick to be named the regular writer on *X-Men*. Amazingly enough, Nicieza and Lobdell took over just a couple of months before Marvel started a massive crossover event throughout the X-Men titles called "X-Cutioner's Song." Talk about being thrown into the deep end!

For the next three and a half years, these two writers (plus their editor, Harras, of course) were the main architects of the X-Men

Universe. Not only that, but since *X-Men: the Animated Series* launched right after Nicieza and Lobdell became the regular writers on the books, for a whole group of fans inspired to reading the comics because of the cartoon series, Nicieza and Lobdell were the only X-Men writers that they had ever known.

Before he began working on *New Mutants*, Nicieza had launched the Marvel comic book series *New Warriors*, about a group of teen superheroes, and the book meant a lot to Nicieza, as he had been on it since the very beginning. So between *New Warriors*, *X-Force*, and *X-Men*, Nicieza's card was quite filled (although he still found the time to launch a Cable spinoff series from *X-Force* and write the first years' worth of stories for the book).

Lobdell, on the other hand, was just writing *Nick Fury, Agent of S.H.I.E.L.D.* (which was wrapping up its run) and stories for Marvel's anthology series, *Marvel Comics Presents*, so he soon became the go-to writer whenever Marvel needed someone to fill in on other X-related titles. He filled in on *Excalibur*, he filled in on *X-Factor*, he wrote Wolverine stories for *Marvel Comics Presents*, he launched the X-Men quarterly series, *X-Men Unlimited*—he was all over the place at Marvel in 1993–94. Lobdell then also launched a brand-new X-Men spinoff series called *Generation X*, about the newest group of mutant students who attended school at the new Xavier Institute, with Emma Frost and Banshee as their headmasters (longtime X-Men hanger-on Jubilee was the main star of the new series, as the X-Men finally seemed to concede that she was probably too young to be hanging out with the X-Men proper).

Following the massively successful "Age of Apocalypse" crossover, Nicieza was fired from *X-Force* and *X-Men* due to a dispute with Harras over the direction of the titles. While initially Mark Waid was going to take over *X-Men*, Waid and Lobdell had problems working together, so Lobdell just ended up writing both titles, with other writers scripting over his plots when needed. In 1997, Lobdell was also let go, as Marvel decided to go in a new direction with brand-new writing teams on both *Uncanny X-Men* and *X-Men*. By this time, the comic book market had collapsed (sales were a seventh of what they were in 1993), so throughout one of the most popular periods in X-Men history, sales-wise, most of the comics were written by either Fabian Nicieza or Scott Lobdell, which is quite a feather in their respective caps.

24 Must Read: "Days of Future Past"

After the great success that he had with his hit film, *The Terminator*, James Cameron was sued by author Harlan Ellison, as Cameron had once mentioned one of Ellison's stories as an inspiration for the film. However, Cameron also mentioned another story that influenced his time-travel classic—that story was "Days of Future Past" by John Byrne, Chris Claremont, and Terry Austin, which ran in *X-Men #141–142* (technically, the title officially changed its name from *X-Men* to *Uncanny X-Men* with *#142*).

"Days of Future Past" is not only influential among time-traveling stories (although, to be fair, Byrne later recalled being partially inspired by an old episode of *Doctor Who*, so obviously everyone influences everyone else), but it also was a major turning point in the history of the X-Men. It introduced the concept of time travel into the X-Men universe and that would eventually be an extremely frequent topic of stories, including some of their most famous stories of all time (including "The Age of Apocalypse").

"Days of Future Past" has a basic setup. We see the X-Men in the future, who have almost all been hunted down and either killed or imprisoned in concentration camps (the John Byrne cover of the *X-Men #141*, with a wall covered with posters of dead or captured X-Men, is one of the most iconic covers in comic book history). The world is a terrible mess, with mutant-hunting Sentinels patrolling the skies at all times. The remaining X-Men come up with a plan. One of their members, Kate Pryde, will have her consciousness sent back in time to when she was a teenaged member of the X-Men and she will help prevent the assassination of the anti-mutant iconoclast Senator Robert Kelly. This is because Kelly's assassination will turn him into a martyr and lead directly to the Sentinels being funded as an anti-mutant deterrent, which will eventually lead to the Sentinels taking over.

Kitty Pryde had just joined the X-Men when she had her future self take over her old body. After some jubilant reunions with long-dead friends, she explains the mission at hand, which is to stop the newly reintroduced Brotherhood of Evil Mutants from killing Senator Kelly. Magneto had a few different Brotherhood of Evil Mutants over the years, but this was the introduction of Mystique's personal group, which included longtime X-Men foe, Blob, plus three new villains: the elderly psychic, Destiny; the one-man earthquake machine, Avalanche; and the British (later Australian) fire-controlling mutant, Pyro. (Byrne actually intended for Pyro to be gay, so he dressed him in flamboyant clothing as a sign. Claremont, though, decided to make him British. It's literally a case of "I'm not gay, I'm European!") This new Brotherhood would hound the X-Men for years after this story. Also of note, when the X-Men clash with the Brotherhood, Nightcrawler is shocked that Mystique is blue and she plays to his doubts to distract him. Years later, it would be revealed that Nightcrawler is, indeed, Mystique's son.

While Kate/Kitty and the X-Men tackle the Brotherhood in the past/present, the remaining X-Men of the future take on the Sentinels and try to stop them, whether Kate succeeds in the past or not. Sadly, the older versions of the X-Men were slaughtered by the Sentinels, with Wolverine actually being fried to just his skeleton. This led to another one of the most iconic covers in Marvel history. John Byrne had actually drawn the original cover for *Uncanny X-Men #142*, but it was not used for some reason. (It might have been delayed in being delivered to Marvel's offices. This was back in the days when original art was delivered by Federal Express. More than one delivery of comic book art was lost over the years). So the inker, Terry Austin, took an interior panel by Byrne and redrew it extra-sized, with the classic caption, "This issue—everybody dies!"

The ending of the issue was one of the many clashes that Byrne and Claremont had with each other during their collaboration process. Once Kate/Kitty and the X-Men successfully saved Kelly's life, Byrne's intent was that Kate would then cease to exist, since her actions would have erased her future and all the X-Men who died in the future would also disappear, since the events that led to their deaths no longer occurred. That's what Byrne drew, but since Claremont was the last one of the two to actually touch the issue (when he added captions and dialogue), Claremont added a caption that noted that Kate (after giving herself a kiss for some reason) returned to her timeline. So Claremont was now establishing that the original timeline still existed, which suggested the logical question of, "So what was the point then?" Claremont would later return to that timeline for more than one story in the future.

25 X-Men Reboot Film Series

Contrary to popular belief, Marvel did not sell the film rights to their X-Men characters in an attempt to raise money to deal with their bankruptcy in the late 1990s (although that likely is the reason that they worked out a movie deal for Spider-Man in 1999). No, their movie deal was signed in 1993, when comic book sales were at a near-all-time high. The reason that people believe that it was done during their most desperate period is that, just like the Spider-Man deal that *was* signed during the bankruptcy period, the X-Men movie deal has terms that are notably unfavorable to Marvel.

For a relatively modest fee, Sony (with Spider-Man) and Fox (with the X-Men) have, in effect, lifetime contracts to make as many movies as they want with the characters. The simple fact of the matter is that even during their boom period of 1992, Marvel did not quite understand the value of their intellectual properties. Part of this, of course, is the fact that very few superhero movies had been hits by 1992. Outside of Superman and Batman, possibly the two most famous comic book characters of all time, very few characters had ever been turned into movies, let alone successful ones. Thus, Marvel signed a bad deal with Fox for the film rights to the X-Men, a deal they have regretted ever since.

The trick is, though, that the only way that Fox can lose the license is if they fail to produce a film using the X-Men characters within a specific period of time (precisely how long is unclear, but it's likely roughly 10 years). That is how Marvel regained the rights to most of their characters for their films and television shows, including at least one character (Daredevil) from Fox. The original

X-Men film franchise began in 2000 and after *X-Men: The Last Stand* was a bit of a box office disappointment in 2006, Fox shifted to solo films, with *X-Men Origins: Wolverine* coming out in 2009. There were plans for an *X-Men Origins: Magneto*, but after *X-Men Origins: Wolverine* disappointed, *X-Men Origins: Magneto* transitioned to a complete reboot of the franchise.

2011's *X-Men: First Class* was about the origins of the X-Men and the Brotherhood, and Fox turned to a familiar face to direct the film: Bryan Singer, director of the first two X-Men films. Singer backed out of the project, but remained on as a producer. Matthew Vaughn, who was the original director on *X-Men: The Last Stand*, took over and also rewrote the script with Jane Goldman. Set in the early 1960s, James McAvoy played a young Charles Xavier, Michael Fassbender played a young Magneto, and Jennifer Lawrence played a young Mystique. The film was a major success, and resuscitated a bit of a flagging film franchise.

The next film cleverly merged the new X-Men and the old with 2014's *X-Men: Days of Future Past*, which saw the returns of Patrick Stewart, Ian McKellen, Hugh Jackman, and Bryan Singer to the franchise, as the X-Men in the future are being hunted down by Sentinels and their only chance is to send the consciousness of one of their own, Wolverine, back in time to his body in the early 1970s, where he has to put together the younger versions of Xavier and Magneto to help him save the life of Bolivar Trask, the creator of the Sentinels. Mystique originally killed him, which turned Trask into a martyr, leading to a future where Sentinels have killed most mutants in the world. In a clever twist that also wrapped up the original X-Men film franchise, Wolverine is *so* successful at his mission that he actually not only prevented the Sentinels future, but he also averted the tragic deaths of Jean Grey and Cyclops that occurred in *X-Men: The Last Stand*, so Singer got to return to the franchise and give his original characters a happy ending.

A poster for 2011's X-Men: First Class. *From left: Jason Flemyng, Nicholas Hoult, January Jones, James McAvoy, Michael Fassbender, Jennifer Lawrence, and Kevin Bacon.* (Twentieth Century Fox Film Corporation/Photofest)

With the original characters now given their proper send-off, the next film entered the 1980s, as Bryan Singer said goodbye to the franchise with 2016's *X-Men: Apocalypse*, which saw the Ancient Egyptian mutant En Sabah Nur try to cause the end of mankind with the help of a quartet of mutants, including Magneto. This

Top Five Biggest Lies/Deceptions by Professor X

5. **Kept the Danger Room's sentience a secret**
   When Xavier updated the Danger Room using Shi'ar technology, he discovered that it was sentient. For some reason, he kept this information to himself. Eventually, the Danger Room went nuts and killed a student.

4. **Didn't tell Cyclops or Havok that they had a brother**
   While it paled in comparison to the other deception revealed in "X-Men: Deadly Genesis," it is still pretty lame that Xavier knew that Cyclops and Havok's long-lost brother was training with Moira MacTaggert and didn't tell them about him.

3. **Faked his death**
   After he found out about an impending alien invasion, Xavier decided that the best course of action was to have a shape-shifting alien fake his death so that he could have time to prepare for the invasion. Instead of just telling the X-Men to, say, leave him alone for a little bit, he just pretends to be dead. It's like his go-to idea at all times is to lie.

2. **Created a second X-Men team, saw them die, and covered it up**
   After the original X-Men were captured, Xavier put together a new team of X-Men to save them. This team was then slaughtered. Not only did he just try again with another new team (the famous All-New, All-Different X-Men) he decided to just never tell anyone what happened, even wiping Cyclops' memories of watching it happen!

1. **Claimed that the X-Men weren't named after him**
   While obviously the whole "lied about the second team" one is truly the worst, we have a special case in our heart for him telling the X-Men that his name was Professor X and they were the X-Men, but the team was named after their "X-Tra powers." That's not even a remotely believable lie! And for such a silly reason! That's what made it tops.

film also introduced younger versions of the main cast of 2000's *X-Men*, with a new Cyclops, Jean Grey, and Storm. With Singer now departed, the screenwriter of *X-Men: Days of Future Past* and *X-Men: Apocalypse*, Simon Kinberg, took over the director's chair for the next film in the franchise, *X-Men: Dark Phoenix*, which will be the second time that the X-Men film franchise has tackled Jean Grey's transformation into Dark Phoenix. And with Disney in the midst of a purchase of Fox in early 2018, the future of the X-Men films is up in the air.

26 Kitty Pryde

If someone asked you to name the greatest basketball player of all time, you'd likely say Michael Jordan. Now, imagine if you found out that Jordan never played basketball but was actually a mathematician. In other words, what if the most famous example of a certain type of person was not actually that type of person at all? That is the case with Kitty Pryde, who is the most famous example of the "everyman point of view" character in comic book history, and yet ceased to be an "everyman" almost right away.

Kitty Pryde was introduced in *X-Men #129* as part of an attempt by John Byrne and Chris Claremont to both breathe some new life into the X-Men and also to recapture the original intention of the X-Men, which was to be a school for mutants (a purpose the series hadn't served in over a decade). Byrne and Claremont originally pitched a brand-new series starring just new mutant students, with Kitty Pryde as one of the possible new students (Byrne named her after an old classmate of his with the same name). Marvel passed on the new series idea, but Kitty was reworked into a new mutant that the X-Men recruited in *X-Men #129* (by Byrne, Claremont, and Austin). Kitty was a "girl next door" from Chicago who was also being recruited by Emma Frost of the Hellfire Club, who wanted Kitty to attend Frost's own school for mutants, the Massachusetts Academy. Kitty eventually chose the X-Men and she formally joined the team following the conclusion of "The Dark Phoenix Saga" (so Kitty's addition to the team came upon the book losing Jean Grey and Cyclops, as Cyclops took a leave of absence from the team after Jean Grey died).

Byrne left the series soon after Kitty joined the book, and in Byrne's absence, Claremont slowly made alterations to the character, with the most notable one being the fact that Kitty was now, in effect, a young genius. Yes, the "everyman" point-of-view character for regular readers to associate with was now a child prodigy. Despite the fact that she really did not fit in to the role almost as soon as she was introduced, Kitty still began to be used as the most notable example of the everyman point-of-view character. That character type soon became a common trope in comic books, with a number of books introducing their own version of Kitty Pryde. (The trend became so famous that Marv Wolfman and George Perez used it to their advantage when they added Terra to the cast of the New Teen Titans. She seemed so similar to Kitty Pryde that people assumed that they were just aping Kitty Pryde like everyone else, but in reality, Terra was a murderous traitor working against the Titans.)

One of the things that Kitty Pryde soon became famous for under Claremont's direction was giving impassioned speeches about bigotry. She gave two in "God Loves, Man Kills" and she gave a particularly notable speech in *New Mutants #45* to a whole high school of students following the death of a young student who killed himself because he was scared that people thought that he was a mutant. During the early 1980s, Kitty Pryde, despite her young age, was the conscience of the X-Men.

Another notable role for Kitty Pryde was being the first example of another popular comic book trope, which was to pair Wolverine with a young girl. Wolverine's gruff exterior contrasted and complemented his young partners, and Kitty Pryde was the first character to have this role (they even costarred together in a miniseries, "Kitty Pryde and Wolverine." In it, Kitty finally picked out a code name that lasted—Shadowcat).

After being written out of the X-Men, Kitty became a founding member (along with her fellow former X-Man, Nightcrawler) of the British superhero team, Excalibur. Kitty served with the team for years, growing from a teen into a young woman. She then returned to the X-Men along with Nightcrawler. After the death of her first boyfriend, her teammate, Colossus, Kitty retired from the team and tried to pursue a regular college degree.

Instead, in Joss Whedon and John Cassaday's *Astonishing X-Men*, Kitty was recruited by Cyclops to be part of a new team of X-Men, who were designed to be the public face of the X-Men. Cyclops needed someone articulate and liked by the public and Kitty Pryde was the perfect choice for the gig. Kitty seemingly sacrificed herself to save the world at the end of Whedon and Cassaday's *Astonishing X-Men*, but she eventually made her way back to Earth and the X-Men.

Most recently, after serving as the coheadmaster (with Wolverine) of the Jean Grey School for Higher Learning and briefly serving as a member of the Guardians of the Galaxy (she was even engaged to Star-Lord for a hot minute), she has returned to serve as the current overall leader of the X-Men.

27 Storm

While the success of the Avengers films have made it so that Black Widow is quite likely the most popular Marvel female superhero to your average person on the street, for a long period of time, that "honor" (quotes because it really is more a statement about how few prominent female heroes Marvel has had over the years than anything else) would likely go to Storm. In fact, when Marvel and DC had a crossover event in 1996 called "Marvel vs. DC," Storm was one of the 26 superheroes who participated in fights between Marvel and DC characters (13 Marvel heroes and 13 DC heroes). Fans would vote on seven of the 13 contests and Storm vs. Wonder Woman was one of the matchups—and Storm actually won! So yes, at one point, Storm was famous enough that she beat Wonder Woman in a popularity contest!

Like most of the All-New, All-Different X-Men, Storm's personality was not really set until after her cocreator, writer Len Wein, left *X-Men* and saw the book taken over by Chris Claremont (working with Storm's other cocreator, artist Dave Cockrum). In Claremont's take on the character, she was half-American (born in New York City) whose parents died during fighting in Egypt. She was trapped in the same blast that killed her parents, and that led to her developing claustrophobia. She grew up as a street urchin in Cairo, where she became a master pickpocket and thief. As a teenager, she ended up in the plains of Africa, where her newly activated mutant ability to control the weather caused the natives to worship her as a goddess. That was the situation Storm was living in when she was recruited to join the X-Men by Charles Xavier.

During her early years with the X-Men, Storm vacillated between two distinct aspects of her personality. She carried herself with a sense of regality, but she had also just been living in Africa as a naked "goddess." So her idea of appropriate behavior sometimes shocked her fellow X-Men. Storm was also beautiful, so a common plot in the early years was the villains would fall in love with Storm and try to get her to marry them. There seriously were three different X-Men foes who tried to make Storm marry them (Arkon, Doctor Doom, and Dracula).

When Cyclops left the X-Men after "The Dark Phoenix Saga," Storm stepped up and became the leader of the team. In this new role, she had to show a different side of herself. She was always known as a kind and nurturing person, but now that was in charge, she had to show that she could be tough too. This was best demonstrated when she fought Callisto, the leader of the Morlocks, in a fight to the death after the Morlocks kidnapped Kitty Pryde. Storm actually delivered a fatal blow to Callisto in the fight, thereby making Storm the new leader of the Morlocks (luckily, the Morlocks had a member with healing powers, so Callisto was able to be saved).

Storm and Kitty Pryde had a sort of mother/daughter relationship, and Storm's increased toughness caused friction in their relationship. This was spotlighted in a story line where Storm got a new look, dressing in black leather with a Mohawk. Kitty Pryde was aghast at the changes (the whole thing was based on how the young daughter of *Uncanny X-Men* editor Louise Jones reacted when Jones' husband abruptly shaved his beard while on vacation). Around this time, Storm also lost her mutant abilities for a couple of years, but she had grown so tough that she remained leader of the X-Men even without her powers.

Throughout the 1990s and early years of the 21st century, Storm remained a major member of the X-Men (when the X-Men split into two squads, X-Men Blue and X-Men Gold, Storm was the leader of the Gold team, while Cyclops led the Blue team). Things changed when Storm actually got married! You see, when she was a young teen making her way in the plains of Africa (before becoming a "goddess"), she befriended a young teenage boy. They spent a lot of time together before parting ways. That boy was T'Challa, who grew up to become the Black Panther, the King of Wakanda. Years later, T'Challa had to find a Queen for Wakanda and Storm ended up being his choice. They had the wedding of the century. For the first time in decades, Storm was no longer a regular X-Men cast member, as now she was part of the *Black Panther* series (they even both briefly joined the Fantastic Four, together replacing another notable married couple, Mister Fantastic and Invisible Woman). Sadly, during the Avengers vs. X-Men conflict, Storm and Black Panther had their wedding annulled by Wakanda's High Priest (who, of course, happened to also be T'Challa).

Storm replaced Kitty Pryde as the coheadmaster of the Jean Grey School for Higher Learning, and when Wolverine died, Storm took over as the sole headmaster. She also became the overall leader of the X-Men when Cyclops died. Storm led the X-Men into a war with the Inhumans and when it ended, she stepped down as leader of the X-Men. She currently remains a member of the team, just under the leadership of Kitty Pryde.

28 Rogue

Over time, it got to the point where every comic book that Chris Claremont was writing for Marvel was X-Men related. However, in the early years of the *X-Men*, when it was just a single comic book (heck, not even a monthly comic book series for the first couple of years), Claremont had to keep busy on a variety of other comic books, including notable runs on *Marvel Team-Up*, *Iron*

Fist, Spider-Woman, and *Ms. Marvel.* On *Ms. Marvel,* Claremont's X-Men collaborator, Dave Cockrum, redesigned Ms. Marvel's costume and gave her a very Cockrum-esque design (Cockrum was the king of sashes) that lasted for decades. Ms. Marvel's ongoing series ended abruptly right before Claremont was about to start a story line involving Mystique, the Hellfire Club, and a young Southern villain that was going to be introduced named Rogue. Instead, Ms. Marvel's series was canceled and she ended up just a member of the Avengers.

Her stint in the Avengers ended in *Avengers #200* when she literally went into Limbo, along with a man named Marcus, who admitted that he had used machines to make Ms. Marvel love him, but the Avengers all thought that it was fine for her to go off to another dimension to live happily ever after with Marcus. A comic book fan named Carol A. Strickland wrote a fanzine article called "The Rape of Ms. Marvel" that led Claremont to write *Avengers Annual #10,* which brought Ms. Marvel back from Limbo and had her tell the Avengers how much they let her down. However, in that same annual, she finally met Mystique's Brotherhood of Evil Mutants, which now included Rogue, who was going to be introduced in Ms. Marvel's own series. Here, Rogue drained Ms. Marvel of her powers entirely. Rogue had the ability to absorb the powers and personality of anyone she made physical contact with, but she typically only made brief contact with people. With Ms. Marvel, she absorbed it all, so she gained all of her powers and all of her personality!

After a few other appearances as a member of the Brotherhood (where artists had a hard time handling the fact that Rogue was a teenager; she had always been drawn with white streaks in her hair, so other artists always seemed to think that she was old because of those), Rogue eventually was forced to join the X-Men because she needed help from Professor X to deal with the literal voice in her head, as while she had Ms. Marvel's strength and invulnerability, she also gained Ms. Marvel's personality.

The other X-Men naturally had a problem with a new team member who had just recently been their enemy (and, in fact, only stopped being their enemy because of selfish personal reasons), but Rogue soon showed her worth. In fact, she became one of the most stalwart members of the team (basically Rogue, Storm, and Wolverine were the only members to remain members of the team from the early 1980s through the late 1980s). Eventually, she was able to free herself of Ms. Marvel's personality (while keeping her powers).

Even without that major obstacle in her life, Rogue still had to deal with the basic problem behind her powers, which is that she cannot touch a person without draining their powers and personality (Rogue was tormented as a child when she kissed her first boyfriend and put him into a coma). This became a major source of drama when she met a new teammate, the Cajun mutant known as Gambit. They entered into a classic "Will they or won't they?" relationship, although in their case, it was almost a case of "Can they or can't they?" As the question really wasn't whether they loved each other but rather whether they could physically love each other. Their relationship has gone through many ups and downs over the last 25 years (they even managed to take their relationship to the physical level on a few occasions when Rogue's powers were canceled out).

Rogue's powers have changed a number of times over the years as well, as she has lost Ms. Marvel's powers, briefly replaced them with Sunfire's powers (it was a very odd point in her career for her to suddenly have fire powers), had no extra powers outside of her power absorption, and then had Wonder Man's powers (which coincidentally were very similar to her classic Ms. Marvel powers). Her level of control has changed as well.

Most recently, Rogue has been the main mutant representative on the mutant/human superhero team known as the Uncanny Avengers. It's pretty amazing to think that a mutant who started off as a die-hard enemy of the X-Men would end up as one of the most public faces of mutant heroism.

29 Must Read: "God Loves, Man Kills"

Outside of a couple of books about the origins of Marvel heroes and villains in the mid-1970s, Marvel had never had much of a presence in the book market, but as the 1980s began, Marvel launched *Marvel Graphic Novel*, a series of high-profile original graphic novels designed for the trade paperback market. They were designed to be oversized, glossy books like the comic "albums" that are so popular in Europe. Their first one was by star writer/artist Jim Starlin and it featured the death of the longtime cosmic hero Captain Marvel.

The books were intended to be a mix between creator-owned material and material set in the Marvel Universe. In addition, some of the books were designed to tie directly in to the Marvel Universe, while others were meant to be read as if they were part of a separate continuity. When Marvel approached legendary artist Neal Adams about drawing an X-Men graphic novel, their original pitch was that it would be outside regular Marvel continuity. This would have been demonstrated by Magneto being killed early in the story. However, Adams was unable to work out a contract with Marvel (the *Marvel Graphic Novel* deals had different author contracts than typical Marvel comics) and so Chris Claremont reworked the concept for the new artist on the book, Brent Anderson, who had recently almost become the new artist on *Uncanny X-Men* following Dave Cockrum's second stint (Anderson drew the first issue of X-Men after John Byrne's departure).

The finished work was a stunning examination of the horrors of bigotry and the dangers of allowing your religious beliefs to serve as a sort of shield from having to question the righteousness of your actions. In the book, Reverend William Stryker has built up a mass following by preaching against the sin of mutantkind. Meanwhile, his private group of "Purifiers" have been hunting down and killing mutants. The book opens with the death of two young mutant children. Both mutant children were black and the pages greatly evoke

Top Five Most Iconic X-Men Covers

5. *X-Men #137*
   While certainly not a bad cover by any stretch of the imagination, this Byrne/Austin cover has become iconic because people know what happens to Cyclops and Jean Grey inside the comic.

4. *X-Men #1*
   Generally speaking, with very few exceptions, the first cover appearances of characters are always going to be one of their most iconic covers.

3. *X-Men #142*
   Amazingly, John Byrne's cover for this issue was not used, so Marvel had Terry Austin just take an interior panel and turn it into a cover and an icon was born.

2. *Giant-Size X-Men #1*
   Gil Kane was Marvel's go-to cover artist in the 1970s, and his cover introducing the All-New, All-Different X-Men makes it clear why he had that honor. The mixture of dynamic art and a historic moment makes for an iconic cover.

1. *X-Men #141*
   In the annals of comic book cover history, one of the most homaged covers of all time is this stunning John Byrne cover that kicked off "Days of Future Past."

The famous image of Reverend William Stryker and Nightcrawler from Chris Claremont and Brent Anderson's "God Loves, Man Kills." (Art by Brent Anderson)

some of the most horrific acts of violence against African Americans during the Civil Rights Movement. When Magneto comes across the dead mutants, he decides to take Stryker out.

Professor X and Cyclops are captured by Stryker after Xavier had just publicly debated Stryker on the issue of human/mutant relations. With their two leaders in custody, the X-Men ended up teaming up with Magneto to rescue Xavier and Cyclops. As it turned out, Stryker was planning on using a machine powered by Xavier to give all mutants in the world cerebral hemorrhages. Naturally, it turned out that Stryker's son had been born a mutant and he had never forgiven himself for that "sin."

In the end, the X-Men confront Stryker on national television, stopping his horrific plan from occurring. Kitty Pryde of the X-Men then gives a beautiful speech about the power of looking beyond one's appearance to see the humanity in people's souls. The demonic-looking Nightcrawler is the centerpiece of this debate (never has Nightcrawler looked less human than when Anderson drew him in this sequence), with Kitty successfully arguing that Nightcrawler might look like a demon, but he's actually one of the purest souls anyone has met.

With Stryker's bigotry exposed in front of the world, he turns and tries to shoot Kitty, but one of the police officers (a human) assigned to provide security for the televised event shoots Stryker before he can fire on Kitty. Stryker is arrested for the crimes of the Purifiers. Xavier offers Magneto a place on the X-Men, but Magneto turns him down (but not before hesitating) and then explains to him that while they have won the battle, Stryker might win the war, as he has already been set up to look like a martyr for his cause.

At the time, the story was not really worked into X-Men continuity, as no one made a reference to the events of the story in the comic until 21 years later, when Claremont wrote a sequel to the story in the pages of *X-Treme X-Men*. The reason for the sequel was because that same year, the second X-Men film, *X2*, was based on the events of "God Loves, Man Kills" (only Stryker is a general rather than a reverend).

30 Grant Morrison

In the United States in the 1960s, most comic book readers were specifically fans of superheroes. That wasn't the case in other countries, where superhero stories were certainly popular, but not the only form of comic book entertainment. Therefore, over the years, it seems like British comic book writers, in particular, have been able to view superheroes with a sense of detachment that American comic book writers have never had. The result often means a brand-new take on superheroes. One of these British writers who helped change the comic book industry was Grant Morrison.

Morrison had begun to make a name for himself in British comic books in the 1980s, including a superhero called Zenith, which was a very clever, postmodern take on the superhero concept. Morrison then broke in to American comics in the late '80s with a best-selling Batman graphic novel, *Batman: Arkham Asylum*, and acclaimed runs on both *Animal Man* and *Doom Patrol*. In the former series, Morrison played with metafictional elements, like literally meeting Animal Man at the end of his run and talking about the influence Morrison's real life had on Animal Man's fictional adventures. In the latter, Morrison took a typical (if somewhat strange) superhero team book and turned it into one of the most bizarre comic books in existence. In 1996, Morrison took his ideas mainstream, when he relaunched the Justice League with a return to the original members of the team in *JLA*. Morrison's unique mixture of off-the-wall ideas and earnest love for the characters resulted in a blockbuster success, making *JLA* DC's best-selling comic book series.

Now a legit comic book superstar (as opposed to just a critically acclaimed indie darling), Morrison was given a chance in 2001 by the new editor-in-chief of Marvel Comics, Joe Quesada, to completely revamp the X-Men line of comic books. Morrison's biggest innovation was to expand the mutant population. In Morrison's *New X-Men*, mutants were no longer a feared minority, they were a feared minority who were threatening to become an eventual majority on Earth! Professor X finally "came out" as a mutant (although it wasn't really Xavier in charge of his body at the time, but really his evil psychic "twin" sister, Cassandra Nova). The X-Men stopped wearing costumes and began wearing outfits more similar to the outfits that they wore in the X-Men films and became more of a mutant outreach team than anything else.

One of the major plots in Morrison's run was to introduce a new mutant named Xorn, who had healing powers. A Chinese mutant with a "black hole for a brain," Xorn quickly proved himself with the X-Men by helping them defeat Cassandra Nova (who had taken control of her twin's body). He then became a popular instructor at the expanded Xavier Institute, whose student population was booming. The tragic twist was revealed at the start of Morrison's penultimate story line in his run—Xorn, this whole time, was secretly Magneto! The mutant had used his magnetic powers and special "nanobots" to make it seem like he was healing people, but it was really the nanomachines that were doing the healing and he was just controlling them with his powers.

At the end of the story, Magneto is killed, but not before he also kills Jean Grey, who Morrison was slowly transforming in his run into having the mutant ability to control the Phoenix Force. So that's why she was chosen to be replaced by the Phoenix Force so many years earlier. At the end of Morrison's run, we see the future of the X-Men, where Jean returns to life 150 years in the future. She actually then goes back in time with her powers to force her widower, Cyclops, to move on with his life with Emma Frost, who Cyclops had cheated on Jean with during Morrison's run.

The biggest problem with Morrison's run is that when he was first hired, Marvel was just coming out of bankruptcy and had, in effect, nothing to lose. They were willing to just give the X-Men line to a guy like Morrison to come in and do what he wanted. When they got back to normal and sales had recovered, they suddenly weren't as willing to let Morrison do whatever he wanted and the clashes eventually led to Morrison leaving the X-Men much earlier than he intended. Morrison headed back to DC Comics, where he began a decade-long run on *Batman*.

31 Gambit

When it comes to a comic book character reaching certain popularity levels, it's often a case of the character just having good timing. For instance, Gambit just happened to be introduced right when Jim Lee was taking over as the regular artist on *Uncanny X-Men* (Lee designed Gambit's costume) and thus, right before comic books were hitting sales levels that they had not seen since the peak of World War II. Then the *X-Men: Animated Series* launched in 1992 and the roster for that cartoon was based mostly on the cast of Jim Lee's 1991 *X-Men* series, which happened to prominently feature Gambit. So within two years, Gambit went from not even being in existence to becoming one of the most famous comic book characters to a whole generation of fans, whether readers of the X-Men comics or viewers of the X-Men cartoon.

This was especially notable because when Gambit was introduced, Chris Claremont actually intended for Gambit to be a bad guy! Well, not necessarily a bad guy, exactly, so much as he was going to be an agent of Mister Sinister, who was going to infiltrate the X-Men for him. This was part of Claremont's original plan for Mister Sinister, which would have involved "Mister Sinister" as being a creation of a powerful mutant who is stuck as a child. Thus, Mister Sinister was his idea of what a supervillain would be like. Gambit, in the meantime, would be his example of what a superhero would be like. They were both creations of the same mind, however. The idea, though, would be that Gambit would ultimately rebel and perhaps remain a member of the X-Men. However, Claremont obviously left the X-Men before he could ever implement this story line, so instead, Gambit was given a brand-new origin.

Instead, Gambit was a member of a special Thieves Guild in New Orleans that was constantly at war with a rival Assassins Guild in the city. He attempted to unite the two guilds by marrying a young woman in the Assassins Guild, but then her brother challenged him to a duel and Gambit killed him. He had to go on the run. During this time, he was hired by Mister Sinister to help put together a group of mercenaries. What Gambit did not know was that this team of mercenaries, the Marauders, were put together to slaughter the sewer-dwelling mutants known as the Morlocks. This was Gambit's secret shame for many years and trying to make up for his role in the "Mutant Massacre" is what drove him to become a superhero.

Gambit's powers allow him to create a kinetic charge in items. He can "charge" items up and then force them to explode. He most commonly would charge up playing cards and then throw them at people, as the cards would then explode on his targets, doing minor damage (the bigger the object he charges, the bigger the explosion would be). Gambit joined the X-Men after he saved a young girl who he ran in to while robbing a home. The young girl turned out to be a de-aged Storm. Gambit agreed to help her back to the X-Men but when he succeeded (and she was then re-aged to adulthood), he agreed to stay on as a team member.

During this time, Gambit fell in love with his new X-Men teammate, Rogue, who could not touch Gambit without absorbing his powers and his personality. This was shown quite often on the *X-Men: Animated Series*. (This included constant sexual innuendos by Gambit—like when he's holding a pool cue, charging the tip of it, and telling Rogue that he has more than enough energy for her to absorb. Yeesh.) He and Rogue have gone through many ups and downs in their relationship, but it always seems like they'll eventually get back together in the end. They're just far too connected to each other.

In the last decade or so, Gambit has mostly served as a solo hero. He has had a number of solo ongoing series and often finds himself working with villains in misguided attempts to protect Rogue. Like when he joined up with Apocalypse and agreed to become his Horseman of Death in the hopes that he could perhaps help tamper Apocalypse's worst impulses. Or when he then joined up with Mystique and Mister Sinister's reformed Marauders so that he could protect Rogue when the Marauders attacked the X-Men. Gambit recently rejoined the X-Men. In his 2012 ongoing series, writer James Asmus intended for Gambit to be revealed to be bisexual, but Marvel ultimately nixed that approach. Gambit recently rejoined the X-Men in the pages of *Astonishing X-Men*.

32 Nightcrawler

If you were to pick out a single member of the X-Men to use as an example to prove the folly of hating and fearing mutants based solely on what they look like, then you could do no better than Kurt Wagner, the German mutant hero known as Nightcrawler. Despite being born looking like a blue-skinned demon (complete with a spade-tipped tail, right out of devil mythology) and having a mutant power (teleportation) that activates with a "Bamf!" and the scent of brimstone (talk about leaning into the devil mythology), Nightcrawler was the sweetest and most fun-loving member of the All-New, All-Different X-Men.

Amusingly enough, if it weren't for a failed pitch, Nightcrawler not only would not have been a member of the X-Men, he wouldn't have even been a Marvel Comics character at all! Before he became the artist on *X-Men*, Dave Cockrum was a very popular artist on DC Comics' "Legion of Super-Heroes" feature in the pages of *Superboy*. Cockrum already famously redesigned most of the costumes of the members of the team (most of his designs became the iconic looks for those characters), but he then wanted to do even more. He pitched DC on a new superhero team that would also be set in the future, like the Legion of Super-Heroes. They would be called the Outsiders and one of the members of the team was Nightcrawler—the same exact design. DC Comics passed and Cockrum eventually went to work for Marvel instead, and when he and Len Wein began to create the All-New, All-Different X-Men, Cockrum brought Nightcrawler with him.

Wein's original take on the character was similar to what you would expect while looking at someone like Nightcrawler—he was bitter due to his appearance. In fact, when we first meet Nightcrawler in *Giant-Size X-Men #1*, he is being hunted by an angry mob who wants to kill him. However, since Wein left the series early on, Cockrum was able to convince the incoming writer, Chris Claremont, to take a different approach with Wagner. Instead of being bitter, Nightcrawler was upbeat and loved his new life as a superhero. He was a born swashbuckler (he grew up as a circus performer) and being a superhero was the perfect setup (you got to wear costumes and fight over-the-top battles against evil). Nightcrawler soon became Cockrum's favorite member of the X-Men and he would routinely push for Claremont to have Nightcrawler more prominently featured in the series (Cockrum also introduced new powers for Nightcrawler, including the ability to turn invisible when in the shadows).

However, even Claremont and Cockrum differed on Nightcrawler a bit, as Claremont wanted to make Nightcrawler religious and Cockrum objected. He didn't see the character as the religious type. When John Byrne joined *X-Men* to replace

Cockrum, Byrne agreed with Cockrum's take. Thus, it would not be until both artists were off the series that Claremont revealed that Nightcrawler was a devout Catholic. (Back when he first suggested the idea, Claremont was leaning toward making him Jewish, but in the meantime, Claremont had introduced another Jewish X-Man, Kitty Pryde, and had hinted heavily that X-Men villain, Magneto, was a Jewish survivor of the Holocaust.) Nightcrawler's religion became a major part of his personality, with Claremont later even having him train to be a priest. Later writers squelched that idea, but he remains a religious person.

After being injured during the X-Men crossover, "Mutant Massacre," Nightcrawler went to England to recuperate (along with his teammate Kitty Pryde) and they ended up forming an X-Men spinoff team in England called Excalibur. Nightcrawler served on that team for many years, until the team disbanded and the two of them rejoined the X-Men.

Throughout the years, Nightcrawler's parentage had gone through a number of different possibilities. At one point, his father was going to be the demonic Nightmare, the Doctor Strange villain. Then–Doctor Strange writer Roger Stern nixed that idea. Later, Mystique was going to be Nightcrawler's father (as she would shapeshift into a man and impregnate her longtime girlfriend, Destiny). That idea was a little too "out there" for Marvel, so Mystique was instead revealed to be Nightcrawler's mother. His father was introduced years later in a much-derided story line called "The Draco," where we learn that Nightcrawler's father is a demonic mutant from another dimension (which could be considered "hell") called Azazel.

After Nightcrawler actually died in battle in 2010, he went to Heaven. However, his father hatched a plan to steal the souls of all those living in Heaven, Hell, and Limbo. Nightcrawler and the X-Men foiled the plot, but in the process, Nightcrawler had to sacrifice his own soul to save the billions of other innocent souls at risk. As part of the deal, Nightcrawler also returned to the land of the living, where he naturally rejoined the X-Men and has been serving with them ever since.

33 X-Men Action Figures

In the early 1990s, comic book sales were reaching numbers that they had not seen since the 1940s (and they were doing so while costing a dollar rather than a dime). However, even with their increased sales figures, Marvel's comic book merchandising was still surprisingly in an effectively dormant state. Sure, there were the standard posters and things like that, but there had not been a company-wide Marvel toy line in almost a decade, not since the relatively unsuccessful (it was popular enough to have more than one series released, but that was about it) attempt at a toy line by Mattel (that did lead to the very successful comic book crossover event that tied in with the toy line called "Marvel Super Heroes Secret Wars"). So when a company called ToyBiz gained the license to make action figures based on Marvel figures in the early 1990s, no one expected much.

Anyone who had low expectations for ToyBiz's Marvel toys would have been still somehow disappointed by the initial releases from ToyBiz. The first group of toys had poor articulation, ridiculous attempts at "powers" (Spider-Man and Nightcrawler both came with suction cups to mimic their "wallcrawling" abilities, but the suction cups were not removable, so you just had a Spider-Man figure who had to walk around with suction cups stuck to him) and outdated designs (Cyclops was wearing a costume he had not worn in a year by the time the toys were released in 1991).

Then a funny thing happened—*X-Men: The Animated Series* debuted. Suddenly, there was a whole new market for X-Men–related action figures. ToyBiz kept doing general figures for Marvel superheroes, but also gave the X-Men their own toy line. This time they spent some time and money on the design and actually had the toys tie in with the comics. The results were a marked improvement and the kids of America went for them big time, especially with the cartoon around to serve as basically a half-hour advertisement for the toys.

The most popular figure, of course, was Wolverine, so ToyBiz managed to find a way to work a different version of Wolverine into each new series of figures that they released. This, of course, meant that they had to delve deep into the history of Marvel Comics to find different versions of Wolverine that could be adapted into new figures.

The weird thing about most releases of anything (action figures, video games, comic books, movies) is that the initial series, the ones that form the backbone of the entire property, rarely are the ones that do the best in sales. This is because no one knew about them before they came out. It is only when that first property is successful that the other items in the series are even released. Thus, the most popular series in the X-Men action figure line was the fourth series, which happened to include an obscure X-Men villain named Tusk. Due to his inclusion in the most popular series of figures, a whole generation of fans probably knows who he is despite the character barely showing up in the comic books.

Originally, the release pattern of the X-Men action figure line was essentially "Whoever we think looks cool," while also slowly working through the main X-Men roster. Through four series, that approach looked like it was pretty brilliant. Then the fifth series came out and things fell apart. The figures in this series included a street-clothes Wolverine, Rogue of the X-Men, two minor Starjammers characters named Ch'od and Raza, a member of Magneto's Acolytes named Senyaka (who was dead in the comics at the time of his toy's release), an obscure member of Excalibur named Kylun, and a member of the Reavers named Bonebreaker. It seemed to be about as random of an assortment of figures as possible. And since the previous series sold so much, the fifth series was preordered at high levels...and the figures just sat on shelves for years. Starting from that point, ToyBiz began releasing their toys based on related themes. No more "Here are just six various X-Men characters."

As the 1990s came to a close, the comic book industry had collapsed, but ToyBiz was still going strong. Marvel had purchased part of ToyBiz and sought to buy the rest of it before they ended up declaring bankruptcy. After a battle between two of Marvel's biggest stockholders, the courts ended up giving control of Marvel to ToyBiz, who were heavily involved in the bankruptcy proceedings because of the importance Marvel meant to their toy line. They were still the controlling interest in Marvel when the company was sold to Disney in 2009.

34 Colossus

After giving up his editor-in-chief position in late 1975, Len Wein soon found himself writing a large chunk of Marvel's major titles at once. Wein was the writer on *Amazing Spider-Man*, *Incredible Hulk*, *Fantastic Four*, and *Thor* all at the same time for years. Had he remained editor-in-chief he certainly would have continued writing on *X-Men*, which was one of two assignments he had during his editor-in-chief gig (*Incredible Hulk* being the other). Had he remained, the All-new, All-Different X-Men would have ended up much differently, and Colossus might have seen the biggest change of all of them.

Wein saw Colossus as, in effect, the star of the series. At the time that the All-New, All-Different X-Men were introduced, there was an unwritten rule in comic books that the biggest superheroes all used primary colors (red, yellow, and blue) in their costumes. Superman used all three, Spider-Man used two and Batman used two (during his yellow oval chest symbol era). It was no surprise, then, that Colossus' costume was also designed using all three primary colors. Colossus was set up to be the main character.

When Chris Claremont took over as the writer of the X-Men, however, he changed things. Colossus first took a backseat to Nightcrawler (during Dave Cockrum's initial run) and then Wolverine (during John Byrne's run and in all runs since). Under Claremont's pen, Colossus' sensitive nature was played up. Here was a young man who wanted nothing more than to be an artist, but was somehow forced to be a superhero instead. During the classic "Proteus Saga" story line (a precursor to "The Dark Phoenix Saga"), Colossus is forced to take Proteus' life (the evil mutant's one weakness was metal and Colossus' power was to transform into living metal) and Proteus' death would haunt Colossus for quite some time.

Soon after she joined the X-Men, Kitty Pryde and Colossus saw their relationship blossom into a romance. While not many people seemed to have voiced any concerns at the time, in retrospect it was pretty clear that having the 19-year-old Colossus date the 14-year-old Kitty Pryde was not going to work out. Therefore, during "Marvel Super Heroes Secret Wars," Colossus had an affair with an alien woman who lived on the Battleworld created for "Secret

Wars." Even though she died at the end of "Secret Wars," Colossus knew he could no longer date Kitty.

Over the years, Colossus became more and more jaded (during the "Mutant Massacre," one of the iconic moments is when Colossus just snaps the neck of one of the Marauders and warns the others that they are next) and also began to make some foolish decisions. After his younger sister, Illyana, passed away from the Legacy Virus (a disease that only affected mutants), Colossus agreed to leave the X-Men and join Magneto's Acolytes.

When that ended up not working out, Colossus eventually returned to the X-Men. Beast then discovered a cure for the Legacy Virus, but in its first form, it needed to be injected into a mutant who then used their powers and thus activated the cure, but in the process, the mutant who activated the cure would die. Rather than wait for Beast to work more on the cure and find a way to avoid it killing whoever used it, Colossus just grabbed it and injected himself with it, choosing to die so that others could live. It was a noble gesture, but still ill-considered.

This being comic books, Colossus turned out to not actually be dead years later in Joss Whedon and John Cassaday's *Astonishing X-Men* run. It turned out that some aliens believed that he was destined to destroy their planet, so they kidnapped him and held him captive. The X-Men then freed him. A now older Kitty Pryde reconnected with Colossus and they had sex for the first time together (it got so intense that Kitty actually accidentally phased through the bedroom floor).

They broke up again when Colossus volunteered to take the place of Cain Marko as the new Juggernaut when Cain was temporarily chosen as one of "The Worthy" during the "Fear Itself" crossover (where a number of hammers came to Earth and possessed the people who found them, Marko included). Kitty was sick of how willing Colossus was to sacrifice himself all the time.

Colossus was one of the five X-Men who were possessed by the Phoenix Force during "Avengers vs. X-Men." Since his possession ended, he has worked hard to make up for his actions while in his possessed state. He has continued to serve with the X-Men, which is a bit awkward now that his ex, Kitty Pryde, is the leader of the team.

35 New Mutants

Following the success of John Byrne and Chris Claremont's X-Men run, the sales on *Uncanny X-Men* continued to rise even after Byrne left the series. The book was slowly moving up the sales charts at Marvel and it became clear to Marvel editor-in-chief Jim Shooter that it needed to have a spinoff series. Claremont decided to revisit an idea that Byrne and Claremont had a few years earlier (which had been rejected by Shooter at the time) to introduce a new batch of students at Xavier's. Shooter now loved the idea and decided to use Marvel's new *Graphic Novel* series to launch the title.

Marvel Graphic Novel #4 (by Chris Claremont and Bob McLeod) introduced the world to the New Mutants. The X-Men had been captured by the evil alien race known as the Brood, and Professor X believed that his students were all dead. Xavier planned on ending the whole "training mutants" endeavor at this point, but a series of peculiar circumstances forced him to change his mind when he suddenly found himself surrounded with a group of young mutants who all clearly needed direction in their lives. So he started the school back up again and these new mutants became his first new class.

The team members were: Cannonball, a shy teen from Kentucky who could turn himself into a living cannonball when he began to fly, which he termed "blasting" because he would leave an energy trail when he flew (he would repeatedly remind everyone that he was "nigh invulnerable when I'm blastin'"); Karma, a Vietnamese teen who could possess people (who had been originally introduced in an old *Marvel Team-Up* story by Claremont and Frank Miller); Psyche (soon referred to mostly by her real name, Dani Moonstar), a Native American teen who could force people to see their greatest fears; Sunspot, a rich and spoiled Brazilian teen who used solar energy to gain super strength; and

Top Five Greatest Solo Wolverine Stories

5. *Wolverine #10* "24 Hours"
   Chris Claremont, John Buscema, and Bill Sienkiewicz reveal that Sabretooth has been tormenting Wolverine every year on Wolverine's birthday for as far back as Wolverine can remember, including one particularly tragic day when Wolverine finally had enough.

4. *Origin #1–6*
   Paul Jenkins, Bill Jemas, Joe Quesada, Andy Kubert, and Richard Isanove delivered a sprawling epic that saw a little privileged boy turn into a man under the most horrible of situations.

3. *Wolverine #66–72, Giant Size Old Man Logan #1* "Old Man Logan"
   In a bleak future, Wolverine is dead and only Logan has survived. Can he find his inner hero before it is too late? That's the question that Mark Millar, Steve McNiven, and Dexter Vines asked.

2. *Marvel Comics Presents #72–84* "Weapon X"
   Barry Windsor-Smith unveiled the story of how Wolverine gained his adamantium skeleton and claws in a brilliant riff on a sort of horror film, as the experiment turns on his tormentors.

1. *Wolverine #1–4*
   Chris Claremont, Frank Miller, and Joe Rubinstein completely redefined Wolverine as a samurai in this historic series that saw Wolverine get his first solo series.

Wolfsbane, an extremely reserved young Scottish girl, raised by an abusive preacher, who could turn into a wolf.

Uncanny X-Men was so popular that *New Mutants* was an instant success, quickly becoming Marvel's second-highest-selling book behind only *Uncanny X-Men*. A year or so into the book's run, Claremont decided to change things up when the series added Bill Sienkiewicz to the creative team. Sienkiewicz was a popular artist who used to draw like Neal Adams. As the years went by, though, Sienkiewicz began to experiment with his art and he developed a brilliant, unconventional style that involved a lot of mixed media art in his work. His work was much darker than the earlier artists on the series, so Claremont made the stories darker to match. The young teens were soon put through quite the wringer.

Five years into the book, Claremont was launching two new X-Men spinoff series, *Wolverine* and *Excalibur*. He left *New Mutants* temporarily to his longtime former editor, Louise Simonson (who had edited *New Mutants* for its first couple of years), but he ended up deciding not to return to the series. By this point in time, Magneto had been named the Headmaster of Xavier's and his relationship with the New Mutants was not a good one. They routinely disobeyed his orders and went on missions against his wishes. Then the team decided to leave Xavier's for good and go out on their own. By this time, they had merged with a team of young heroes from Simonson's *X-Factor* run called the X-Terminators.

The mentor-less New Mutants soon found themselves with a new leader when they ran into the mutant mercenary known as Cable. Cable debuted in *New Mutants #87*, which was one issue after Rob Liefeld joined the series as the new artist. The young artist's dynamic art style soon began to draw a lot more attention to the series, and soon Liefeld would be coplotting the series with Simonson. With *New Mutants #98*, Liefeld took over the main plotting duties from Simonson, with Fabian Nicieza coming on board as the new scripter over Liefeld's plots.

By this time, it was clear that Liefeld planned to take the book in a dramatically different direction. Slowly but surely, members of the team were leaving the book, through death or some other means. Sunspot, Dani Moonstar, Wolfsbane, and most of the X-Terminators all left the book. Of the rather large cast of characters in the book when Liefeld joined in *New Mutants #86*, the only two members of the team who made it to the end of the series were Cannonball and Boom-Boom (one of the X-Terminators). Liefeld introduced a few new members and then turned the New Mutants into X-Force.

The original New Mutants crew later reformed as a team years later, when they were all now young adults and a whole other generation of mutants had come and gone. The New Mutants are set to have their own film adaptation released in 2018.

36 Joss Whedon/John Cassaday

When Grant Morrison left the X-Men, he left very big shoes to fill. Luckily for Marvel, they were able to replace Morrison with a writer who was actually much more famous than Morrison…just not in terms of being a comic book writer. Joss Whedon came from a sceenwriting family (his father was a successful screenwriter and producer) and by the mid-1990s, he was a successful screenwriter himself, although mostly working as a "ghostwriter," someone who would be hired to re-write a script to improve it but not get credit in the end. Whedon was especially known for his dialogue, so he was often hired to make the dialogue in a film better (one of his most notable ghostwriting assignments was *Toy Story*). He famously added some dialogue for the first X-Men film. Anyhow, while not working in film, he was busy creating one of the most iconic fantasy series of the 1990s with *Buffy the Vampire Slayer*, a clever twist on the horror genre where the beautiful cheerleader-looking girl is actually the hero of the story.

Chris Claremont's X-Men work was a clear influence on Whedon's *Buffy* and when Whedon agreed to take over from Morrison as the main X-Men writer (Marvel would launch a new series, *Astonishing X-Men*, for Whedon, rather than literally have him take over from Morrison on *New X-Men*), he wore his influences on his sleeve. He brought Kitty Pryde back to the X-Men and made constant references to past X-Men story lines.

Whedon was joined on *Astonishing X-Men* by John Cassaday, an artist who rose to prominence on his long run on *Planetary* with writer Warren Ellis. In that series, a group of interdimensional archaeologists investigate unusual phenomena. Each of these unusual phenomena, of course, are thinly veiled versions of notable pop culture figures, like Doc Savage, the Hulk, Lone Ranger, Tarzan, etc. Cassaday had to handle a whole pile of different styles and designs and did so smoothly. His realistic artwork was especially great for character-driven work, as he was really good with character's expressions.

In Whedon and Cassaday's first arc, they introduced a possible cure for being a mutant. That same arc revealed that Colossus had not really died back when he cured the Legacy Virus. Colossus reunited with the X-Men as they took down the alien who had faked Colossus' death and kidnapped him (and used the Legacy cure to come up with a mutant cure).

In their second arc, they revealed that the X-Men's Danger Room was now a sentient being and wanted revenge on the X-Men—and especially Charles Xavier—for keeping it captive for so many years. In their third arc, they had Emma Frost seemingly rejoin the Hellfire Club and turn on the rest of the X-Men (memorably reverting Wolverine's mentality to what it had been before he learned of his mutant powers, which was that of a posh young child). Kitty Pryde, who had never trusted Emma Frost's hero turn, got to do her own version of Wolverine's classic "You had your chance. Now it's my turn!" pose from *X-Men #132,* when Emma Frost forced her to phase through to the caverns below the X-Mansion.

Finally, Whedon and Cassaday finished out their run by taking the team into outer space to face off against the aliens who had captured Colossus so long ago because they believed that he was destined to destroy their planet. As it turned out, they had a plot to destroy Earth and it involved a giant bullet. Kitty seemingly sacrificed herself by phasing the entire bullet through Earth, but in the process she was trapped on a giant bullet hurtling through space without any chance of stopping.

What was so notable about *Astonishing X-Men*, other than the content in the comics, of course, was the fact that Whedon and Cassaday were the only creative team on the entire series. Almost no comic book series have the same creative team on the entire run anymore. Granted, to achieve this effect, *Astonishing X-Men* had to go on a very gradual release schedule (with practically a year for the final couple of issues to come out), but still.

Whedon and Cassaday also introduced the alien-protective branch of SHIELD, led by Abigail Brand, called SWORD. SWORD has become a major part of the Marvel Universe and might even be adapted into the *Agents of SHIELD* TV series in the future, which would bring everything full circle for Joss Whedon.

37 Apocalypse

In their last story arc as the creative team on *X-Factor*, Bob Layton and Jackson Guice introduced a new evil mutant team called the Alliance of Evil. They fought against X-Factor and kept referring to their mysterious master. Layton's original plan was for their mysterious new leader to be a revamped version of the old Daredevil villain, the Owl (having been mutated so much that he barely resembled his original design).

However, before he could get a chance to make this revelation, *X-Factor* editor Bob Harras removed Layton from the series. Harras then hired former *X-Men* and *New Mutants* editor Louise Simonson to take over the series. She now had to finish Layton's story line. She had Guice redraw the silhouette of the villain at the end of *X-Factor #5,* and in *X-Factor #6* we met the actual leader of the Alliance of Evil—Apocalypse! Apocalypse's whole deal was the idea of natural selection. He wanted to test mutantkind to see who were the most fit to rule the world.

With Apocalypse now introduced, Simonson had more time to think about the character and she had him slowly make guest appearances working behind the scenes in X-Factor (by this point, Simonson had begun working on the series with her husband, Walter Simonson, who took over from Guice on art duties on the book, paired with inker Bob Wiacek). Apocalypse recruited a trio of mutants and genetically manipulated them to some unknown result. Meanwhile, X-Factor member Angel had tragically lost his wings after they were seriously injured during the "Mutant Massacre." Angel seemingly then killed himself. However, it was soon revealed that those three mutants had been given new abilities to become three of Apocalypse's Four Horsemen—the fourth Horseman, Death, turned out to be Angel, who Apocalypse had now given deadly metal wings.

It was at this point that we first learned that Apocalypse had actually been around since Ancient Egypt and that he might be the oldest living mutant on Earth (his real name is En Sabah Nur). He often entered periods of long hibernation and only came out of his hibernation when something interesting was going on in the world. This time around, it was the rise of the modern mutant race that drew Apocalypse out of the shadows and into conflict with X-Factor. The team eventually broke Angel free of Apocalypse's programming, with Angel keeping the metal wings and renaming himself Archangel.

Apocalypse became X-Factor's most notable foe and the team clashed with the ancient mutant again in a story where Apocalypse infected Cyclops' son with a techno-organic virus with no known cure in our time. Therefore, to save his life, Cyclops sent his son into the future to have his virus cured. The baby grew up to become Cable, who was Apocalypse's greatest foe in the future. (A healthy clone of Cable was captured by Apocalypse, who planned on taking over that body when his current one got too old. The clone eventually became Stryfe, head of the Mutant Liberation Front.)

After the original X-Factor team merged back into the X-Men, Apocalypse followed them to become a general X-Men villain. He has tangled with the X-Men many times over the years, with one of his most famous clashes being in the story line, "The Twelve," where 12 mutants who were apparently designed to destroy Apocalypse were instead part of a plot by Apocalypse to gain a new, more powerful host for his consciousness. After failing to take over the body of X-Man, a refuge from an alternate reality where Apocalypse ruled the world, Apocalypse ended up possessing Cyclops. Eventually, Jean Grey and Cable forced Apocalypse out of

Cyclops' body as well, seemingly killing Apocalypse. He was resurrected and was killed a few other times.

Eventually, a group of worshipers of Apocalypse decided to start over with a cloned child version of Apocalypse. A newly formed version of X-Force encountered the child and debated whether it was fair to kill the child before it actually did anything. In the end, Fantomex (of X-Force) shot and killed the child. Fantomex later cloned the child and then tried to raise him in an idyllic virtual reality world, trying to prove whether he made the right decision to kill the original clone (was nature more important than nurture?). The clone grew up to be a heroic member of the X-Men by the name of Genesis (of course, Genesis continues to be haunted by fears of turning evil).

What's amusingly fascinating about Apocalypse is that he is obsessed with the idea of survival of the fittest for mutants (and humans, too) but he tries to defeat the X-Men all the time and he never wins—so are we even sure that Apocalypse is one of the fittest at this point?

38 The X-Over

Comic books had been having crossovers ever since the 1940s, when a fight between Namor and the Human Torch spilled into each of their respective features in *Marvel Mystery Comics*. Then Otto Binder did the first true modern crossover with the epic "Monster Society of Evil" event in the pages of all of the Captain Marvel comic book series in the mid-1940s. (Binder was the writer on all of them, so it was easy for him to coordinate it all.) However, for the most part, comic book crossovers were a rarity. Batman and Superman only shared a handful of panels in a few issues of *All-Star Comics* despite literally sharing a comic book series for over a decade. Their first true crossover was a major event.

When Marvel Comics debuted in the 1960s, Stan Lee essentially invented the idea of a continual shared comic book universe. Again, the fact that Lee was the writer (or cowriter) for more or less every Marvel Comic title made it easier for Lee to have, say, a *Daredevil* issue lead into a *Fantastic Four* issue. Even after Lee stopped writing comics regularly, it was a regular occurrence for other writers to cross their titles over. Steve Englehart famously crossed over two titles that he was writing in the early 1970s, *Avengers* and *Defenders*, for a multi-part crossover called "The Avengers/Defenders War." However, even something as elaborate as "The Avengers/Defenders War" was still only a two-book crossover. Even as the 1980s began to see larger intracompany crossover events like "Marvel Super Heroes Secret Wars" and "Crisis on Infinite Earths," these were not interconnected stories. The comic book world, then, changed forever (for better or for worse) with the "Mutant Massacre."

In 1986, *Uncanny X-Men* and *New Mutants* were written by Chris Claremont. His longtime former *X-Men* and *New Mutants* editor, Louise Simonson, was writing *X-Factor*. She was also writing *Power Pack*, a series about four young siblings who had superpowers (their last name was Power, naturally). Meanwhile, Simonson's husband, Walter Simonson (Louise Simonson edited under her previous married name, Louise Jones, and wrote comics under her current married name), was drawing *X-Factor* and also writing *Thor*.

The three of them (Claremont and the Simonsons) were close friends. Claremont had an upcoming story that involved a major turning point in the history of the X-Men, with two longtime members (Nightcrawler and Kitty Pryde) being written out and new members (Psylocke, Dazzler, and Longshot) joining the team. Claremont and the Simonsons decided to celebrate this major event by trying a unique story approach where each of them would tell the same basic story, just from different perspectives.

Uncanny X-Men told the main event. The evil Marauders entered the tunnels that contained the sewer-dwelling Morlocks and began slaughtering them. When the X-Men showed up to save the Morlocks, they suffered heavy losses, as well. In *New Mutants*, Magneto tried to protect his younger charges from the events of the Massacre, while X-Factor, Thor, and Power Pack all encountered the Marauders as well (with Angel of X-Factor getting hurt so badly that he lost his wings). All of the titles could be read without the others, but together they told a massive story.

The event was a gigantic sales success, so Marvel insisted that they do another one the following year. "Fall of the Mutants" had a similar approach to "Mutant Massacre," with *Uncanny X-Men*, *New Mutants*, and *X-Factor* each telling parallel stories with similar themes that did not actually overlap. (In *Uncanny X-Men*, the X-Men are seemingly killed saving the world, while in *New Mutants*, one of the team members is killed for real, and in *X-Factor*, Angel is remade as Death of Apocalypse's Four Horsemen.)

Things were so successful that the next X-Men crossover, "Inferno," spread throughout the Marvel Universe, with multiple other titles tying in to the event. This time around, *Uncanny X-Men* and *X-Factor* were one continuous story, with Claremont and Simonson cowriting the event. The next event, "The X-Tinction Agenda," saw, for the first time, all three titles (*Uncanny X-Men*, *X-Factor*, and *New Mutants*) tell one continuous crossover event. (Chapter 1 was in one book, Chapter 2 in another, and on and on.)

By now, massive crossovers were commonplace in comic books, but the X-Universe still took it one step further with 1992's

"X-Cutioner's Song," which was a massive 17-part crossover event between four different titles (*Uncanny X-Men*, *X-Men*, *X-Force*, and *X-Factor*) that told one continuous story (amusingly, this led to an issue of *X-Factor* that featured none of their regular characters in the issue). That was it for the mega-crossover event for over a decade, until "Messiah CompleX" and "Second Coming" brought the tradition back in 2007 and 2010, respectively.

39 Deadpool

Very often, you will hear people talk about how a character was a surprise success. Deadpool, on the other hand, is an unusual case of a character being an instant success but still being somewhat of a surprise success as well!

Deadpool debuted in 1990's *New Mutants #98* (by Rob Liefeld and Fabian Nicieza). He owed his origins, oddly enough, to Todd McFarlane's run on Spider-Man. McFarlane and Liefeld were such good friends that they had a brotherly bond. However, it was very much a big brother/little brother relationship, with the older McFarlane being the big brother who would often give his little brother a hard time. When McFarlane was working on his best-selling *Spider-Man* series, Liefeld was working on *New Mutants*, a book with a large cast of characters. McFarlane joked that he had it easy, since he didn't even have to draw Spider-Man's face, since he wore a full face mask, while Liefeld had to draw multiple faces each issue! Thus, Liefeld decided to introduce a character with a full face mask, just like Spider-Man. In fact, Spider-Man was even more of an influence, as Liefeld intended for Deadpool to be sort of

Ryan Reynolds (as Wade Wilson/Deadpool), Stefan Kapicic (as Colossus), and Brianna Hildebraand (as Ellie Phimister/Negasonic Teenage Warhead) in 2016's surprise smash hit Deadpool. (Twentieth Century Fox Film Corporation/ Photofest)

an evil version of Spider-Man—a wisecracking character who just happened to be a bad guy.

Deadpool showed up as a mercenary sent to capture Cable, the new leader of the New Mutants. He was defeated in the issue by Cable's old friend, Domino, who arrived in that issue to join up with the new team Cable was forming. The character was so well received that when the book ended with *New Mutants #100* and relaunched as *X-Force #1*, *New Mutants/X-Force* editor Bob Harras insisted that they get Deadpool back into the series as soon as they could. So Liefeld and Nicieza brought him back in *X-Force #2*, but since *X-Force #1* was already written, they had no way to get

Deadpool in there, so they added a spotlight page on Deadpool in *X-Force #1*.

Deadpool continued to be a prominent guest star in *X-Force* and other titles for the next few years, including starring in a pair of miniseries. However, after Liefeld and Nicieza had both moved on from *X-Force*, Deadpool fell by the wayside for a few years. When he was given his own ongoing series in 1997 by Joe Kelly and Ed McGuinness, it was a big surprise.

The "little book that could" revamped the character, with Kelly making Deadpool more of a humor-driven book, including, most notably, Deadpool breaking the fourth wall a number of times. This included an iconic 11th issue where Deadpool traveled back in time…to a 1966 issue of *Amazing Spider-Man* (Kelly and artist Pete Woods spent the issue mocking the now outdated references in the Steve Ditko/Stan Lee issue). However, while the series was critically acclaimed, it was not a big sales success (but it had loyal fans, which played a role later on). It was canceled twice during Kelly's tenure, once after issue *#25* and once after issue *#33*. Luckily, fan outrage led to it getting uncanceled both times. Kelly remained the first time, but the second time around he left the book. That series lasted until 2002.

Nicieza returned to the character in 2004 with a series teaming up Deadpool with his old nemesis Cable, in *Cable/Deadpool*. Nicieza ramped up the humor, especially the breaking the fourth wall aspect of the series (each issue would open with Deadpool talking directly to the reader). That series ended in early 2008 and it seemed like Deadpool just wasn't working as a character.

Then Daniel Way changed everything in late 2008 when he had Deadpool guest star in an arc in *Wolverine: Origins*. Up until this point, Deadpool was appearing strictly in the comic book equivalent to PG and PG-13 stories. *Wolverine: Origins*, on the other hand, was the comic book equivalent of an R-Rated film and the darker humor really served Deadpool well. The guest appearance led to Way soon writing a new *Deadpool* ongoing series in 2009 that was R-rated. Deadpool hasn't had a title canceled since Way's new take debuted.

The R-rated take on Deadpool led to a 2016 film adaptation starring Ryan Reynolds (who had appeared as a horribly misguided version of Deadpool in *X-Men Origins: Wolverine* back in 2009) that fully embraced the R-rating and turned the film industry on its ear by becoming a surprise blockbuster. Its success has opened up the R-rating for superhero movies in the future (the next Wolverine film, 2016's *Logan*, became the first Wolverine film to be rated R). Deadpool is set to appear in a series of upcoming films and is now one of Marvel's most famous characters.

40 The Original X-Factor

As the X-Men grew in popularity, one of Chris Claremont's biggest worries was that other comic book writers would want to use the members of the X-Men that Claremont was not actively using in *Uncanny X-Men* at the time. Claremont wanted to keep the X-Men characters under his control. He always intended on working characters in and out of the book. However, even though Claremont had delivered the *New Mutants* in 1983 as the first *X-Men* spinoff, sales were so strong that Marvel wanted a second spinoff. Claremont protested the addition of another spinoff, so Marvel just moved forward without Claremont's involvement.

At the time, the status of the original five members of the X-Men were as follows: Jean Grey was dead; Cyclops had recently been pushed off the X-Men to go be in Alaska with his new wife, Madelyne Pryor, and their new baby; and Iceman, Angel, and Beast were teammates in a revamped Defenders team in *New Defenders*. Therefore, Marvel saw a perfect opportunity to bring the original X-Men together in a new series. The issue, though, was what to

Top Five Oddest Cases of X-Men Characters Retroactively Knowing Each Other

5. Banshee/Deadpool
Since he was older than the other All-New, All-Different X-Men and had fewer stories written about his past than the others, Banshee was a go-to character when you wanted to reveal that, oh yeah, he totally knew Deadpool back in the day.

4. Cable/Sunfire
When Cable traveled from the future, he arrived a number of years earlier than necessary, so he spent the remaining time as a mercenary and seemed to run into everyone, including seemingly random mutants like the Japanese mutant Sunfire.

3. Sage/Professor X
For years, the hero who would become known as Sage was better known as just Tessa, the assistant to Sebastian Shaw, head of the Hellfire Club. Then Claremont revealed that she had been undercover this whole time and she actually met Xavier before any of the other original members of the X-Men.

2. Cable/Rogue
In the world of coincidences, Cable showing up in the past at just the right time to cut off a mob after Rogue following the first manifestation of her powers (while kissing the boy next door, absorbing his personality, and putting him into a coma) is pretty high up there.

1. Banshee/Omega Red
As noted, Banshee's age made it easier for him to tie in with other older characters, but whoever thought it made sense to tie in the Irish hero with the origins of the Russian mutant assassin (and later Wolverine rogue), Omega Red, was probably not thinking straight.

do with the fifth spot? After Bob Layton and Jackson Guice were hired to create the spinoff, the plan was for Dazzler (who had not yet joined the X-Men) to be the fifth member of the team. Instead, a unique plot idea changed everything.

The idea was actually coined by a fan named Kurt Busiek (who was just transitioning into comic book writing at the time), who had told the idea to Roger Stern at a comic book convention around the end of "The Dark Phoenix Saga" in 1980. Stern told John Byrne the idea and when Byrne heard about the new X-Men spinoff using the original members of the X-Men, he passed the idea along to editorial.

The idea? Reveal that Jean Grey never actually died in "The Dark Phoenix Saga." Show that the Phoenix Force cut a deal off-panel in *X-Men #100* and the deal was that the Phoenix Force would take Jean's place and Jean would go into suspended animation. Then the Phoenix, inspired by Jean's memories, would go on to sacrifice itself in "The Dark Phoenix Saga," leaving the real Jean hidden somewhere. Marvel loved the idea, and in a crossover involving Stern's *Avengers* and Byrne's *Fantastic Four*, the Avengers and the Fantastic Four would team up to discover the very-much-alive Jean Grey in a cocoon at the bottom of the bay that the Phoenix had popped up out of way back in *X-Men #101*.

Chris Claremont, naturally, was aghast at the idea of his famous story line being undermined with the launch of a new series he didn't want to exist in the first place. At the last moment, he pitched an idea to Marvel to have Jean Grey's sister, Sara, be the fifth member instead. It was too late. As a last-minute concession, Claremont was allowed to rewrite large pieces of *Fantastic Four #287* (which introduced the now-alive Jean Grey) to at least fit in with Claremont's view of how the Phoenix Force worked.

The original five members of the X-Men reunited in *X-Factor #1* (by Bob Layton and Jackson Guice), as they came together to celebrate Jean's seeming return from the dead. The trick, though, is that Jean's love of her life, Cyclops, was now married with a kid. So, in another move that Claremont hated, Cyclops ditched his wife and child to go be with Jean and his friends. Magneto had just become the new headmaster of Xavier's, so they decided not to return Jean to the X-Men. Instead, they formed a new team called X-Factor. The idea was that they would play off of anti-mutant hysteria by pretending to be mutant hunters. They would charge people to hunt down mutants, but then they would take in the mutants that they "hunted down" and train them how to better use their powers. It was an odd setup that would not last for long.

After just five issues, Layton was replaced by Louise Simonson, who had been Claremont's editor on *Uncanny X-Men* and *New Mutants*. She quickly revealed that the anti-mutant idea was a plot designed by Angel's business manager, Cameron Hodge, who turned out to be an evil mutant hater. X-Factor broke free of the constraints of their "mutant hunting" agenda and just began to out-right train a new generation of mutants (sort of like a counterpoint to the New Mutants). Once that was out of the way, however, it was increasingly difficult to explain why they didn't team up with the X-Men again, and eventually, after over five years, that's precisely what happened, as X-Factor merged with the X-Men. The series continued with a new cast, who used the X-Factor name as a government-sponsored mutant strike force.

41 Sabretooth

It is very common for characters to retroactively find themselves connected to each other. Heck, those retroactive connections are very much a staple of the X-Men line of comic books. However, it is far less common to have a situation that existed with Sabretooth. Introduced in 1977's *Iron Fist #14* (by Chris Claremont and John Byrne), Sabretooth was invented by Claremont and Byrne specifically to have a connection to Wolverine...and yet the two characters did not meet until 1986!

When the character first showed up as an assassin who Iron Fist has to stop, the intent was for Sabretooth to eventually be revealed as Wolverine's father. In fact, while working on Iron Fist, Byrne had taken a go at designing what Wolverine looked like under his face mask (he did not take off his mask in his *Incredible Hulk* appearances or his first five *X-Men* appearances). As it turned out, Dave Cockrum had just come up with what Wolverine looked like without his mask (it appeared in his sixth *X-Men* appearance, in *X-Men #98*), so Byrne's facial design was instead used for Sabretooth. When Byrne then took over art duties (and then coplotting duties) on *Uncanny X-Men*, he and Claremont planned on Wolverine and Sabretooth having a confrontation where Sabretooth would kill Wolverine's fiancée, Mariko, and then Wolverine would be forced to kill his own father.

Byrne left the book before that plot could be implemented, and instead, Sabretooth was brought back to the pages of *Power Man and Iron Fist* (Power Man and Iron Fist's series merged with each other and became a team-up book featuring the two disparate heroes) as a recurring foe, forming a partnership with a villain called the Constrictor. Sabretooth's reputation as a villain took repeated hits during his appearances in *Power Man and Iron Fist* and the ultimate blow was when he guest starred in *Spectacular Spider-Man* and was beaten nearly to death by the Black Cat!

Claremont finally got to bring Sabretooth over to the pages of *Uncanny X-Men* with the "Mutant Massacre," where Sabretooth and a team of villains called the Marauders decided to slaughter the sewer-dwelling mutants known as the Morlocks under the orders of the mysterious Minster Sinister. The X-Men showed up to stop them and Wolverine and Sabretooth had two epic battles with each other.

We soon discovered that Wolverine and Sabretooth had some sort of strange connection to each other. In *Wolverine #10* (by Chris Claremont, John Buscema, and Bill Sienkiewicz), we learned that Sabretooth shows up on all of Wolverine's birthdays to beat him up, just to show him that he is stronger than Wolverine. During one of those occasions, he killed Wolverine's lover, Silver Fox, just to show that he could do it. These, of course, were more hints that Sabretooth was meant to be Wolverine's father.

You might be confused as to how Sabretooth could defeat Wolverine so easily while having trouble with Power Man, Iron Fist, and Black Cat. Claremont had an answer all ready to go for that, but he never got a chance to use it in a regular Marvel Comic book story. He planned that the weaker versions of Sabretooth were clones designed by Mister Sinister and the real Sabretooth did not make his debut until the "Mutant Massacre."

Over time, like many of Claremont's other intended plots, other writers went in a different direction. In a story line in the pages of *Wolverine* toward the end of Claremont's stint on *Uncanny X-Men*, it was revealed via a SHIELD DNA test that Sabretooth was not Wolverine's father.

The two characters continued to have a strong connection, however, especially when it was revealed that the two used to work as secret agents together along with a few other veterans of the Weapon X program. As it turned out, they had even formed a proto-version of the X-Men at one point.

During one memorable story line, Sabretooth was captured by the X-Men and kept prisoner in the X-Mansion, as Professor X believed that it was possible to rehabilitate Sabretooth. Wolverine believed otherwise and he attacked Sabretooth and finally got the drop on him and popped his claw through Sabretooth's brain. Sabretooth survived, but seemingly was now brain damaged and harmless. That, of course, was a ploy. He nearly killed Psylocke when he made his escape from the X-Mansion.

Years later, a magical spell "inverted" the major Marvel heroes and villains, turning good characters evil and evil characters good. Sabretooth was one of the characters affected by the spell, but was one of only a few characters who remained inverted when everyone else was cured. The now-good Sabretooth joined the Uncanny Avengers and then a Magneto-led X-Men team.

Beast

In recent years, it has become more in vogue for comic book heroes to serve on multiple superhero teams (for a time there, Wolverine was a member of two Avengers teams, two X-Men teams, and the leader of X-Force). For years, though, the path that Beast took was quite unusual, as he was a prominent member of three of Marvel's most famous superhero teams—the X-Men, the Avengers, and the Defenders.

Hank McCoy began his comic book career as one of the five original members of the X-Men. His giant hands and feet were part of his mutant ability to essentially be superhumanly faster, stronger, and more agile than a normal person. When he was first introduced, though, that pretty much was all of his character traits—that he looked like a beast and had powers like a beast and was named the Beast. A few issues into the *X-Men* series, though, Stan Lee came up with the idea to play the Beast against type. This was done by revealing that the Beast was actually a genius. He was both the brains of the X-Men and the brawn of the X-Men!

When the X-Men ceased coming out with new adventures in 1970, Beast was the first member of the team to get his own solo series. On Roy Thomas' direction, Gerry Conway introduced a Beast feature in *Amazing Adventures #11*, where Beast was transformed into a werewolf-looking creature. That look evolved into a blue-furred creature in the rest of the short-lived feature, which was soon taken over by Steve Englehart, in his first Marvel Comics regular writing assignment. The Beast was distraught over no longer appearing human.

Englehart then took over one of Marvel's biggest titles, *The Avengers*, and he eventually brought the Beast over to join the Avengers (oddly enough, Beast did not actually join the Avengers until after *Giant-Size X-Men #1*). Englehart had the Beast return to his wisecracking X-Men days, while still continuing to mope over his lot in life. It was not until Jim Shooter took over the series that Beast had a moment of realization that, for all of his moping, he was now a member of the most famous superhero teams in the world and where he saw a monster, everyone else saw a superstar hero. He then embraced his blue-furred self and his newfound fame.

Eventually, though, Beast felt that he was not living up to his potential with the Avengers, where he was always destined to be the guy in the background. He was never going to be the smartest guy on the team (not with Tony Stark on the team) and he was never going to be the leader of the team (not with Captain America on the team) so he instead joined the Defenders, where he became the leader of the odd superhero team (that, up until this point, was more of a hang-out group that wandered into trouble than a traditional superhero team). Beast then recruited two of his old X-Men teammates, Angel and Iceman, and they formed a new version of the Defenders.

That team broke up just in time for Jean Grey to turn out to be alive and the original X-Men members formed a new team called X-Factor. They initially pretended that they were mutant hunters. The problem with having a famous blue-furred mutant Avenger as a "mutant-hunter" was solved when Beast was returned to his human form in Bob Layton's first arc on the series. Layton was soon replaced by Louise Simonson, who began a long subplot that resolved itself with the Beast returning to his blue-furry self.

After X-Factor merged back into the X-Men, Beast became one of the most prominent members of the X-Men, as he was the go-to scientist character in the series. When mutants began to contract a deadly virus for mutants known as the Legacy Virus, Beast went to work on the disease and actually ended up curing it!

Soon after, a secondary mutation saw Beast transform again into a feline-style monster, patterned after the Beast from the 1946 Jean Cocteau film adaptation of *Beauty and the Beast*. Beast now had to struggle just to learn how to pick up a pen again. He kept worrying whether he would continue to mutate into a mindless Beast.

More recently, the Beast had been working with the Inhumans to come up with a cure for M-Pox, a deadly disease for mutants that was caused by exposure to the Terrigen Mists on Earth. (The Terrigen Mists are the special chemical reaction that gives Inhumans their abilities—their former leader, Black Bolt, had exposed the world to the Mists rather than let the evil Thanos get his hands on the Terrigen Mists.) After he failed, the X-Men went to war with the Inhumans.

43 Must Read: "Age of Apocalypse"

In the early 1990s, there was a magazine devoted to comics that was called *Wizard: The Magazine for Comics*. *Wizard* soon became so popular that it sold better than most of the comic books that it wrote about within its pages. In 1994, its popularity helped Marvel with some stealth advertisement. Rumors kept popping up in *Wizard* that Marvel planned to cancel all of the titles in their X-Men line, which had increased at the time to a staggering *eight* titles (*Uncanny X-Men, X-Men, X-Factor, X-Force, Excalibur, Cable, Wolverine,* and *Generation X*). This was before the internet was in widespread use for comic book news, so people did not know all of the plans for a comic book line eight months in advance. So when "The Age of Apocalypse" began, the *Wizard* articles helped fans believe that what they were seeing was going to be for real and what they were seeing were every X-Men comic coming to a close at the same time!

It all started when Professor X's son, Legion, who suffered from mental illness, used his astonishing psionic powers to actually travel back in time to when Charles Xavier and Erik Lensherr were young men and still good friends. Legion planned on killing Lensherr to save Legion's father, Xavier, from ever having to deal with Magneto in the future, with the (deranged) thought process being that without Magneto to fight against, Xavier would have had time to spend with Legion as a boy.

A handful of X-Men ended up getting sucked into the past with him (Storm, Psylocke, Iceman, and Bishop). The X-Men fought against Legion to keep him from killing Lensherr, but he was ultimately too powerful for them. He was all set to kill Lensherr when the Xavier from the past stepped in front of the deadly blast meant for Lensherr. Xavier died 20 years in the past, but more importantly, the epic battle between Legion and the X-Men and Xavier and Lensherr ended up waking Apocalypse out of his hibernation years before he was originally set to wake up. Thus, Apocalypse was able to conquer the world before superheroes ever started showing up on Earth. Lensherr, though, promised his dying friend that he would take over his dream in his honor.

Thus, every X-Men title was "canceled" and replaced with a new book set in an altered reality where Apocalypse ruled the world and the only real threat to his control was a rogue group of heroes known as the X-Men, led by Magneto. *Uncanny X-Men* became *Astonishing X-Men*, *X-Men* became *Amazing X-Men*, *X-Factor* became *Factor X*, *X-Force* became *Gambit and the X-Ternals*, *Excalibur* became *X-Calibure*, *Cable* became *X-Man*, *Wolverine* became *Weapon X*, and *Generation X* became *Generation Next*.

While many of the original X-Men were still X-Men in this new reality, there were a few notable changes. Cyclops, Havok, and Beast all served Mister Sinister, one of Apocalypse's most loyal lieutenants, and former X-Men foes Exodus, Changeling, and Sabretooth were members of the X-Men. Sabretooth, in particular, was a noble figure who had a relationship with the young mutant hero known as Blink (who had died in her first story in the original Marvel continuity) that was very similar to Wolverine and Kitty Pryde's relationship in the original continuity. Wolverine was around, but was called Weapon X and had only one hand, as Cyclops had blasted the other one off. Magneto and Rogue were married and had a young son.

Since Bishop was a time traveler from the future whose whole reason to traveling to the present had been erased by Legion's accidental murder of Xavier, he managed to survive the changeover as a sort of "man out of time." He explained to Magneto and the X-Men that what they needed to do was find and fix the M'Kraan Crystal, the crystal that controlled all reality. It had been broken by Legion's murder of Xavier and Bishop believed that he could use it to return to the past to prevent Legion from doing the act. So while Magneto and the X-Men were helping him on this mission, they were also trying to break down a force field around Apocalypse's headquarters. The issue is that the remaining humans still on Earth had decided that when the force field went down, they were going to drop all of their nukes on the city, killing Apocalypse and the X-Men. So time was of the essence.

Luckily, Bishop succeeded on his mission and seemingly killed Legion in the past. However, before he could do so, a few people from this altered reality ended up in the regular Marvel Universe (namely the evil version of Beast, a villainous geneticist known as Sugar Man, the version of Cable from this altered reality called X-Man, and one of Apocalypse's deadliest soldiers, known as Holocaust.

44 The Danger Room

In the early days of the X-Men, there really was not a whole lot to make the book stand out. Oh, sure, there was the novelty of the fact that they were all mutants instead of getting their powers from cosmic rays, Gamma bombs, or radioactive spiders, but other than a simpler origin story, being mutants was not as big of a deal back in the early days. No, the two things that really stood out early on were Magneto, who was one of the top villains of the era, and the Danger Room.

The Danger Room was the X-Men's training center (introduced in *X-Men #2*). There really was not anything like it in comics when it was introduced. The closest approximations would be Superman's Fortress of Solitude, the Fantastic Four's Baxter Building, and the Flash's Flash Museum, none of which are really all that similar. The idea of a futuristic place where heroes could go to train themselves was a novel concept by Jack Kirby and Stan Lee and they milked it a lot early on in the series (sometimes it seemed almost as if there were so many training scenes because Kirby and Lee didn't know what else to do with the X-Men).

When the All-New, All-Different X-Men debuted, the Danger Room remained, only it was now a lot more high tech, with lasers and robots pushing the X-Men to their highest levels. One of the common plot points back then (and in future stories as well) would be that the Danger Room's safety settings were accidentally turned off. The X-Men really did not have a very good system for safety since it seemed like the safety settings would get turned off constantly. This would lead to the X-Men suddenly having to prove themselves against obstacles with weapons set to "kill" instead of "stun."

After the X-Mansion was destroyed in the early 1980s (one of the many times that the X-Mansion was destroyed over the years), Professor Xavier rebuilt it for his new students (the New Mutants), only he now incorporated alien technology from the Shi'ar Empire into the Danger Room (being the consort of the Shi'ar Empress has its benefits). Debuting in an early issue of *New Mutants*, the Danger Room now used holographic technology (mixed with force fields so that the holograms would be solid) to be able to replicate any environment on Earth or other planets (heck, it could even create fictional landscapes). Of course, being the Danger Room, its' very first appearance in its new form left the New Mutants stranded in the room with the safety settings accidentally turned off.

The Danger Room would continue to be a mainstay of X-Men comics over the years, although as time went on, a little bit of the novelty wore off as the concept of a high-tech training center was now omnipresent in superhero comic books. Every superhero team had their own. However, it was not too late for the Danger Room to still surprise fans!

In the second story arc on Joss Whedon and John Cassaday's *Astonishing X-Men* series, titled (appropriately enough) "Danger," two young mutants were inside of the Danger Room when one of them, a recently de-powered mutant named Wing, was tricked by the Danger Room into jumping off a holographic cliff, killing himself. As it turned out, the Danger Room was sentient! The first death within the Danger Room triggered a procedure that allowed the consciousness of the Danger Room to actually escape within a robotic body.

The X-Men fought against the Danger Room, who continued to be able to project detailed holograms to fool them. However, it continued to do everything it could to not actually kill anyone. It was then revealed that Professor X had discovered that the Danger Room was sentient soon after the Shi'ar technology caused it to become sentient, but since he didn't know what else to do, he just chose to do nothing.

Eventually, the Danger Room (now calling itself Danger and identifying generally as a female) stopped being so angry at the X-Men and agreed to help them. She began to serve as a member of the team for a few years. When Wolverine reopened Xavier's school as the Jean Grey School for Higher Learning, he incorporated non-sentient Shi'ar technology to turn the entire X-Mansion into a Danger Room, so classrooms could turn into whatever the teachers wanted them to become.

Most recently, the original Danger Room has begun to work with the X-Men Blue team as their primary mode of transportation, typically taking on the form of the X-Men's famous Blackbird jet.

45 Cable

Many X-Men characters have complicated backgrounds within the comics and a number of X-Men characters have complicated backgrounds behind the scenes. However, no character can boast the levels of complication in both fields as Cable, the time-traveling mutant warrior with more parents (in the comics and outside the comics) than just about any character in history.

The behind-the-scenes origins for the character began when Rob Liefeld joined writer Louise Simonson as the creative team on *New Mutants*. The title had recently seen the group of young mutants break free from their ostensible mentor, Magneto, while also merging with another team of young mutants from the pages of *X-Factor*, the X-Terminators. So the cast of the group had grown, but without a leader or a real base of operations (the X-Mansion having been destroyed in one of its routine destructions), the team was in a state of disarray. So *New Mutants* editor Bob Harras decided that the team needed a new leader. He wanted the new leader to have more of a military attitude than their previous leaders, to give the book a new approach.

Before joining *New Mutants*, Rob Liefeld had designed a number of possible new characters for the series. One of the characters that he had designed was a cyborg character that Liefeld recalled was essentially a mix between Bruce Willis from *Die Hard* and Arnold Schwarzenegger from *The Terminator*. He had a number of possible names written down for the character. When he pulled the design out for *New Mutants*, he chose the name "Cable."

However, since both Liefeld and Simonson were told of the new direction by Harras, then Simonson naturally was *also* developing a militaristic leader for the team. Therefore, there is some dispute between the two over who gets credit for creating Cable. Liefeld clearly designed the character on his own, but there is some debate over how much of a role Simonson had in the early personality of the character. She clearly wrote his first appearance in *New Mutants #87*, so either way; she officially gets credit as cocreating the character. Harras' role, though, is reminiscent of the impactful role that Roy Thomas had in the creation of Wolverine, though both editors always seem to be left out of creator credits for their respective characters.

Simply put, the only thing that anyone knew about Cable when he showed up was that he was a time traveler, he was a cyborg of some sort, and he was a badass. Once he was introduced, Simonson and Liefeld kept him a mystery for a few issues (although they revealed that he had history with Wolverine, but then again, everyone seems to have history with Wolverine). Once Liefeld took over full control of the plotting of the series, he had a few different ideas for the character. One of them was that he would be a grown version of Cannonball, the leader of the *New Mutants*. Another one was set up by the ending of the final issue of *New Mutants* (by Liefeld and Nicieza). In that issue, the villainous Stryfe, who showed up with the Mutant Liberation Front at the same time that

Top Five Most Emphatic Kitty Pryde Speeches

5. *Astonishing X-Men #22*
While the fate of the X-Men and Earth itself were up in the air, Kitty made a great speech to Colossus about how things are always going to be crazy, and you have to make time to grab the things that will make you happy.

4. *All-New X-Men #13*
After Havok bizarrely said that he felt that the word "mutant" was offensive and that he thinks we shouldn't care as much about what makes us different, Kitty tore that argument apart by comparing her mutant identity with her similarly "invisible" Jewish identity. Suffice it to say that she is proud to call herself both a Jew and a mutant.

3. *New Mutants #5*
After a high school student kills himself after being accused of being a mutant, Kitty gives a speech about how there are so many ethnic slurs that could be used to tear people down, but we have to look past them and treat everyone like a person.

2. *Marvel Graphic Novel #5* ("God Loves, Man Kills")
In front of a large anti-mutant audience at Madison Square Garden, Kitty makes a heartfelt argument that Reverend William Stryker is the real monster on the stage, no matter how much he tried to cast her friend, Nightcrawler, as the monster.

1. *Uncanny X-Men #210*
When an injured Nightcrawler finds himself unable to teleport and suddenly surrounded by a large anti-mutant mob, Kitty comes to his defense and makes an eloquent speech that manages to convince the angry mob to disperse and leave well enough alone.

Cable debuted, took off his helmet and appeared to be…Cable! Liefeld's idea was that Stryfe would be an older version of Cable who turned evil at some point in time. So Cable's greatest foe would be himself.

However, Liefeld soon left Marvel to cofound Image Comics, and thus he was no longer in control of Cable's background. Marvel decided to go in a different direction. Cyclops previously had sent his infant son, Christopher Nathan Summers, into the future to save his life after he had been infected with a techno-organic virus by Apocalypse. During "X-Cutioner's Song," it was revealed that either Stryfe or Cable was the grown version of that infant and the other one was a clone. At first, it seemed like Cable was going to be the clone, but then it turned out that Cable was the original (he was a cyborg as a result of the techno-organic virus ravaging his body before being put under control) and Stryfe was a clone without the virus who was then captured by Apocalypse with the intent of Apocalypse using Stryfe as a host body.

So Cable was now older than his own father, Cyclops. The issue was even weirder when you consider that Cable's birth mother was Madelyne Pryor, a clone herself of Jean Grey, who then died. When Cyclops married Jean Grey, Cable got to see who, in effect, *should* have been his parents. Cable has been a valuable member of the X-Universe ever since, leading many versions of X-Force and also being part of a number of X-Men teams.

46 Psylocke

Even in terms of X-Men characters, Psylocke's history is a bit of a tangled mess of different writers taking her in wildly different directions before she found a home in, of all places, another person's body!

In the mid-1970s, Marvel launched Marvel UK, a British subset of Marvel, which mostly reprinted Marvel stories but also did original content, starting with *Captain Britain*, created by Chris Claremont (who was actually born in England) and Herb Trimpe. In the eighth issue, we met Captain Britain (Brian Braddock)'s sister, Elizabeth, who had some sort of mental abilities (originally the power to see the future). When we next saw her, she was now working as a professional model. Then writer Alan Moore and artist Alan Davis took over the Captain Britain feature. They reintroduced Psylocke and made a few major changes to the character.

First off, they dyed her hair purple. Secondly, she was now "Betsy." Thirdly, they had her now working for the British equivalent of SHIELD, STRIKE, as one of their psi-operatives. She became a regular supporting cast member for her brother, working alongside him and other heroes (sadly, her lover was also in STRIKE and he was murdered). Her last major change during this era was when Alan Davis took over writing duties on Captain Britain and had Betsy fill in for her brother as the new Captain Britain. She was beaten badly by the villainous Spymaster, with her eyes being torn from her skull.

That was how she was left off in Marvel UK, but then Davis was wooed over to American comic books and Claremont got him to work on the X-Men with him. Psylocke moved to the United States, complete with new robotic eyes created by the villainous Mojo (who intended to use them to spy on the X-Men), and ended up joining the X-Men. She was given a new costume with a special suit of armor to help protect her in battle. Psylocke was a member of the X-Men when they sacrificed themselves to defeat the Adversary. The British magical being known as Roma resurrected the team and gave them a magical device known as the Siege Perilous, a sort of "get out of jail free" card. Most of the X-Men eventually ended up taking the Siege Perilous, including Psylocke. When Wolverine ran into Psylocke a few issues later, she was now Asian!

Yes, in a story that saw a number of rewrites over the years (at first her body was magically altered, but then it became a mind-swap situation), Psylocke found her mind transferred into the body of an Asian ninja (with a Jim Lee–designed costume that evoked Frank Miller's famous ninja, Elektra). The character went from being a minor member of the X-Men to being one of their most popular members of the team (Jim Lee's penchant for drawing her in skimpy bathing suits in a number of issues likely played a major role in her increased fame—even her regular costume was little more than a skimpy bathing suit).

Psylocke began to date her teammate Archangel (they bonded over the fact that they both grew up in rich families). After Psylocke was almost killed by Sabretooth, Archangel and Wolverine found a magical item known as the Crimson Dawn that merged with Psylocke. It brought her back to life, but it also gave her magical powers, like the ability to teleport in and out of shadows (she also gained a magical facial tattoo). She later used up all of her powers to trap Shadow King in her mind (she was originally going to be killed off in the story, but Joe Kelly and Steve Seagle decided to just write her off).

Chris Claremont brought her back to the X-Men when he returned to the series in 2000. When he launched *X-Treme X-Men*, Claremont intended to briefly kill her off, just to bring her back without the confusing Crimson Dawn aspects of her powers, but Marvel had just implemented a brief "Dead is Dead" rule, so characters could not be brought back to life for a few years. So Psylocke remained dead far longer than Claremont intended. Eventually, once the "Dead is Dead" rule was dropped, Claremont managed to pull off his delayed story line, bringing Psylocke back to her "normal" Asian ninja state.

In recent years, Psylocke has mostly been a member of various versions of X-Force, the black ops X-Men team, dealing with the fact that she is willing to kill but hating that aspect of her personality. However, she can't deny that she has that side within her and she has still continued to kill when she felt it was necessary.

47 X-Force

X-Force is the name of a variety of prominent teams related to the X-Men, who were generally quite different in tone from each other, but shared one major thing in common—their willingness to work outside "the line."

The first X-Force was the logical extension of the New Mutants being given a new, militaristic leader in Cable. Slowly but surely, Rob Liefeld got rid of most of the members of New Mutants and replaced them with tougher, more "extreme" characters like Shatterstar, Feral, Domino, and Warpath. Only Cannonball and Boom-Boom remained from the original New Mutants, and Boom-Boom was mostly used as comic relief. The team was driven by Cable, who apparently felt it was his duty to get Cannonball and the others ready for a dark future by turning them into an elite paramilitary unit (Domino was important for this job, since she had formerly worked with Cable on precisely that sort of unit when they were both mercenaries together).

When Cable disappeared on the group (Cable has always been very prone to disappearing on people, typically through some sort of time-traveling adventure), Cannonball took over the reins of the team. Slowly but surely, more and more of his New Mutants teammates were working their way back to the team, like Sunspot and Rictor and then Dani Moonstar (Siryn also joined the team pretty early on—she was a bit more of an old-school hero, so she did not fit that well with the "extreme" heroes like Feral and Shatterstar). Eventually, X-Force just became the New Mutants under another name.

Right before the original X-Force ended, they were revamped to be more of a black ops team, working with Pete Wisdom (a British operative) and Domino. When that series ended with the whole cast of the book seemingly dying, they were quickly replaced with the strangest version of X-Force yet. The new X-Force was a group of reality-show-style heroes, whose adventures were constantly being recorded, and they were treated like rock stars. The original X-Force contested the use of the name and eventually this X-Force renamed themselves X-Statix.

After a few reunions of the original Cable-led version of X-Force, the next big step for the group was when Cyclops decided that the X-Men should have their own secret black ops team. They would be a team that could go out and eliminate threats to the X-Men before they attacked the X-Men. In effect, Cyclops created his own little secret murder squad. Wolverine, Warpath, Wolfsbane, Domino, Archangel, and X-23 were the main members of the team, with Elixir serving as essentially their medic through his healing powers, and the Vanisher their transportation through his teleporting powers. One of the most offensive aspects of it is that one of the team members was X-23, a mutant who had come to the X-Men for help with her urges to kill (she had been cloned from Wolverine and raised to be an assassin), so to see Cyclops turn

X-Force #1 from August 1991, written by Rob Liefeld and Fabian Nicieza, with illustratrions by Liefeld. (Cover art by Rob Liefeld)

around and use her worst impulses to help his murder squad was dispiriting.

Eventually, Wolverine decided that X-Force could no longer follow Cyclops' direction. Rather than shut the team down, however, he restarted the team as an independent team using the same basic agenda that they had under Cyclops' rule, just with the agenda being set by themselves and not Cyclops. The team was made up of Wolverine, Psylocke, Archangel, Deadpool, and Fantomex. On their first mission, they encountered a young child who was a clone of Apocalypse and destined to take over as the new Apocalypse eventually. The team was torn on whether it was right to kill a child before they became a villain. Psylocke stood against her teammates to try to keep them from killing the kid, but Fantomex ultimately managed to shoot the kid in the head. The problem was that with the clone out of the way, the next step was to use Apocalypse's hidden programming to turn Archangel into the next Apocalypse. Eventually, X-Force were forced to kill their own teammate.

After that team broke up, two rival versions of X-Force debuted—one led by Cable and made up of mutants on the run, including Colossus (who felt guilty over his actions when he was possessed by the Phoenix Force), and another led by Storm and Psylocke and trying to keep up the original mission of the previous Wolverine-led X-Force. Ultimately, the two teams merged into one. When that merged series ended, that has been the last X-Force comic for the last few years.

48 X-Men Redemption

One of the hardest things about creating a really cool supervillain is the fact that you really can't use villains all that often. Superheroes get to appear in comic books every month, but you can't do the same thing with supervillains, because it would become far too repetitive (back in the 1940s and '50s, there were three to four stories in every issue of, say, Batman, so it was a lot more acceptable for the Joker to show up every other issue). Therefore, the obvious temptation for writers is to turn cool supervillains into superheroes so that they could be used more often. That's a temptation that X-Men writers have found very difficult to avoid caving to over the years.

The most famous X-Men redemption case is clearly Magneto. When he was introduced along with the original five X-Men way back in *X-Men #1*, he was about as clear cut of a villain as you could ever see. He was essentially "What if Hitler was a supervillain?" as his belief was that mutants were superior to humans and should therefore rule over them (although, more specifically, he should rule over everyone). Magneto was quite willing to destroy entire countries early on through the use of nuclear weapons. He would go on to fight against most of the other major Marvel superheroes, including Thor, the Avengers, and the Defenders.

When Chris Claremont brought Magneto into the pages of *X-Men* to fight the All-New, All-Different X-Men, he seemed like the same basic villain that he had always been for the first couple of times that he faced them. However, *Uncanny X-Men #150* changed everything. Magneto had established his own sovereign island and, after declaring his sovereignty, he was attacked by the Soviet Union. Magneto sunk an entire Soviet nuclear submarine, killing all those aboard, and the X-Men were sent in to stop him. Though when Magneto was about to (perhaps fatally) attack Kitty Pryde, he realized that she was Jewish. This led him to reveal that he was a victim of the Holocaust.

From that point forward, Claremont began to write Magneto more sympathetically, as a man driven to extremes from his damaged past. We also learned that he and Charles Xavier were once good friends but his past led him to a darker path. After aiding the X-Men during "God Loves, Man Kills" and "Marvel Super Heroes Secret Wars," he eventually took over as the head of Xavier's after Xavier was injured and had to take a leave of absence. Magneto later returned to villainy, only to return to serve with the X-Men on a number of occasions.

Emma Frost was another notable success story, as she was also introduced as a vicious killer. Over the years, though, her character was mellowed out to the point where she was named the coheadmaster of Xavier's spinoff school for mutants (which used to be her own school for mutants back when she was evil and training mutants to be agents of the Hellfire Club). She later became a prominent member of the X-Men during Grant Morrison's run and was the cohead of the X-Men with Cyclops for a number of years. Recently, she has taken a bit of a turn for villainy, but she still sees herself as doing good…just on her terms.

Sabretooth and Mystique have been harder subjects. When the speculator's boom hit big in the early 1990s and Wolverine was the hottest character in comics, any Wolverine-related characters were hot properties and Sabretooth was the most popular Wolverine-related character. The issue is that he was just so evil that any redemption story line for him just fell flat, as he was just too evil to redeem. For a time, he and Mystique were both forced to work for the government-sponsored mutant superhero team, X-Factor, under the direction of X-Factor leader, Forge. That wasn't really redemption, though.

For Sabretooth, it took literal magic to fix his issues, as he was "inverted" by a magical spell that turned the heroes of the Marvel Universe into villains and the villains into heroes. When the spell was reversed, a few characters remained inverted and Sabretooth was one of them.

Mystique, meanwhile, has had so many secret motivations over the years that it is difficult to ever really know what her deal is. She has aided the X-Men a number of times and turned out to be secretly working against them but other times has legitimately helped them. She's just too secretive to ever be truly redeemed.

49 The Byrne/Claremont Feud

The most acclaimed run in X-Men history was when Chris Claremont and John Byrne worked together in the late 1970s/early 1980s. Byrne started the series as purely the artist on the book, but he had so many ideas for the series that he quickly moved up to co-plotting status. By the end of Byrne's run on the series, Byrne was doing the lion's share of the plotting, with Claremont mostly doing the scripting of the series. The problem, though, as far as Byrne saw it, was that no matter what Byrne did on the book, the simple fact of the matter was that the last one between the two to work on the comic book was Claremont. So Byrne could do whatever he wanted to on his end, but Claremont could just change it on his end and the book would then go to print with whatever Claremont wanted. (Unless, of course, their editor insisted on Claremont changing things, but especially with the way that comic book deadlines worked, it was very difficult to expect an editor to have dialogue rewritten so late in the game.)

Since this would happen so frequently, it often seemed like Byrne was getting very angry over minor issues, but to Byrne, each issue was just symptomatic of the larger problem. Of course, on the other side of the coin, Claremont was irritated that Byrne kept complaining all of the time. The final straw turned out to be the opening of *X-Men #139*. The issue opened with Byrne drawing Colossus tearing out a tree while doing some yard work on the X-Mansion estate. Byrne drew Colossus easily tearing the tree out of the ground. Claremont, however, added captions that noted that Colossus strained with all of his might to tear the tree out of the ground. In Byrne's mind, the changes now weren't even matching the actual drawing in the comic book. So Byrne quit the book (by the time *X-Men #139* came out and Byrne saw what Claremont had done, Byrne had already done the next few issues, so he just had to finish up *Uncanny X-Men #143*).

Byrne then took over *Fantastic Four* as the writer and artist. Now that Byrne was in control of his own title, though, he began to use the book to express some of his issues with Claremont. The first shot was an obscure one in *Fantastic Four #240*, where Byrne had Black Bolt use his mighty powers to move the Inhumans' home of Attilan from Earth to the moon. The feat came with a caption that noted that they weren't going to insult their readers by adding a special-effect noise here. That was a direct response to an earlier *X-Men* issue when Byrne was irritated that a special-effect noise was added that covered up his drawing of a volcano erupting.

Byrne's biggest irritation was when Claremont would use "his" characters in the pages of *Uncanny X-Men* without clearing it with Byrne. Claremont had Doctor Doom team up with Arcade to fight the X-Men in a couple of issues, and in one of them, Arcade lit his cigarette by striking a match against Doom's armor. Byrne then had an issue of *Fantastic Four* when he revealed that that Doom was not the real Doctor Doom, but rather one of Doom's special Doom-bots that he used to fill in for him at times (he made sure to destroy that Doom-bot, as clearly it was defective if it allowed someone to strike a match on it).

Claremont was not shy about firing back. When Byrne did a story line in *Fantastic Four* where Mister Fantastic saves Galactus' life under the theory that Galactus was a force of nature, Claremont was irritated. He had to kill off Dark Phoenix because she killed a planet, but Galactus killed multiple planets and we're saying that he was okay? So Claremont wrote a bit into an *Uncanny X-Men* issue where Shi'ar Empress Lilandra found out what Mister Fantastic did and showed up as a hologram in the Baxter Building to threaten him. An irate Byrne then wrote an issue of *Fantastic Four* where

Mister Fantastic was tried for his "crime" of healing Galactus and everyone came to the conclusion in the end (including Lilandra) that he was right to have done so.

Since neither Claremont nor Byrne actively work on Marvel Comics anymore, there has not been an update in the feud in many

Top Five Worst Things Cyclops Has Done

5. Killed Professor X

This one is tricky since he was technically possessed by the Phoenix Force at the time, and that certainly could have had some effect on his thinking. Still, he murdered his own mentor after Xavier tried to prevent him from turning into Dark Phoenix. That's not good.

4. Cheated on Jean Grey with Emma Frost

After being married to Jean Grey for a few years, Scott began to have a psychic affair with another telepath, Emma Frost. In their tawdry sex dreams together, he even had Emma dress up as Dark Phoenix. It was super awkward when Jean Grey used her powers to discover them.

3. Tried to leave wife and child

After his wife gave birth to their son, Cyclops still felt it was his duty to leave his family to take over control of the X-Men (who had suddenly been put in the hands of Magneto). Cyclops challenged Storm to a duel for the leadership of the X-Men. He lost and he looked *so* upset over having to stick around with his wife and infant son.

2. Put X-23 in X-Force

The X-Men, generally speaking, are about helping people. So when a young mutant named X-23 came to them to help her get over her addiction to killing, you would think it would be very messed up to then put her on your own private squad designed to kill off your enemies. And yet, that's precisely what Cyclops did.

1. Left his wife and child

Once Jean Grey turned out to be alive, Cyclops couldn't wait to fly from Alaska to New York and ditch his wife and kid. When he came back, they were gone. You have real Father of the Year material here.

decades. Although you could probably count Byrne agreeing to script Jim Lee and Whilce Portacio's plots in the early 1990s after Claremont was pushed out as writer on *X-Men* in favor of Lee and Portacio as a sort of shot at Claremont.

50 Mister Sinister

Even in the world of superhero comic books, where two of the most famous characters are unironically named Mister Fantastic and Doctor Doom, Mister Sinister is one of the sillier-sounding supervillain names. However, unlike many other characters with silly names, in the case of Mister Sinister, his silly name was actually part of his original history, a history that never managed to make its way into the actual comic books.

As originally envisioned by Chris Claremont, Mister Sinister was the creation of a mutant child who was unable to physically age even as his mind continued to age. He turned into a villain, but since he was stuck in the body of a child, he needed something a bit more imposing when interacting with other people. Still being, in effect, a grown-up child, he came up with the idea of using his power to create a new character named "Mister Sinister" (the sort of name that a child would think of for a villain).

Claremont actually went so far as to write a few backup stories in the pages of *X-Men Classic* (a reprint series that also added backup stories with original material that would fill in the blanks in the old stories) that showed this child, named Nathan, who lived in the same orphanage that Scott Summers ended up in after his parents apparently were killed. It was here, then, that Sinister's obsession with Scott Summers began. Originally, Claremont intended for that same child to go do the same thing as he did with Sinister with a heroic character who would join the X-Men, as part of a plan to strike at the X-Men from within. That character? None other than Gambit! In the original version of the story, Gambit would end up breaking free from the control and possibly became his own heroic individual person. Obviously, this is not what ended up happening in the comics.

Instead, with Claremont gone, it was not until 1996 that Mister Sinister gained an origin. Now, he was revealed to be Doctor Nathaniel Essex, a doctor in the late 19th century that was obsessed with genetics, especially when the firstborn son to he and his wife died at birth. He began doing rather disturbing experiments when his wife became pregnant with their second child. He even dug up their first son! When he was visited by En Sabah Nur (Apocalypse), he was offered a chance at immortality to continue his experiments. He actually ended up deciding to give up his work and devote himself to his wife and unborn child, but when he returned home to tell his wife his decision, he learned that she had discovered his subjects and freed them all. The shock/stress had also caused her to suffer a miscarriage and she died from loss of blood. As she died, she explained to him that he was "sinister." So he was forced to accept Nur's offer, which transformed him into the disturbing-looking being that is Mister Sinister.

Mister Sinister has been particularly obsessed with the DNA of Scott Summers and Jean Grey. When Jean Grey seemingly died in "The Dark Phoenix Saga," Sinister created a clone of her named Madelyne Pryor and arranged it so that Madelyne and Scott Summers would cross paths, fall in love, and a have a child. That child, Nathan Summers, was destined to become Cable, the ultimate nemesis to Apocalypse, who Sinister wanted out of the way for his own reasons (at least part of which is because he still bore a grudge for being transformed into a freakish being that will never die).

Mister Sinister also organized the Mutant Massacre, as he discovered that the Morlocks (an underground race of mutants) had been genetically altered using his own techniques (as it turned out, they were created by the Dark Beast, an alternate reality version of the Beast who was trained by the Sinister of that reality). He could not deal with any competition, so he put together the Marauders to kill the Morlocks for him. He has always made sure to continue to keep clone bodies of each of the Marauders in case they were killed in battle (he could always just use one of their clones).

Sinister is mostly obsessed with genetics in general, so when the first mutant born on Earth after M-Day showed up, he tried to get his hands on her. He worked out a deal with Mystique, but she betrayed and killed him. He next showed up in a cloned female body, now calling himself Miss Sinister. Once he returned to his original body, he also later tried to cure the M-Pox effects from the Terrigen Mists on Earth, but he failed (for such a great scientist, he seems to fail all the time).

51 Rob Liefeld

The odds are that you probably know at least one teenager when you were younger (or perhaps even now) that delivered pizzas or worked construction or some other such job but insisted that they were a really good artist that should be drawing for Marvel or DC Comics. Ninety-nine percent of these folks never actually do anything...but that 1 percent...that 1 percent can, as they say, change the world. That was the case with Rob Liefeld, one of the most significant X-Men–related comic book creators of the 1990s.

After graduating high school in the mid-1980s, Rob Liefeld worked odd jobs while sending samples of his comic book artwork to various small press comic book publishers. A self-taught artist, Liefeld's early work was rough, but showed promise. He would attend comic book conventions and show his artwork to representatives from the various comic book publishers. Mark Gruenwald actually offered him a short story at Marvel after seeing his work at a San Francisco convention, but Marvel ended up having another artist redraw the story (Liefeld still got credited in the issue for his earlier work on the story). Then DC's Dick Giordano (who saw Liefeld at the same convention that Gruenwald saw him) asked for more samples of his work. Liefeld complied and soon, while only 20 years old, Liefeld was assigned a miniseries for DC Comics that introduced a brand-new Hawk and Dove.

The series caught the comic book industry by surprise and Marvel was contacting Liefeld before the series was even over to offer him more assignments. They all went well and soon, Liefeld was being offered his pick of available comic book series. One of the first series he was offered was *Alpha Flight*, which was set to get a new creative team and direction (amusingly enough, the new writer on the series ended up being Liefeld's future collaborator Fabian Nicieza). By this time, Liefeld had already starting creating tons of new characters. He was bubbling over with new ideas. He was planning on bringing his new characters to whatever series he took over next. It could have been *Alpha Flight*. Cable could have been some sort of Maple Leaf–themed character. The only problem was that Liefeld was only willing to join *Alpha Flight* (which was nearing 100 issues at the time) if they would agree to reboot it. They said no, so he instead took the only available X-Men–related title at the time, *New Mutants*.

Liefeld joined the current writer on the series, Louise Simonson, and right away, Liefeld began introducing some of the characters he'd created in his sketchbook (mostly as villains called the Mutant Liberation Front). At the same time, *New Mutants* editor Bob Harras asked for a new leader for the New Mutants, an older, more militaristic character who would take the New Mutants in a new, edgier direction. One of the characters in Liefeld's sketchbook matched the concept perfectly, so Liefeld brought him to the series and named him Cable. *New Mutants'* sales suddenly started to rise significantly and Liefeld's early issues became hot items on the back-issue market (his second issue, *New Mutants #87*, the first appearance of Cable, even got a rare second printing at a time when Marvel did not give books multiple printings very often).

Liefeld was doing so well on the book that Bob Harras gave the book to Liefeld entirely, with Simonson moving to DC Comics to launch a new Superman title. Liefeld was now the sole plotter for the series, as well as the artist. Fabian Nicieza came on board as the scripter of the book. Their first issue together was *New Mutants #98*, which set the stage for the ending on *New Mutants*, as Liefeld planned to relaunch the series as a new, edgier book. *New Mutants #98* introduced a new second-in-command for the team in Domino, a new villain (who would help write Sunspot out of the book) in Gideon…oh, and a mercenary with quite a mouth named Deadpool.

With *New Mutants #100*, the book ended and Liefeld and Nicieza launched *X-Force*, with two other new Liefeld creations, Shatterstar and Feral, being introduced in the final *New Mutants* issue. *X-Force #1* was bagged with trading cards and was, at the time, the highest-selling single comic book series of all-time (Jim Lee soon passed its sales numbers with *X-Men #1*). Liefeld was so famous that he even starred in a Levi 501 jeans commercial directed by Spike Lee! *X-Force* was a huge success, but before a year was up, Liefeld left Marvel to help form the independent comic book company Image Comics. He worked on the X-Line of comics for less than four years but changed it dramatically in that short period of time.

52 Emma Frost

Obviously, no comic book creators ever truly know what will happen to their characters after they create them. There is surely no way that Stan Lee and Jack Kirby thought that a generic wood monster from an issue of *Strange Tales* (that acted like every other monster in every other issue of that series) would become something special, and yet Groot is now one of Marvel's most famous characters. However, it probably still surprises Chris Claremont and John Byrne to see just what has happened to their creation of Emma Frost since her introduction as a member of the Hellfire Club in "The Dark Phoenix Saga."

The Hellfire Club was based on an episode of the British TV series *The Avengers* (no relation to the Marvel comic book series with all of the assembling) where the female lead on the series, Emma Peel (played by the beautiful Diana Rigg), had to go under cover in a secret criminal society as the "Queen of Sin" wearing just a high boot, lace, and corset. Shockingly, this episode stuck in the memories of both Byrne and Claremont and when they introduced the evil mutant secret society known as the Hellfire Club, they included their White Queen, Emma Frost, who dressed in similar fashion (she was a powerful telepath, to boot).

When she was introduced, Emma Frost, who was running a rival school for young mutants, tried to recruit Kitty Pryde. She lost out on Kitty Pryde but managed to capture the X-Men briefly. Frost was so evil early on that she had some of her men killed after they failed in their first attempt to capture the X-Men. The X-Men had been captured right afterward, but that was not good enough for her!

Emma Frost became a recurring foe of the X-Men over the years and especially in the pages of the *New Mutants*, where we met the Hellions, some of Frost's prized pupils at her Massachusetts Academy who were trained as enforcers for the Hellfire Club or, more simply, as the evil versions of the New Mutants. Tragically, in an attack orchestrated by Trevor Fitzroy, a villain from the future, almost all of Frost's Hellions were murdered by Sentinels and Frost herself was put into a coma. She remained in the custody of the X-Men while in her coma. She finally came out of it using a body swap (she had done so once before with Storm) with Iceman. She also showed him how he could use his powers more effectively.

While she was staying with the X-Men recovering from her coma, Xavier gave her a chance at redemption. He would move his Xavier's School to her now-abandoned Massachusetts Academy and entrust Emma as the coheadmaster of this new school, along-side former X-Men member Banshee. She agreed and she was happy to get back to teaching young mutants, even if her methods were sometimes a bit extreme (that was why Banshee was around, to balance her out). Eventually, this school shut down after Frost's own sister tried to blow up the school (one of the students died in the explosion). Emma killed her own sister to avenge her fallen student.

Emma then ended up in Genosha, which was brimming with mutants after the Legacy Virus (which was decimating the mutant island's population) was cured. Tragically, another Sentinel attack (this time organized by Cassandra Nova) killed almost all of the mutants on the island. Emma was one of the only survivors, as she had developed a secondary mutation of being able to turn into diamond. Emma joined the X-Men and quickly was drawn to the "Boy Scout" nature of Cyclops, who contrasted her well. The two began a psychic affair. After Jean Grey died, Jean was resurrected in the distant future and she actually used her Phoenix powers to go back in time and push Cyclops and Emma Frost to begin a relationship.

Cyclops and Emma Frost became both a couple and the new coheads of Xavier's. First, they ran a school for mutants, but after the mutant population was reduced to roughly a thousand mutants on Earth, they also coled the X-Men's retreat to their own island, dubbed Utopia. Following "Avengers vs. X-Men," Cyclops and Emma went rogue before reconciling with the rest of the X-Men. After Cyclops died of the deadly M-Pox (produced by the Inhumans' Terrigen Mists), Emma used her powers to make everyone think that Cyclops was still alive and pushing for a war with the Inhumans. After her ruse was uncovered, Emma Frost went on the run and formed her own version of the X-Men.

53 Must Read: "Wolverine"

One of the most popular independent comic book series of the 1980s was a small parody series created in 1984 by two young men, Kevin Eastman and Peter Laird. The series specifically parodied the work of two comic book creators of the era, Chris Claremont and Frank Miller. From Claremont, the series made fun of mutants (the X-Men) and teenagers (the New Mutants), while with Frank Miller, they made fun of his repeated usage of ninjas in his work

(Daredevil and his creator-owned series, *Ronin*). The series in question was the *Teenage Mutant Ninja Turtles*, which quickly became much more than a parody comic and was soon an empire. The only major project that both creators who inspired *TMNT* worked together on was *Wolverine*, a 1982 miniseries that served as the first solo series for a member of the All-New, All-Different X-Men and also a chance for Claremont and Miller to mix mutants with ninjas themselves.

At this point in time, the word best used to describe Wolverine was probably "berserker," as the character was a walking pile of rage, but that had served him well so far in his life. (This series introduced the classic Wolverine catchphrase, "I'm the best there is at what I do, but what I do best isn't very nice." Miller's cover for the first issue is one of the all-time most iconic Wolverine images—the sight of him smirking and gesturing to the reader to just try him. He knows he's the best at what he does.) However, Miller and Claremont (who co-plotted the series together, with artist Joe Rubinstein doing finishes and inks over Miller's breakdowns) introduced a new facet of Wolverine's personality—they developed him from berserker to the beginning of being a bit of a samurai.

During one of the earliest Byrne/Claremont story lines in *X-Men*, the X-Men were believed to be dead and had to travel across the world to get back home. One of their stops on the way back was in Japan, where they helped stop the evil Moses Magnum from destroying the island nation. Wolverine fell in love with a Japanese woman named Mariko Yashada while the X-Men were there. Now that some time had passed, Wolverine had come back to Japan to discover why Mariko was no longer responding to his letters. As it turned out, her father Shingen Yashada, the head of a vast criminal empire, had married his daughter off to an abusive husband just to repay a debt. Wolverine, naturally, could not deal with this situation and so he tried to solve the problem by killing Shingen.

The cover of Wolverine #3 from the historic miniseries. (Cover art by Frank Miller and Josef Rubinstein)

However, he easily defeated Wolverine using just a wooden stick, as Wolverine's berserker rage was useless against Shingen's trained skills. He dismissed Wolverine as no more than an animal.

While Wolverine was at his lowest, he was aided by a young woman named Yukio, a Ronin (a rogue samurai) who helped save Wolverine from an attack by the Hand, the evil ninja organization that Miller had famously introduced as villains during his Daredevil run. In a breathtaking two-page spread in *Wolverine #2*, Wolverine faced off against an army of Hand ninjas, with only Yukio's help to escape alive. Wolverine and Yukio begin a torrid affair, wild and crazy, more like animals than people.

Eventually, Wolverine realized that the only way that he could possibly defeat Shingen is if he became a better person, one more focused and less filled with constant rage. The simple fact of the matter is that up until now, up until Mariko, he never had a person who he felt was worth becoming a better man for, or a person who made him feel like he could become a better man. He let Yukio down easily (and learned that she had been a double agent this whole time, sent by Shingen to take care of Wolverine, but Wolverine's goodness had forced her to change her allegiances).

Shingen had dishonored his family name and in the final issue of the series, Wolverine challenges him to a rematch and this time, the "animal" was the better man and Wolverine won their second fight, killing Shingen and elevating Mariko to the head of the Clan Yashada. This also opened the way for Wolverine and Mariko to marry, which would be dealt with in a future issue of *Uncanny X-Men* (it did not end well for Wolverine). Back in those days, miniseries were rarely completely independent stories. They often tied in to continuity. Claremont, in particular, tried valiantly for years to work all of Wolverine's solo series into the X-Men comic book series continuity. In other words, when Wolverine had a solo series, Claremont would write him out of the main book for a few issues. This eventually became impossible when Wolverine gained an ongoing series.

54 X-23

While not quite as popular as the original 1990s *X-Men: The Animated Series*, *X-Men Evolution* (which debuted in the fall of 2000 following the success of the first X-Men movie earlier that year) was still a popular series. The concept of the show was to revisit the original setup of the X-Men comic book series, with a group of teens working together as a team, only with the teen characters being a mixture of X-Men from different eras of the team's history (including a few new characters, like Spyke). There were a few other adult mentors/teachers other than just Professor X. The two main adult mentors were Storm and Wolverine. Of course, with Wolverine an adult on the show, that left open room for a younger version of the character, and in stepped writer Craig Kyle, who introduced the world to X-23.

Debuting in a third season episode (cowritten by Kyle's writing partner, Christopher Yost), X-23 was a young female clone of Wolverine created by Hydra to be an assassin. She hated Wolverine because she blamed him for what she had become. Kyle described her as a version of Pinocchio, where instead of a puppet learning how to be a real boy, X-23 was a killing machine that was learning how to be a real girl. The character was popular enough that she was quickly adapted into the comic book universe in 2004.

X-23 debuted in the comics during a miniseries called *NYX* (by Joe Quesada and Joshua Middleton), which was about a group of young mutants trying to make their way through the streets of New York City. They ran into X-23, who was working as a prostitute, specializing in sadomasochism. She constantly cut herself. It was a very odd way of working the character into the comics and it was quickly abandoned.

Instead, Chris Claremont worked the character into the X-Men after she hunted down Wolverine to get some answers about her past from the man she was cloned from. As it turned out, those answers would be supplied by the man who invented her! Craig Kyle cowrote (with Christopher Yost) two miniseries that revealed X-23's origins. She was the result of an experiment by a mysterious project at cloning Wolverine that kept failing because their original DNA source was poor, so they kept failing to replicate the Y chromosome. A brilliant doctor, Angela Kinney, suggested that they just make the clone female instead. After 22 failed tries, the 23rd try, using Kinney's idea, was a success. However, the project director, irritated at her idea being used against his wishes, insisted that Kinney be the surrogate for the baby.

Angela soon grew attached to the baby, whom she named Laura, but the project quickly turned Laura into a killer. They took out her claws, covered them with adamantium and then put them back into Laura in both her arms and her feet. They also developed a "trigger scent," which would cause her to go berserk and kill anyone in her path. Angela worked out a way to get Laura free that involved killing the director. She pulled it off, but she did not know that the director had earlier doused Angela with the trigger scent. Laura then killed her own mother. As she died, Laura helped send her to Charles Xavier for help.

The problem with X-23 when she ended up finding the X-Men and working with them was that Cyclops soon found himself needing X-23's skills as an assassin to help supplement his recently-created black ops team, a revamped version of X-Force. So despite Laura coming to the X-Men to help cure her killing ways, Cyclops decided to user her as a killer as well.

After serving with X-Force for a while, Wolverine kicked her off of the team because he saw what the situation was doing to her.

Eventually, she left the X-Men to enroll in Avengers Academy, where she tried to learn how to better deal with other people. At this point in time, Laura was extremely shy around other people. She rarely spoke at all. She was as close to a killing machine as possible. She was making progress when tragically she was kidnapped, along with a bunch of other students from around the world, and forced to hunt each other down in an "Arena" created by the villainous Arcade.

She was so damaged from the experience that when the surviving students were rescued, she ended up losing her memories. She ended up hooking up with the time-displaced X-Men, who were under the direction of Kitty Pryde. Laura began a relationship with the Angel from the past. Around this time, Wolverine died and Laura decided to take over as the new Wolverine, a role she currently maintains.

55 Neal Adams

In the 1970s, Stan Lee and John Buscema released a book called *How to Draw Comics the Marvel Way.* They were not misleading people, as there really was a "Marvel Way" to draw comics for most of the 1960s and early 1970s (with some notable exceptions, of course, like Steve Ditko, Jim Steranko, and Gene Colan) and that was to draw like Jack Kirby. However, after a generation of artists who all tried to draw like Jack Kirby, there was soon a generation of artists who all tried to draw like someone else. That person? Neal Adams.

For an artist who would eventually define the look of comic books in the late 1960s/early 1970s, it is interesting to note that

Top Five Best Last-Page Magneto Reveals

5. *Uncanny X-Men #148*
Cyclops and his lady friend, Lee Forrester, had found themselves shipwrecked on a mysterious island in the middle of the ocean. After getting themselves somewhat settled, they discover whose island it is—Magneto's!

4. *X-Men #17*
All throughout this early X-Men issue, the individual members of the X-Men are picked off, one by one, by some shadowy bad guy who was hiding in the X-Mansion to attack them after they got back from visiting Iceman in the hospital. At the end of the issue, Angel's parents make a surprise visit to the X-Mansion, only to be greeted at the door by...Magneto!

3. *X-Men #111*
The villainous Mesmero had hypnotized the X-Men into thinking that they were part of a traveling carnival. Beast showed up to rescue his friends and seemed about ready to do so when he was struck down from behind by someone. Then, when the rest of the X-Men managed to break free of Mesmero's control and confront him, Mesmero is suddenly knocked out and his attacker is revealed as Magneto (who then took the X-Men prisoner himself).

2. *New X-Men #146*
A mysterious new pacifist healer on the X-Men named Xorn had quickly made a name for himself on the team through his kind actions. He became a beloved teacher, with many students devoted followers of his. He then took off his mask and revealed himself to be none other than Magneto, taking over the school right out from underneath Xavier!

1. *X-Men #62*
This is a twist on the typical Magneto reveal, as Angel was rescued on a mission to the Savage Land by a mysterious older man. At the end of the issue, we realize what Angel does not know—that this man is secretly Magneto (who had never been seen without his helmet before now)!

when Neal Adams first tried to break into comic books in the late 1950s, after he first got out of school, he had a hard time finding any assignments outside of some short story work for Archie Comics. In 1962, he transitioned to comic strip work and soon began drawing the popular *Ben Casey* comic strip that tied in with the TV series of the same name. The strip came to a close in 1966 and Adams could have easily found another comic strip gig, but Adams wanted to get into commercial art, so he decided not to pursue any more comic strip assignments.

However, Adams found commercial work difficult to get, so he decided to draw comic books again in the meantime, while waiting for his commercial art career to take off. He was just starting to get a foot in the door at DC Comics when they had a change in management and Carmine Infantino was placed in charge and Infantino was all about Neal Adams. He soon made Adams DC's unofficial comic book cover artist and Adams was transcendent in the role, drawing some of the most memorable comic book covers of the era. Neal Adams' covers were the best marketing tools any DC Comics series had at its disposal.

Back in the 1960s, there was an unwritten rule that if you worked for DC Comics, you did not work for Marvel Comics as well. Of course, the rule was nonsense, since multiple DC Comics artists were doing work for Marvel Comics. However, they were doing the work under pseudonyms. Mike Esposito was Mickey Dimeo, George Roussos was George Bell, Gene Colan was Adam Austin, and so on and so forth. Adams, though, did not care and just asked Marvel Comics for assignments while continuing working for DC Comics. Simply put, Adams was too popular for DC to do anything about it. Adams has always been a major proponent for creator rights, so he thought it could help other artists also make the move. And it did, as the days of pseudonyms quickly came to an end.

Adams' first issue of *X-Men* was in early 1969, working with writer Roy Thomas and inker Tom Palmer. The two men clicked instantly and soon began plotting their issues together. They went from an epic Sentinels story line (with Cyclops' brother, Havok, officially joining the team—Adams designed one of the greatest X-Men costumes of all-time with his cosmic rings costume he gave Havok) to a striking Savage Land story line which brought Magneto back to the series.

During the Savage Land arc, while Adams redesigned Angel's costume, the artist made an even more memorable change when he became the first artist to ever draw Magneto without his helmet. The distinct haircut that Adams gave Magneto made him look similar to his former Brotherhood of Evil Mutant charge, Quicksilver. This led to a number of fans (and Marvel Comics writers) who determined that the two characters were related, which eventually came to pass. In Adams' final issue, #65, he actually wrote the issue without Thomas (Denny O'Neil scripted it) and that issue brought Professor X back to the series (after Xavier was seemingly killed a couple of years earlier). Adams and Thomas' brief run was considered a contemporary classic, with the duo receiving the 1969 fan-voted Alley Awards for Best Writer and Best Artist (with Palmer also being named the Best Inker).

After continuing his work with Thomas (and Palmer) on the *Avengers* in 1970's "Kree-Skrull War," Adams went back to working primarily for DC, revamping Batman and his rogues gallery in 1971. His commercial art career then took off and that has been how he has spent most of his career for the last 30 years. Major X-Men artists like John Byrne, Bill Sienkiewicz, and Alan Davis were all heavily influenced by Adams, who changed comic book art for generations. Adams recently returned to the X-Men for a miniseries (with writer Christos Gage) called *The First X-Men* about a proto-version of the X-Men.

56 X-Men Video Games

In the late 1980s and early 1990s, one of the quickest ways to determine where a particular character stood in the popular culture was a very simple question, "How many video games do they have?" If you weren't appearing in multiple video games in that era, then you clearly were not someone that was part of the cultural zeitgeist. Luckily, since the X-Men were, in fact, very much part of that cultural zeitgeist, they were all over the world of video games, including some of the most notable video games of the era!

The X-Men made their video game debut with 1989's Uncanny X-Men for Nintendo. The problem with the game was the same one with most licensed video games of the 1980s—it was terrible. It was confusing, the graphics were bad, it was too difficult, it was just an all-around mess. And yet…it was the first time that the X-Men were appearing in a video game and so every kid just had to have the game, no matter how awful it was to actually play.

That was similarly the case with Wolverine's solo video game debut in 1991's Wolverine for Nintendo. It arrived with a striking Jim Lee cover (a variation on his classic *Wolverine #27* cover that graced many a Marvel licensing product in the early 1990s) but little else, as it was also a poorly designed game, but at least it sort of looked like Wolverine, which wasn't even something that the 1989 Uncanny X-Men game could say for its poorly pixelated characters.

Then the 1992 X-Men arcade video game from Konami was released and everything changed. Konami actually put some thought and effort into their game and the graphics were stunning for the time period. The X-Men roster was based on the team in the ill-fated 1989 "Pryde of the X-Men" cartoon pilot, so it included some outdated characters, like Dazzler, but that was a minor inconvenience for a video game that looked like the real X-Men and the characters had powers like the real X-Men. This game also holds the record for the most players who can simultaneously play the game, as most standard versions of the game allow four players at once but special versions allow a shocking six players to play the game all at the same time!

While the arcade game was the cream of the crop, Acclaim released a very popular home console video game at the same time that crossed over the X-Men with Spider-Man in Spider-Man/X-Men: Arcade's Revenge, which saw the heroes all plunged into one of Arcade's murder traps (which conveniently already worked sort of like a video game) and the players would alternate rounds between Spider-Man and members of the X-Men (Wolverine, Cyclops, Gambit, and Storm). Released on all of the major platforms of the time (Super Nintendo, Genesis, and GameBoy), the game was a huge hit.

Capcom, the makers of the smash hit video game series, Street Fighter, licensed Marvel characters for a few video games in the mid-90s, including the very well received X-Men: Children of the Atom arcade game in 1994 (that was also adapted to home consoles). A fighting game much like Street Fighter, the game added a number of interesting innovations, like a really cool "super jump" feature. The game was such a huge success that it soon led to the true game-changer, 1996's X-Men vs. Street Fighter, which crossed over the two popular franchises for one of the best arcade games of the era. The game famously allowed tag-team fighting for the first time ever.

Throughout the rest of the '90s, X-Men video games remained on the forefront of video game development, with notable achievements like 1994's Wolverine: Adamantium Rage being one of the first video games to have a character's health meter get regenerated (inspired by Wolverine's healing powers, but it soon became a common feature in most video games) and 1997's X-Men: The Ravages of Apocalypse being the first superhero video game to be a first-person shooter game (it was literally built on the famous first shooter video game, Quake, to the point where you would have to first own Quake to even install the X-Men version).

In recent years, though the X-Men have certainly continued to have video games released, they are only really released as tie-ins to X-Men or Wolverine films, and even with that, there has not been a new one since 2014's Uncanny X-Men: The Days of Future Past. Similarly, Marvel continues to use the X-Men characters occasionally in Marvel Universe games (like Lego Marvel Superheroes), but in recent years they won't even use them there. For instance, the X-Men are not in the latest Marvel vs. Capcom video game, despite X-Men vs. Capcom being so famous.

57 Paul Smith

It's hard to imagine nowadays, but when Paul Smith took over as the artist on Uncanny X-Men in 1983, there were two very important things that were not yet true regarding the X-Men. First, being the artist on Uncanny X-Men was not yet a "star-making" gig and second, Uncanny X-Men was not yet Marvel's most popular series. Yes, while John Byrne's run on X-Men with Chris Claremont and Terry Austin raised the sales on the series a lot (and the death of Phoenix in X-Men #137 was a particularly strong-selling issue), the book was still at best the third or fourth best Marvel title, behind some combination of Amazing Spider-Man, Fantastic Four, and The

Avengers. Amusingly enough, when John Byrne left *X-Men* to take over *Fantastic Four* as the writer/artist, he actually was going to a higher-profile title.

When Paul Smith took over *Uncanny X-Men* following Dave Cockrum's second departure from the series, though, the book had enough of a buzz about it that people were interested in Smith solely because he was "the new *X-Men* artist," which would soon become a regular experience with later artists like Marc Silvestri, Jim Lee, and Joe Madureira, but was a new phenomenon at the time. As for the sales, it is hard to explain precisely why, but for whatever reason, Smith's debut on the series coincided with *Uncanny X-Men* finally becoming Marvel's highest-selling title, a distinction it would generally maintain for the rest of the decade (sales continued to increase even after Smith left the series).

While we don't know for sure why the sales on *Uncanny X-Men* exploded when Smith took over (Smith was generally still an unknown artist at the time, with few credits to his name, so it seems hard to believe that it was solely because he took over as the artist on the book), we do know that Smith's art was very well received, and with good reason. Smith was one of the most dynamic artists working in superhero comic books at the time. This was evident very soon into his run, when Storm had to fight the leader of the Morlocks, Callisto, in a knife duel to the death. (Normally, this would be the sort of thing that Wolverine would handle, but he was then currently starring in his first miniseries and back in those days, Chris Claremont was so intent on having the continuity work out that he took Wolverine out of *Uncanny X-Men* whenever he was featured in a solo series.)

Their fight scene is so dynamic you can almost convince yourself that the panels are literally moving. Credit must also be given to the great Bob Wiacek, who inked Smith throughout his run on *Uncanny X-Men.*

Wolverine returned to the series in a two-parter where the X-Men visited Japan to celebrate Wolverine's wedding. However, the X-Men were poisoned and only Wolverine and new recruit Rogue were left standing (Wolverine due to his healing powers and Rogue due to the abilities she absorbed from Carol Danvers, the former Ms. Marvel). Rogue had joined the team just an issue earlier and had formerly been an enemy of the X-Men, but she proved herself against the villains Viper and Silver Samurai (sadly, Wolverine's fiancée stood him up at the altar). The 2013 film, *The Wolverine*, essentially just transferred the brilliant fight that Smith drew between Wolverine and Silver Samurai directly into the film.

Smith's time on the series also marked the first time that the visuals for the characters would be permanently altered since they debuted. Cockrum and Byrne had both come up with new costumes for Wolverine during their respective stints on the book, but Cockrum's costume lasted roughly one issue and Byrne's Wolverine costume was essentially just a brown and tan version of his original costume.

During the aforementioned trip to Japan, though, when Storm was poisoned along with her teammates, she managed to escape while still in a poisoned haze. She befriended Yukio, an assassin friend of Wolverine, and the two women spent a night in Japan together. Storm was inspired to change her style from her original, regal outfit to a punk look, complete with a black leather outfit and a Mohawk. When Smith was told that they were going to change Storm's haircut, he worked up a number of options, with the Mohawk look included just as a joke. He was shocked when they told him that they were going to go with that one. Their reasoning was that fans were going to get mad at her new haircut no matter what, so why not go big?

Fewer than 10 issues after becoming the artist on *Uncanny X-Men*, Smith departed the series in *Uncanny X-Men* #175, with incoming artist John Romita Jr. drawing the second half of the book after Smith drew the first part. While his run was short, Smith produced three classic stories in his brief stint ("Professor X is a Jerk!" in *Uncanny X-Men* #167, the Callisto/Storm fight, and the X-Men in Japan arc) and left the series with a redefined look and a newfound spot at the top of Marvel's sales chart.

58 The Death of Thunderbird

One of the ways that the first generation of comic book fans to become comic book writers changed the comic book industry is that they were the first comic book writers who grew up with the same experiences as the other comic book fans who were reading comic books in the era. In other words, whatever interested a typical fan in 1960 would likely also interest, say, Len Wein or Marv Wolfman.

When Jim Shooter broke in to comics in the mid-1960s—*when he was only 14 years old!*—his whole appeal as a writer to DC Comics editor Mort Weisinger was that Shooter knew what the fans were interested in because he was one of them. Shooter famously wrote the first Superman/Flash race, for instance, because he knew that that was precisely the sort of thing that comic book fans had been talking among themselves about for ages.

Since these writers knew what fans wanted to see, they were also acutely aware of the common complaints of fans of the era and one of the biggest ones was the relatively low stakes of superhero adventures. There never really seemed to be all that much danger involved in any given superhero adventure because you always knew that everyone was going to make it out all right. This is why, when Jim Shooter became the writer on *The Legion of Super-Heroes* in 1966, he soon killed off a member of the team by the end of his first year on the book (he chose a character that he had introduced earlier in his run, Ferro Lad, because he wanted Ferro Lad to be black and Weisinger wouldn't let him, so when it came time to kill someone off, he went with Ferro Lad out of spite). Ferro Lad's death was a big deal at the time.

Those comic book conventions were very much on the minds of Len Wein and Dave Cockrum when they invented the All-New, All-Different X-Men and came about devising the almost instantaneous death of one of their new members, the Apache hero known as Thunderbird.

Thunderbird's demise had its origins in a very different sort of plot for the introduction of the new group of X-Men. Originally, Wein and Cockrum were planning on the introduction of the new X-Men to be, in effect, an entrance exam. In *Giant-Size X-Men #1*, the new group was recruited to rescue the original X-Men, who were all captured by a mysterious mutant (who turned out to be a giant mutant island). However, in their original plans, the original X-Men were not actually captured. Instead, they were pretending to be captured. The whole thing was a ruse created by Professor X to work as an entrance exam to see if the new X-Men could make the grade. Wein and Cockrum felt that a couple of the new team should flunk the exam. Originally, it was going to be Banshee and Sunfire. However, both of those characters were established heroes and they felt that that was too predictable (plus, they both grew to like Banshee). So Thunderbird was set to join Sunfire. Cockrum, though, thought Thunderbird looked too cool to not let him make the team. So they just rewrote the story as a legitimate rescue mission and they all made the team (and Sunfire just quit because he's a jerk).

The idea of a surprise failure, though, stuck with Wein and he thought that superhero teams gelled just too quickly. There never seemed to be any real conflict between teammates. Yes, there were interpersonal issues, like Human Torch and Thing fighting and playing pranks on each other, but once the battle started, everyone fell into line. Wouldn't it make sense, though, that some heroes just never manage to become team players? Similarly, Wein knew the conventions of the superhero genre well; he knew no one would expect them to kill a member of the team on their second mission, so he decided to kill off Thunderbird.

Cockrum would later recall there being a debate whether Thunderbird or Wolverine be the one to go (as they were both abrasive personalities), but Wein always insisted that Wolverine was never in any danger of being the object lesson of the importance of teamwork. So as Cyclops trains the new team members in *X-Men #94*, Thunderbird keeps going rogue and thus, when they fight Count Nefaria over the next two issues, Thunderbird decides to foolishly attack Nefaria's plane by himself in *X-Men #95* and it explodes, killing the hardheaded Apache hero. Comic book readers were shocked and X-Men solidified itself as a comic book that was going to be different from all the other ones on the market, a distinction it held true to for many years to come.

59 Wolverine's Healing Factor

With certain superheroes, their abilities are often extrapolated from the slightest bit of information that one writer gave years ago in their first appearance that later writers then took to mean a whole other thing than the original writer ever intended. A good example of this is some writer along the way noting that Captain America's shield was strong and then a later writer determining that that meant that Captain America's shield was indestructible (despite Lee and Kirby repeatedly showing it breaking during the early 1960s). A perfect example of this is Wolverine and his famous (and ever-increasing-in-capability) healing factor.

When Len Wein created Wolverine, besides increased speed and agility, his take on Wolverine's powers were basically nothing more than that he was really tough. Tough enough that he could bounce back from a fight with the Hulk. In other words, it was unclear if Wein really intended for Wolverine to even have a special "healing power." Wein had modeled Wolverine after actual wolverines, who are marked by their tenacious fighting ability, as they often attack animals much larger than them and are so tough that they are surprisingly able to hang with the larger animals in those fights. So that was what Wein had in mind—not really superhuman healing at all.

That, then, is more or less what Chris Claremont and Dave Cockrum included in their comics. In the first couple of years of X-Men comic books, Wolverine doesn't show any notable healing abilities. The first time that Wolverine showed anything resembling a "healing power" was during a fight with the Shi'ar Imperial Guard in *X-Men #107*, the introduction of the Shi'ar Imperial

Guard. Cockrum wanted to give Wolverine a brand-new costume (odd, since he knew that he was leaving the book with that issue, so it seemed like a strange time to debut a brand-new costume for a major character), so he had one of the Imperial Guard burn Wolverine's costume off of him and Wolverine remained in fine shape (and then stole a costume off of another Guard member that was going to be his new costume).

John Byrne joined Chris Claremont on *X-Men* the following issue and they started a long story line where the X-Men traveled the globe trying to get back home after being believed to be dead by everyone. Their journey began in the Savage Land (the mysterious prehistoric jungle land hidden in the middle of the Antarctic) and in *X-Men #116*, Wolverine killed a dinosaur as it bit down on his arm. Storm was concerned for his injury, but he told her not to worry, that he heals fast. Here, then, was the first real sign of the healing factor and even here it could be easily argued that Wolverine was simply trying to keep Storm from worrying about his injury!

Soon, though, Claremont and Byrne decided to specifically increase Wolverine's healing abilities. This attempt, though, was met with resistance by Marvel editorial. This led to a hilarious edit in *X-Men #133* when Wolverine was strafed by machine-gun fire and when the guard goes to confirm his kill, Wolverine turned out to be uninjured! Jim Shooter thought that was too extreme of a healing power for Wolverine (hilarious considering how far Wolverine's healing would go in the future), so he had them change the dialogue so Wolverine mentions that he was only "grazed" by a bullet despite the art clearly showing him getting hit by a few bullets in his midsection and his costume torn all through that section!

Over time, Wolverine's healing powers got stronger and stronger, especially as other writers began to take over the character instead of Chris Claremont. Wolverine's powers reached the height of absurdity during a "Civil War" crossover in 2006. In the story, Wolverine is hunting down Nitro, the villain (with the ability to explode his body and then recorporealize) who infamously blew up during a fight with the New Warriors in Stamford, Connecticut, killing most of the Warriors and hundreds of innocent people (including dozens of children). Wolverine tracked Nitro down, but Nitro then blew up again and turned Wolverine into just a skeleton! Wolverine somehow healed from this shocking injury!

Wolverine's healing power was also used to explain why Wolverine lived for so long after being born in the 19th century. Wolverine's luck ran out in 2014 when an alien virus ended up canceling out his healing powers and then he was killed by a former Weapon X scientist who ironically wanted Wolverine to help synthesize his healing factor for new experiment subjects! Wolverine killed the scientist, but not before the scientist knocked over a container of molten adamantium, coating Wolverine with the molten material, killing him almost instantly.

60 Must Read: "E is for Extinction"

In the late 1990s, Marvel went through bankruptcy, which was a shocking result for a company that was rising so high just a few years earlier. What most fans don't realize, though, is that while Marvel's sales certainly had taken a huge hit between 1993 and 1995, the real reason that the company went through bankruptcy is because Marvel's biggest shareholder, Ronald Perelman (who had purchased the company outright in 1989 and then took it public in the early 1990s), was trying to spend even more money (he had already spent over $700 million in acquiring companies like Fleer and the comic book distributor Heroes World) by buying the remaining shares of the toy company ToyBiz, a company Marvel already partially owned, and then pushing to license their characters into movies and TV shows.

The stockholders objected, so Perelman declared bankruptcy in an attempt to go around the stockholders. He ended up getting challenged by another major stockholder, Carl Icahn, and their feud ended up with neither man being in control of Marvel. Instead, ToyBiz was given control of the overall company in late 1998 and they eventually put the head of Fleer, Bill Jemas, in charge of Marvel Comics. Jemas hired Joe Quesada as the new editor-in-chief of Marvel in 2000 and the two took a bold approach to reimagine Marvel Comics by bringing in acclaimed writers outside of Marvel's usual stable of writers and giving them a great deal of freedom.

That, then, explains why Grant Morrison was allowed so much freedom when it came to his reinvention of the X-Men franchise with his classic first story line, "E is for Extinction." Morrison had so much control he even designed a new logo for the flagship X-Men series (which he also renamed *New X-Men*). Along with Morrison on this journey was artist Frank Quitely (working with inker Tim Townsend), who had worked with Morrison previously on *Flex Mentallo* and *JLA: Earth 2* for DC Comics. The pair debuted on *New X-Men #114* for the first part of the three-part "E is for Extinction," and within three issues they had completely revamped the X-Men universe.

When Morrison took over, the Legacy Virus had recently been cured, leading to the mutant island nation of Genosha (with 16 million mutants, most of whom had been ill from the disease) becoming a superpower under the control of Magneto. The X-Men had just defeated Magneto and brought peace to Genosha. That peace was sadly short-lived. In *New X-Men #114*,

Top Five Best Ragtag Temporary X-Men Teams

5. Phalanx Covenant Team

When Banshee returned from a vacation, he slowly realized that the entire X-Men team had been taken over by shape-shifting aliens called the Phalanx. The only real people were Emma Frost in sick bay, Sabretooth in the X-Men's brig, and Jubilee locked in his room. The quartet made an unlikely team as they fought back against the Phalanx and saved the next generation of mutants from the evil aliens.

4. Planet X Team

After Xorn was revealed as Magneto, Magneto quickly took over all of New York City, keeping Professor X hostage as his prize. Magneto had recruited the best students at Xavier's to serve him, but Cyclops then put together a team of the students Magneto underestimated and they teamed up to take Magneto down and save New York.

3. New Mutants Graduation Team

When the X-Men were temporarily transformed into baby versions of themselves by Mojo, the evil reality show producer from another dimension, the New Mutants had to temporarily take over as the main X-Men team to save the day.

2. Iceman and his Amazing Friends

When Bastion convinced the United States government to allow him to start capturing all mutants, the X-Men were captured quickly. Luckily, Iceman was on a leave of absence, so one of the most unlikely of leaders found himself first saving mutants from capture and then turning them into a makeshift team.

1. Muir Isle Team

After failing to eliminate the X-Men in Australia, the evil cyborgs known as the Reavers decided to kill all the mutants living on the Muir Isle research facility. Banshee and whichever mutants could fight on the island formed a makeshift team and were luckily aided by the arrival of Forge and Freedom Force to help save the day.

Cassandra Nova was introduced. She manipulated one of the Trasks (the creators of the Sentinel program) into giving her access to the Sentinels and in *New X-Men #115* she launched an attack of Sentinels on Genosha that almost completely wiped out the nation's 16 million mutants!

When the X-Men investigated the attack, they discovered that the telepath Emma Frost had survived the attack through another one of Morrison's innovations, the concept of the "secondary mutation," as many mutants gained additional powers. In Frost's case, she learned that she could turn into nearly indestructible diamond. Beast, however, was further mutated into an even more bestial (feline-esque) body with paws instead of hands. He managed to work through it and discovered in the wake of the attack that mutants were actually destined to completely replace humanity on Earth within a few generations!

Nova was revealed as Professor X's psychic twin and she tried to take over Xavier's body. Emma Frost seemingly defeated her by snapping her neck, but it turned out that she had already switched bodies with her brother. In Xavier's body, she then had Xavier publicly out himself as a mutant!

Meanwhile, Morrison and Quitely completely revamped the design of the X-Men. Gone were their traditional superhero garb and in their place were new team uniforms that made them look more like peacekeeping workers, which was not an accident, as Morrison saw them as being more of a mutant outreach group more than anything else (it did not hurt, too, that the X-Men film of the previous year had also taken the X-Men out of their traditional costumes).

Morrison also introduced marital problems between Cyclops and Jean Grey, theorizing that a relationship that began when they were both teenagers might be built more on familiarity and friendship than with actual passion (Cyclops was also dealing with the effects of having recently been possessed by Apocalypse).

Morrison's acclaimed run lasted until *New X-Men #154* (once Marvel's sales recovered, the same freedoms suddenly were no longer present and Morrison exited the book and returned to DC Comics), but it really only took those three issues for Morrison to change nearly everything about the X-Men.

61 Claremontisms

Simply put, every writer has their own particular tics and common phrases that pop up in their work (heck, we bet that you have already noticed some go-to phrases often repeated by this writer). Therefore, it is not a knock on Chris Claremont whatsoever to note that he had a few phrases that he would often reuse in his writing over the years (again, do note that the guy was the main writer on the X-Men universe for roughly 17 years, so he had a lot more opportunities than other writers to repeat phrases). However, there is repeating phrases and there is repeating phrases when you're writing the most popular comic book series in the entire comic book industry for well over a decade. You do the former and a couple of people might notice. You do the latter and it becomes a whole to-do, and thus, the concept of Claremontisms was born. Claremontisms are common themes and phrases that would routinely pop up in Claremont's X-Men work over the years.

When they were introduced, the All-New, All-Different X-Men were very intentionally an international team. Of course, within the written word, you cannot hear accents, so the approach that Claremont used to get across to the readers where each of the character was from is that they would each have a few go-to phrases in their original language (or from their original culture) that they would sprinkle into their dialogue (usually exclamations, as superheroes were quite often being surprised by something). For the Russian Colossus, he would often call people his "Tovarisch" (friend) and he would shout, "By the White Wolf!" The German Nightcrawler would shout out, "Mein Gott!" ("My god!") and mix in a number of other German phrases, and the African Storm would shout out, "By the goddess!" Interestingly, the Canadian Wolverine never got any "Canadian" phrases (although he did say "bub" a lot).

One of the most common plot points in Claremont's work was characters being mind-controlled by the villains. That's not that uncommon, period, as most superhero comics work in mind control plots every once in a while (it's a great way, for instance, to get two superheroes to fight each other), but Claremont had his own particular spin on it. For one, very often the controlled character would begin to dress in bondage gear to denote their mental bondage. Secondly, the controller would often use the phrase "body and soul," as in, "You're mine, body and soul."

Nowadays, a lot of comic books have quick recap pages for new readers. That did not exist during Claremont's time writing the X-Men, so he often had his characters use dialogue that would also explain their powers. The issue with this was that sometimes the phrases used were so detailed that hearing a character repeat the same phrase over and over got to be a bit ridiculous. The most famous example of this was Psylocke, who gained the ability to turn her psionic powers into a "psychic knife." When she started using this new power, she would always introduce it as the "focused totality of my telepathic powers." Similarly, the New Mutants hero Cannonball had the ability to turn himself into, in effect, a human cannonball when he flew (his flying would create an energy effect that it made it look like he was propelled by an engine blast, like a space shuttle). When "blastin'," Cannonball could not be injured, so he would constantly remind people that he was "nigh invulnerable when I'm blastin'!"

Wolverine was popular enough that he got his own Claremontisms, like his famous catchphrase, "I'm the best there is at what I do, but what I do best isn't very nice." Wolverine and Colossus also worked on a maneuver where Colossus would pick up Wolverine and throw him at an enemy so that Wolverine's claws could do long-range damage. They called it the "fastball special," and it became popular enough that Wolverine eventually had other teammates also pull off the move. (Heck, other superheroes even got into the action over the years. Wolverine is very throwable.)

Other notable Claremontisms are when new members join the X-Men, they're told on the cover, "Welcome to the X-Men… hope you survive the experience!" Also, when characters would battle, they would note that "No quarter was asked…and none given" and when one of them would win the fight and have the other at a disadvantage, they would point at them and say, "Bang—you dead." Cyclops and Jean Grey had their own unique Claremontisms, as they would always tell each other that they loved one another "With all my heart." The X-Men were so popular that Claremontisms became a fun shared experience of a whole generation of fans.

62 Death Is Not the End

A common "Claremontism" was when a character showed up that other characters believed to be dead, he or she would quickly retort, "I got better." The line is meant as a joke, since the idea is that the "dead" character did not actually die, but was only believed to be dead. (It's basically a spin on the famous Mark Twain line, "The reports of my death were greatly exaggerated.") However, the truth of the matter is that in the X-Men universe, the characters sometimes legitimately do just "get better."

The impermanence of death was established in the X-Men comic rather early. Before ending his initial run on *X-Men* back in the 1960s, Roy Thomas first killed off Professor X, with the idea being that his death would force the X-Men to grow up in his absence. This move did lead to some notable stories, especially after Thomas rejoined the series with artist Neal Adams. However, before the series was effectively canceled with *X-Men #66*, they decided to give the book a happy ending and reveal in *X-Men #65* that Xavier had faked his death to prepare to repel an impending alien invasion.

One of the most famous deaths of the 1980s, that of Jean Grey, was also one of the most famous death reversals in comic book history. Marvel brought Jean Grey back in 1986, revealing that the Jean Grey who died in "The Dark Phoenix Saga" was actually a copy of Jean Grey created by the Phoenix Force when it wanted to try experiencing what humanity was like. Years later, the real Jean Grey was discovered in a cocoon in the bay where the Phoenix first showed up in *X-Men #101*.

Before Grant Morrison took over the X-Men franchise, former *Uncanny X-Men* writer Scott Lobdell was brought back to resolve some plotlines, including the elimination of the Legacy Virus, the disease that plagued the mutant population. Lobdell had Beast come up with a cure, but the twist was that the only way it would work is if a mutant activated the cure by powering up after injecting the cure. The process, though, would kill the subject. Colossus, whose sister Illyana had died of the Legacy Virus, felt that was a fair price, so he sacrificed himself.

Joe Quesada had implemented a "Dead is Dead" rule soon after he took over as the editor-in-chief of Marvel Comics in 2000. The first exception to that rule was in the opening arc of Joss Whedon and John Cassaday's *Astonishing X-Men* run, where it was revealed that Colossus' death had been faked by some aliens who needed Colossus in custody because of a prophecy that he would one day destroy their planet. Illyana, by the way, also eventually came back to life.

Chris Claremont ran afoul of the "Dead is Dead" rule when he killed off Psylocke in 2001, with the intent of bringing her back to life soon after, just without some of the extra plot points that had followed her along the way (like her magic Crimson Dawn powers). When he was told that he couldn't bring her back, he had to rewrite a number of his X-Treme X-Men plots to accommodate her absence. A few years later, Claremont had returned to *Uncanny X-Men* and now that the "Dead is Dead" rule was, well, dead, Psylocke was able to return from the dead at the hands of her reality-altering brother, Jamie Braddock.

One of the most shocking death reversals was definitely that of Magneto. At the climax of Grant Morrison's *New X-Men* run, he had Magneto kill Jean Grey in *New X-Men #150* and then Wolverine decapitated Magneto in retaliation. A few weeks later, Claremont launched a new version of *Excalibur* set on the Sentinel-ravaged Genosha, seeing the few survivors try to form a new society. The book starred Professor X and...Magneto?!? Yes, just a few weeks after being killed off, they revealed that the Magneto who died in *New X-Men #150* was an impersonator.

During an attack on the X-Men in the crossover event "Second Coming," the young mutant known as Hope Summers was the target. Nightcrawler and Rogue were assigned as her personal bodyguards. However, they were tracked down by the evil (and powerful) Bastion and Nightcrawler sacrificed himself to buy time for Hope and Rogue to escape. Nightcrawler actually made it to Heaven, but had to return to Earth (and life) to prevent an assault on the afterlife led by his evil father, Azazel.

X-Men characters continue to be killed off, only to return later. So it will be interesting if one of the most famous members of the X-Men to currently be dead, Cyclops (who died in 2015), remains dead or if he, too, "gets better."

63 Wolverine's Adamantium Claws

Marvel has some of the most famous characters in the world, so naturally, their intellectual property is very valuable. They hold a number of federal trademarks on the distinctive names of their characters, like Spider-Man, the X-Men, and Wolverine. However, their characters are so famous that Marvel has even officially registered a federal trademark on a pair of sound effects related to their characters! Yes, two of Marvel's sound effects are so famous and so distinctively associated with just Marvel Comics that Marvel has a trademark on them! That means that no one else can use the sound effects on commercial products that would confuse people into thinking that it was made by Marvel. It applies to t-shirts, posters, stuff like that. One of the sound effects is "Thwip!," which is the sound that Spider-Man's web shooters make when they are used. The other sound effect? None other than "Snikt!," the famous sound when Wolverine's adamantium claws are popped out of his body. You know that something is really famous when just the sound that it makes is famous!

As famous as Wolverine's adamantium claws have become today, when Len Wein invented Wolverine in 1974, his take on the claws was that they were part of a glove that Wolverine wore (remember, Wein didn't see Wolverine as being anything else but just really tough. No healing factor and no unbreakable skeleton). In fact, even after Wein left the title, there was really nothing to tell us either way what the deal was with Wolverine's claws over the next few issues, since he always wore his full costume! There was no way to tell if the gloves had claws on them if he would never take the gloves off! That changed in *X-Men #98* (by Chris Claremont, Dave Cockrum, and Sam Grainger) when we finally saw Wolverine in his civilian clothes. When he, Jean Grey, and Banshee were captured by Sentinels later in the issue, Wolverine broke through his restraints by shocking everyone (especially Jean Grey and Banshee) and revealing that his claws were part of him and not in the gloves!

After establishing that Wolverine had adamantium claws in his body, it was only a matter of time until we learned that Wolverine's entire skeleton was made out of adamantium, increasing Wolverine's power set by now making him practically unbreakable (while never explicitly stated, the simple fact that his skeleton always remains together suggests that it comes with some sort of adamantium connecting links for the bones, which is why Wolverine cannot be torn in half).

The fact that Wolverine's skeleton had been covered in adamantium years in the past was a major problem since adamantium had only been invented in a 1969 issue of *The Avengers*, so how could it have been around so much earlier? It was revealed that a Japanese scientist secretly invented adamantium many years earlier and the formula was stolen from him. His daughter vowed to punish those who stole from her father, and she somehow considered Wolverine to be one of those thieves, even though he clearly did not put the adamantium inside of himself! She ended up giving herself adamantium claws and became the villainous (but at least conflicted in her villainy) Lady Deathstrike.

One of the problems with a character being covered in metal is that it was always a bit of a stretch to see how Wolverine could pose much of a threat to Magneto (Colossus, too, for that matter). When the various writers of the X-Men titles were brainstorming ideas for their 1993 "Fatal Attractions" crossover event, Peter David (writer of *X-Factor*) joked that they should just have Magneto pull Wolverine's adamantium skeleton out of his body. Everyone suddenly looked at him and he realized that he had inadvertently inspired a shocking plot twist! In *X-Men #25*, the people of Earth created a force field designed to keep Magneto on his Asteroid M base and off of Earth. He responded to this action by hitting the Earth with a gigantic Electro Magneto Pulse, killing a number of people in plane crashes and things like that. So the X-Men traveled to Asteroid M to take him down for good. During the battle, he used his powers to tear Wolverine's adamantium skeleton in sort of liquid form out of his body through Wolverine's pores!

Wolverine's healing factor was barely able to keep him alive. Then, in another shock, he discovered that the claws were part of his skeleton the whole time! The Weapon X project just coated his actual bone claws when they gave him claws! Wolverine used the bone claws for a few years until Apocalypse decided to turn Wolverine into his Horseman of War and kidnapped Wolverine and recoated his bones in adamantium.

64 X-Men Time Travel

When a comic book property has been around for more than 50 years, like the X-Men, then certain plots are just naturally going to be used a lot, including some very common plot ideas for fictional stories, like time traveling. However, when it comes to time travel, the X-Men took things to a whole other level.

The iconic image that kicked off "Days of Future Past," Uncanny X-Men #141. (Cover art by John Byrne and Terry Austin)

It all started with the classic time-travel epic "Days of Future Past," by Chris Claremont, John Byrne, and Terry Austin, which saw a future where Sentinels have conquered the world and mutants are hunted down and kept in concentration camps. One of the few surviving X-Men, Kate Pryde, is sent back in time by a mysterious mutant named Rachel, to Pryde's younger self, the then-new X-Men member, Kitty Pryde. The older Kate helped her old teammates stop the assassination of an anti-mutant senator whose death would have made him a martyr and caused the Sentinel program to go nationwide.

However, even after Kate succeeded, Claremont revealed that that timeline continued to exist (John Byrne was very angry, since the ending of the story was originally supposed to be Kate disappearing into nonexistence, but Claremont added a line to say that she survived). We met the young mutant who sent Kate back in time, Rachel. She turned out to be Rachel Summers, daughter of Cyclops and Jean Grey. She ended up going back in time as well, and then merged with the Phoenix Force and became the new Phoenix (this was before the revelation that the Phoenix Force had never merged with Jean Grey, but rather had taken her place). She had to deal with the dark truth that her mother was dead in this timeline and it seemed as though she would never be born!

Claremont followed up on Rachel's past with "Days of Future Present," which saw an adult Franklin Richards travel to the present as well. This time, the future world had grown so sick of people going back in time to stop their reality that they empowered a mutant-hunter known as Ahab to go back in time to stop Franklin. It turned out, though, that it wasn't Franklin at all, but one of his "dream selves" that he had created as he had died in the future. It eventually went away, but gave Rachel some sort of closure with Franklin, her boyfriend in the future (her past).

One of the most notable time-traveling X-Men characters was Cable, who was the son of Cyclops and Madelyne Pryor (a clone of Jean Grey), who Cyclops had to send into the future when the infant was infected with a techno-organic virus that could not be cured in the present. In a bizarre twist, years later, on their honeymoon, Cyclops and Jean Grey actually traveled into the future themselves into new bodies and helped raise the young baby Nathan, inspiring him to become a freedom fighter against Apocalypse's rule in the future. He then traveled back to the past to take the fight to Apocalypse in the present day. Cable then lived on Earth for a number of years and helped form X-Force.

When Whilce Portacio became the artist on *Uncanny X-Men* (and the coplotter of the entire X-Men line of comics, along with Jim Lee), he wanted to introduce a Filipino superhero. However,

Marvel's marketing department said that they really could use a black team member, so Portacio's Bishop turned out to be a black law enforcement agent from the future who traveled back in time to chase a deadly criminal from the future named Trevor Fitzroy. Stranded in the past, Bishop joined the X-Men and proved to be a valued member of the team.

Years later, though, when Hope Summers was born, Bishop recalled a prophecy about a baby being born like Hope and it being responsible for the terrible future Bishop was from. So he decided to kill her (he is one of those people who would be willing to kill Hitler as a baby). Cable had to take baby Hope into the future and Bishop then traveled after them and they had a cat-and-mouse game throughout the centuries using time travel. They returned to the present when Hope was now a teenager. Bishop eventually apologized for his poor behavior and was given a chance at redemption (the X-Men love to let people redeem themselves).

Really, no matter the year, the odds are that the X-Men have either traveled to in the past or they will travel to it in the future.

65 Jim Shooter and the X-Men

When Jim Shooter took over as the editor-in-chief of Marvel Comics in 1978, he became the most involved editor-in-chief that Marvel had ever had outside of Stan Lee (who was also writing most of Marvel's titles at the time, so he was a special exception). Most Marvel editors-in-chief took a hands-off approach to their fellow creators, with most notable Marvel writers (Len Wein, Marv Wolfman, and Roy Thomas) actually editing themselves on their own titles. Shooter quickly put an end to that tradition, which

Top Five X-Men Characters Who Have Had the Worst Crimes Forgiven

5. Quicksilver

Few characters have flipped back and forth between good and evil as much as Quicksilver. Usually, some excuse will be used to explain it away (typically mind control). However, after he lost his powers and stole the Inhumans' Terrigen Crystals to give himself powers, he killed a guard and has never had to pay the price for the murder. (He used the old "It was a Skrull, not me" excuse and it has been mostly accepted.)

4. Bishop

When Bishop learned that the X-Men had found a mysterious baby that they named Hope, Bishop flashed back to his youth when he was told a story about how a baby named Hope was responsible for the terrible future that Bishop was from. He then tried to kill her. Even after Cable took her into the future, Bishop followed them for years. He got back to the present and basically apologized and he's now back to normal.

3. Forge

After discovering that there was another dimension that was set to invade our dimension, Forge decided that a good way to stop it would be to trick the X-Men into going to that world and fighting them for everyone else. He just went crazy out of nowhere. Cable later "fixed" his insanity and he was accepted back as a hero.

2. Magneto

Magneto formed his own island and declared his island to be his own sovereign nation. The Soviets sent a sub after him and Magneto sank it, killing over 100 seamen. Everyone has forgiven him, under the theory that it was a wartime decision. That really doesn't fit, but that's how people have written off Magneto's actions when they want to like him as a hero.

1. Emma Frost

In her first appearance, Emma Frost flat-out murdered a few of her underlings because they failed her on a mission. This has never been explained away. Everyone just sort of got used to her being a hero despite her being an outright murderer.

ultimately drove both Wolfman and Thomas to DC Comics within two years of Shooter becoming Marvel's editor-in-chief (Len Wein had already been wooed with promises of being able to write the main Batman ongoing series). Shooter was very hands-on, which his critics have said caused the creators unnecessary aggravation and his supporters have pointed to as a reason for the great critical and commercial success that Marvel saw during Shooter's tenure.

One book that Shooter was especially hands-on with was *X-Men*. The book was an up-and-coming title and Shooter wanted to make sure that it stayed that way. Chris Claremont and John Byrne, however, found Shooter's declarations about the book to be too mercurial. For instance, when Claremont and Byrne pitched Shooter on having a new group of students in *X-Men*, Shooter turned them down, only to ask Claremont a couple of years later to…introduce a new group of students.

As the series went on and the book became more and more popular, Shooter was involving himself more and more into how the book was made. The most famous example, of course, happened at the end of "The Dark Phoenix Saga." Claremont and Byrne had planned for Jean Grey to receive, in effect, a telepathic lobotomy by the Shi'ar in response for her actions as the Dark Phoenix. They would remove her powers to render her no longer a threat. The story had been approved by *X-Men* editor Jim Salicrup, but Shooter insisted that Salicrup never told him about the ending.

Shooter wouldn't allow Jean Grey to survive the actions of Dark Phoenix (like destroying a planet of billions of sentient life-forms), so he made Claremont and Byrne rewrite it. He was okay with her living, but she had to be severely punished (we're talking tortured-in-an-interstellar-prison levels of severity). Claremont and Byrne huddled up and decided that in that case, they would prefer to just kill her off. Shooter loved the idea and the end result was one of the most iconic moments in the history of comics. So did

Shooter micro-manage the situation? Yes, but you could argue that the story was improved as a result, and to many, that is all that matters.

Shooter didn't stop with the ending of "The Dark Phoenix Saga." Soon after, he believed that Wolverine would be better off if people didn't know when he might snap and attack them, so he had Claremont and Byrne add a scene in *Uncanny X-Men #143* where Wolverine almost stabs Nightcrawler when Nightcrawler sneaks a kiss from Wolverine's girlfriend, Mariko, under the mistletoe.

Oddly enough, though, Shooter then determined that Wolverine had never actually ever killed anyone. This was at odds with *X-Men #133*, where Wolverine cut his way through the Hellfire Club's guards. (Shooter made another edit in that issue where Wolverine was cut down by machine-gun fire to his torso, but his healing power allowed him to survive. Shooter thought that made Wolverine's healing power too strong, so had them change a line to say Wolverine was only grazed by the bullets, despite the art clearly showing the bullets hitting him dead on.) However, Shooter was the boss, so in a later story (after Byrne left the book), Claremont revealed that all of the Hellfire Club guards that Wolverine supposedly killed all survived as cyborgs.

Once Byrne left *X-Men* and began writing and drawing *Fantastic Four*, Shooter soon had a new role—referee between Claremont and Byrne! Byrne would complain about Claremont using one of his characters without asking the editor of *Fantastic Four* and Shooter would tell him to take his complaints and work them into the comics. Byrne would do so and then Claremont would complain and Shooter would tell him to retort and so on and so forth.

Shooter was pushed out as editor-in-chief in 1987 after a failed attempt to buy Marvel himself (with a group of investors). Whether Claremont and Byrne would credit Shooter or not, their best work on the X-Men all happened under Shooter's tenure, so he still remains an important part of the history of the X-Men—even if it's only for Jean Grey's death!

66 *Legion* the TV Show

After a number of years, it started to become clear that there was a whole lot that we didn't know about Professor X's early years. Like the whole "was friends with Magneto back when they were young men" revelation in *Uncanny X-Men #161* (by Chris Claremont, Dave Cockrum, and Joe Rubinstein). In that same issue, we learned that after World War II, Charles Xavier traveled to Israel, where he helped people who had suffered trauma during the war.

One of these people was a young woman named Gabrielle Haller, whose parents were killed in front of her when she was in a concentration camp during the war. It left her in a state of catatonic schizophrenia. Xavier used his telepathy to break through the walls that she put up and helped break her out of her catatonia. The more time that they spent together, Haller began to seek out a romantic relationship with Xavier. The issue was that Xavier, being a telepath, knew that she did not really love him but instead she was so grateful for Xavier's help that she perceived that to be love. Despite him knowing otherwise, Xavier decided to let the relationship continue, as he was very attracted to Haller. Their relationship eventually ended when Xavier left Israel to ultimately form the X-Men, but they parted on good terms. As it turned out, though, their time together left Haller pregnant. She decided not to tell

Xavier of the child and she raised him on her own, not even telling her son (named David Haller) about his birth father.

The problem was that, as the son of one of the most powerful mutants on Earth, David also had mutant powers, but they were kicked into existence in a horrific fashion. A bomb meant for Gabrielle (who had become a political figure in Israel, including becoming the Israeli ambassador to the United Kingdom) exploded, killing David's stepfather and causing David's mutant powers to manifest. He wiped out the minds of the terrorists, but ending up adding the personalities of some of the victims, as well as one of the terrorists, to his own, giving him, in effect, dissociative personality disorder. The trauma also put him into a coma. Haller brought her son to Moira MacTaggert at Muir Isle to see if she could help with David.

Eventually, Haller had to turn to Xavier to help with David. When probing David's mind, Xavier realized that he was his son, but he also unleashed David's full powers. Every time he added a new personality, he also added an ability for that personality. When he used one of the abilities, that personality would take over David's body. When he used them all at once, he became, truly, Legion. Since he had literally an unlimited supply of powers, Legion was one of the most powerful mutants on Earth. He just couldn't control the personalities that went with the abilities.

The idea of a superhero who struggles with mental illness fascinated TV writer and producer Noah Hawley, who, following the success of the first season of his TV series adaptation of the Coen Brothers' film, *Fargo*, was given an opportunity to adapt an X-Men character for the first FX Network series based on the X-Men. Hawley had his pick of concepts and a popular idea at FX was to adapt the Hellfire Club. Hawley, though, went for Legion.

The series stars Dan Steven as David Haller, who has been confined to a psychiatric hospital since he was a child, when he was diagnosed with schizophrenia. What David doesn't know, however, is that he has mutant abilities. When his telepathy and telekinesis kicked in, he could not differentiate his powers from mental illness. The TV show does an amazing job depicting both his powers and his mental illness, which remains even when his powers are revealed to him. He was freed from his most recent hospital by a mysterious group called Summerland that tries to help troubled young mutants like David.

In the show, David has multiple personalities as well, and his friend Lenny Busker (played by Aubrey Plaza) ends up in his mind after she's killed. Hawley sets it up as though David's power set is the same as in the comics. However, by the final episode, there is a major twist—Lenny is not there as part of David's power, she is there due to the Shadow King, a powerful malevolent telepathic force that David's birth father tried to protect David from by putting him up for adoption. However, a bit of the Shadow King managed to still get into David's mind and is now trying to control him through personalities like Lenny. It will be interesting to see where they go with Season 2.

67 Wolverine's False Memories

Like so many other famous aspects of Wolverine as a character, his inability to remember his past (a conflict that drove many comic book stories over the years, as well as the first two X-Men films and *X-Men Origins: Wolverine*) was not something that was present in the early days of Wolverine as a character. Wolverine never even hinted at having difficulties remembering his past. Sure, he would occasionally run into someone from his past that he had never mentioned before, but it was presented simply that he was meeting someone that he knew from his past that he just did not talk about, not that he had any problems with remembering them in the first place. In fact, the first issue of the Wolverine miniseries, which was released nearly a decade after Wolverine debuted, included a line that Wolverine even knew who his father was!

That, however, was not going to be the case for long. You see, while Wolverine had long talked about being friends with James Hudson and his wife, Heather, it was not until 1986's *Alpha Flight #36* that we learned that when Wolverine first met the Hudsons, he stumbled out of the woods like a wounded animal. After the Hudsons took him, he had no idea who had given him an adamantium skeleton and claws. Note, though, that the amnesia Wolverine had was specific to the events that gave him the adamantium. Even as he explained to Heather how he could not remember what had happened to him, he continued to remember other events from his past.

Then 1991 saw the release of the "Weapon X" story line in *Marvel Comics Presents* by Barry Windsor-Smith. The story finally revealed how Wolverine gained his adamantium. Following that story line, Larry Hama then revealed in *Wolverine #48–50* that much of what Wolverine believed that he remembered about his past were actually false memories implanted in his mind by Weapon X. This was not to say that everything that he remembered about his past was a lie, as obviously he had run in to plenty of old friends over the years, but mixed along with those legitimate memories were a number of implanted ones. For instance, one of Wolverine's saddest memories was when Sabretooth murdered Wolverine's girlfriend, Silver Fox, on Wolverine's birthday...just to prove that he could do whatever he wanted to Wolverine and Wolverine couldn't stop him. As it turned out, Silver Fox had never actually died. It was all a false memory created by Weapon X and Silver Fox was actually a Hydra agent (Sabretooth then killed her for real).

Now that it had been established that Wolverine's memories could not be trusted, this opened the door to whole new stories of adventures featuring Wolverine that he never remembered before. For instance, we learned of an elite Weapon X strike force that both Wolverine and Sabretooth had been members of (along with a German mutant named Maverick). Wolverine's past was now a blank slate for anyone to interject whatever story that they felt like doing.

In a roundabout way, this led to a major work, 2001–02's *Origin*. You see, with the success of the X-Men film, Marvel quickly realized that the filmmakers were probably going to eventually want to reveal Wolverine's actual background, and since there was not yet one created for the comics, they feared that the movie folks would just come up with their own origin for Wolverine (like how the films came up with a real first name for Rogue on their own and then the comics had to retroactively work that name into the comics, just with a twist, as the comics went with Anna Marie while the movie was simply Marie). So Joe Quesada, Bill Jemas, Paul Jenkins, Andy Kubert, and Richard Isanove revealed Wolverine's actual origin, which had been blocked from Wolverine's mind by the memory implants for over 100 years.

As it turned out, Wolverine was actually the son of John Howlett, a rich plantation owner in Canada, but it is possible that the Howletts' rugged groundskeeper, Thomas Logan, was his actual father. Initially, it was hinted that the groundskeeper's son, Dog Logan, was going to turn out to be Wolverine, but it was instead the pampered son of the Howletts, James. James' mutant powers first manifested when Thomas Logan killed John Howlett in front of everyone. His claws popped out and he mindlessly stabbed Logan to death. His healing powers then "healed" the traumatic memory by blocking it from his mind.

At the end of the crossover "House of M," Wolverine's memory implants were finally removed and Wolverine remembered everything about his past.

68 Plot Danglers

One of the interesting side effects of Chris Claremont being the main writer on *Uncanny X-Men* as it went from being just one of Marvel's many titles to being the centerpiece of essentially its own line of comic books is that Claremont wrote the book basically the same way that he did when it was "the little book that could" as he did when it was the king of the mountain. His approach was to introduce a number of different plots and then slowly address them all over a long period of time. The only problem was that things had changed from the early years and Claremont did not have nearly as much control over how things would play out as he once did when there was only a single X-Men series. When Claremont left the series, the writers who followed him tried to evoke Claremont's style, but they had even less control than Claremont (and also had much shorter runs). The end result was a whole lot of what we like to call "plot danglers."

A plot dangler is a plot that was introduced and then never actually resolved. These sorts of things happen frequently in comics, as writers are removed from projects before they get a chance to finish their stories and the incoming writers are not interested in finishing the work of their predecessors. For the most part, those sorts of plots are minor things. However, there were also a lot of major plots that were left dangling for years before writers eventually got around to addressing them.

In the "Mutant Massacre," for instance, the Marauders were directed by Mister Sinister to slaughter the Morlocks. Why did Mister Sinister want them to do that? Claremont never gave a reason why at the time and no one else came up with an explanation until about a decade later, when it turned out that Sinister recognized them as his own work, and since he knew he didn't create them, then it meant that someone else had copied his work and he couldn't leave knockoffs of his work around (the copier turned out to be the Dark Beast, a student of Sinister from the "Age of Apocalypse" universe).

When Jim Lee and Whilce Portacio took over as the plotters of both *X-Men* and *Uncanny X-Men*, one of their earliest stories was revealing that, at some point in the future, one of the X-Men would turn out to be a traitor and appear to kill most of the original X-Men. Bishop, a new recruit to the team, knew this because he saw the security footage of the incident from the future. Lee and Portacio never revealed who the X-Traitor was and they left the X-Books after roughly a year, leaving the story just hanging there in the wind. Ultimately, Scott Lobdell revealed that the X-Traitor was a possessed Professor X, whose psionic powers (mixed with Magneto's mind, which had been hanging around in Xavier's mind after Xavier had wiped out Magneto's mind during a fight) had transformed into the powerful being known as Onslaught. Bishop's presence in the past, however, changed the future and he saved the X-Men.

Another notable one was "the Twelve." A number of characters from the future showed up in the present and referred to "the Twelve," which was "the dozen mutant humans who will one day rise up and lead all of mutantkind in war against Homo sapiens in the twilight of Earth." Many characters were rumored to be part of the Twelve, including Cyclops, Storm, Cable, Franklin Richards, and Psylocke. It became an interesting guessing game for years as to who would be part of the Twelve. When the Twelve finally did come together, it was revealed that the whole prophecy had been a plot by Apocalypse to trick them into helping him get a new body to possess.

For years, there were hints that Gambit and Mister Sinister had some sort of connection to each other (likely left over from

Claremont's original plan that they were going to be created by the same person), until finally we learned that Gambit had been hired by Sinister to put together a group of mercenaries (who became the Marauders) and also to find out the location of the Morlocks. Even there, though, Sinister paid Gambit with a mysterious vial whose importance has somehow still never been explained! So resolving a notable plot dangler created an even longer-lasting plot dangler!

Luckily, for the most part, major plot danglers are much less common nowadays, as writers just don't have the same freedom these days that Claremont did to wander around and eventually resolve his plots. Still, it's always fun to see if future writers will revisit any other unresolved danglers.

69 Must Read: "Weapon X"

In 1970, Roy Thomas managed to convince Stan Lee that it made sense to pay the licensing fee to make comic books based on one of Robert E. Howard's pulp novel characters, Conan. Lee was wary of the endeavor, so much so that he refused to approve the use of John Buscema to draw the series. Buscema was one of Marvel's most popular (and highest-paid) artists and he loved to draw sword and sorcery books like *Conan*, but Lee felt that he was too valuable on their superhero titles. Instead, Lee insisted that they use a cheaper artist.

So Thomas went to an unheralded young artist named Barry Windsor-Smith, a British artist who was calling himself simply Barry Smith at the time. Smith had worked with Thomas on a couple of *Avengers* issues and had actually made his debut on an issue of *X-Men* in 1968. Smith turned out to be a revelation and *Conan* soon became one of Marvel's highest-selling comic book titles, with Smith becoming one of the most popular artists in the industry. Despite his popularity, Smith left the series after just three years, choosing to abandon comic book art entirely.

After working as a fine artist for a number of years, Smith decided to make a triumphant return to comic books in 1983, working on a few projects for Marvel. In 1984, he drew "LifeDeath," a one-off issue of *Uncanny X-Men* written by Chris Claremont, which saw Storm holed up in the high-rise apartment of the mutant inventor known as Forge. Forge had developed a weapon that could temporarily take away mutant abilities. A government agent turned the power all the way up and tried to use it on Rogue of the X-Men. Forge pushed him to prevent the agent from blasting Rogue, but instead the blast hit Storm, robbing her of her powers. Forge nursed her back to health, but when she found out that he was the inventor of the device, she rebuked him and left.

The issue was very well received. A year later, Smith returned to do a sequel to "LifeDeath" (a third part was started but then Smith decided to take it himself and do it as a creator-owned story). One year later, Smith drew a stunning one-off issue with Wolverine being hunted down by Lady Deathstrike and the cyborgs known as the Reavers. Then, finally, one year later, he did a fairly generic fill-in issue following "Mutant Massacre." While his work was sporadic, Smith was still one of the most acclaimed artists in the business and his annual *Uncanny X-Men* issues were highly anticipated events.

Before leaving Marvel a second time to go work for Valiant (a comic book company launched by Jim Shooter after he got pushed out by Marvel), Windsor-Smith decided to tackle Wolverine's origins. In a serialized story in *Marvel Comics Presents #72–84*, Marvel's biweekly anthology series, Windsor-Smith wrote, drew, and lettered the 13-part story, "Weapon X," which told the story of how Wolverine was given his adamantium skeleton and claws.

Windsor-Smith truly is one of the top comic book artists of all time. His sense of storytelling meshes wonderfully with his detailed and layered character work. And not only was "Weapon X" full of that breathtaking artwork, the story was unique in that it was mostly told from the perspective of three of the people who worked on the project: the mysterious "Professor," Abraham Cornelius, and Carol Hines. Cornelius and Hines, especially Hines, are the closest that the story has to protagonists, as they at least seem a little bit reluctant to mind wipe a complete stranger and inject him with a pile of adamantium.

The story, for the most part, plays out like a thrilling horror film, as the bad guys are ultimately done in by their own hubris when the monster that they have just created manages to turn on them in the end. In the aforementioned Wolverine vs. Lady Deathstrike issue that Windsor-Smith drew, he was especially good at drawing Wolverine in a messed-up state, and the design he has of Wolverine covered in tubes and a virtual reality helmet has become an iconic look for Wolverine in the years since.

Windsor-Smith, by the way, was friends with Chris Claremont and he didn't want to step on Claremont's toes, so he asked Claremont if he had any plans as to Wolverine's origins. At the time, Claremont was planning on having Apocalypse being involved in Wolverine's origins (another "plot dangler" that was never followed up on), so Windsor-Smith threw in a scene where the Professor is on the phone with a mysterious person who was his secret boss. The idea would be that you could just assume it was Apocalypse on the other end of that line.

70 Mystique

This surely comes as no surprise, but comic book writers tend to be partial to characters that they themselves created. Therefore, whenever you see an older character brought into a comic book seemingly out of nowhere, odds are good that the writer of that comic had something to do with the creation of the character. No writer in comic book history, however, has been quite as loyal to his creations as Chris Claremont. If Claremont invented you, there is a very good chance that he found a way to work you into an X-Men comic book story at some point. A perfect example of this is Mystique.

Introduced toward the end of Ms. Marvel's ongoing series, the shape-shifting Mystique clearly had some sort of elaborate plot all set to go against Ms. Marvel. However, the series was canceled before Claremont could get to that story. It would have involved the introduction of Rogue. A couple of years after *Ms. Marvel* ended, Claremont then brought Mystique into *X-Men* for "Days of Future Past," where she formed a new Brotherhood of Evil Mutants consisting of herself, Blob, Pyro, Avalanche, and Destiny. Destiny was an older woman and she and Mystique had an extremely close relationship. This was back in the days when Marvel would not allow openly gay couples in their comics, but Claremont did his best to allude to Mystique and Destiny's close friendship being something deeper than that.

In fact, after Claremont was rebuffed in his initial attempt at revealing that Nightcrawler's father was the Doctor Strange villain Nightmare, Claremont's next idea was to have Mystique and Destiny be revealed to be Nightcrawler's parents, with Mystique having shape-shifted into a man and impregnated Destiny. When Mystique first met Nightcrawler, she heavily hinted that she was his mother. Soon afterward, however, Mystique introduced another "child," with Rogue making her delayed debut as a member of the Brotherhood of Evil Mutants in *Avengers Annual #10*. Rogue was the foster daughter of Mystique.

After Rogue joined the X-Men (because Professor X could possibly help Rogue control her powers), Mystique transitioned the

Top Five Best Young Female Friends for Wolverine

5. Armor
The young mutant with psionic armor was a good contrast to Wolverine because she was a noble, heroic type and Wolverine was more of a down-and-dirty hero.

4. Katie Power
The youngest member of the Power Pack worked really well with Wolverine because she was such a sweet, innocent kid who kept looking for the good in Wolverine, even when times were awfully dark (like when she ran into him on a school field trip when he was being hunted down by Lady Deathstrike and the Reavers).

3. X-23
Oddly enough, Wolverine and his clone, X-23, never had all that many scenes together when Wolverine was alive. Since his death, though, flashbacks have shown that their relationship was a lot closer than we had ever known before. They had an adorable, almost father-and-daughter relationship.

2. Kitty Pryde
The hero who all the others were inspired by, the only reason that Kitty doesn't get number one is the fact that she stands out so much on her own, so the whole Wolverine/Kitty relationship is not as important to her.

1. Jubilee
Jubilee, on the other hand, is still mostly known for her time as Wolverine's sidekick (with her outfit hilariously using the same color scheme as Batman's sidekick, Robin).

Brotherhood of Evil Mutants into the first government-sponsored mutant strike force, with the team receiving full pardons and now becoming Freedom Force. They were used by the government frequently, including in a story where the Avengers were accused of being traitors and became fugitives from justice. Freedom Force managed to capture the combined forces of the Avengers and West Coast Avengers!

Then Destiny died during a mission and Mystique had a mental breakdown over the loss of one of the greatest loves of her life. This slowly set up a sort of redemption arc for Mystique, where Forge took her into his home following her breakdown because he felt responsible for the death of Destiny (Forge had asked for Freedom Force's help to rescue a group of mutants on Muir Isle from an attack by the evil cyborgs known as the Reavers and during the battle, Destiny and one of Freedom Force's newer recruits were killed). Forge recruits Mystique and Sabretooth for a new version of X-Factor (controlling them through explosive devices placed in their skulls) and Forge and Mystique ultimately begin to date.

That situation obviously ultimately fell apart and she went on the run. Soon afterward, the X-Men movie came out, with Rebecca Romijn playing Mystique, who now is covered with blue scales. Mystique's look was changed in the comic books to match her scaly look in the films. She also went back to being a traditional villain, once again trying to kill senator Robert Kelly (which she first tried to do in her debut X-Men appearance).

Then she received her own ongoing series by Brian K. Vaughan (launched at the same time as Vaughan was launching *Runaways* for Marvel), where Professor X recruited Mystique to work for him as a secret agent, as no one would believe that she was secretly working with the X-Men. That series did not last that long, and soon Mystique was back to her villainous ways. One of her most diabolical plots saw her pretend to join the X-Men, only to get other villains on to the team so that they all turned on the X-Men at once. Her actions during this period led to Wolverine hunting her down and seemingly killing her.

She survived, of course, but then Mystique was portrayed in the X-Men reboot films by Jennifer Lawrence and became more of a heroic character, so suddenly Mystique was once again a member of the X-Men, this time a part of Magneto's team of proactive X-Men, consisting of characters that weren't afraid of getting their hands dirty. Mystique is a perfect shape-shifter, as her plots and characterizations have changed many times over the years.

71 M-Day

Ever since she debuted in *X-Men #4*, Scarlet Witch (Wanda Maximoff) has been one of the most misunderstood mutants in the Marvel Universe. We're not even talking about how she debuted as a member of the Brotherhood of Evil Mutants and was not actually ever evil (heck, later stories even bizarrely revealed that she wasn't actually a mutant, but that's neither here nor there for this discussion). No, we're taking about how the Scarlet Witch's powers have befuddled comic book writers for over 50 years now. When she first fought against the X-Men with the Brotherhood of Evil Mutants, her power was a "hex" that would cause bad luck for whoever she targeted with the hex. What "bad luck" meant in any given situation was seemingly random. It might mean that a wall abruptly collapsed on her opponent, it might mean that they trip out of nowhere; it was really up in the air. This was always a difficult thing for artists to depict, so they eventually just gave her generic energy blasts that they called "hex bolts."

During his run as the writer/artist on *Avengers West Coast*, however, John Byrne decided to further develop her powers. He theorized that if she was giving people "bad luck," then what she was really doing was altering reality itself by making "bad luck" occur. So Byrne took that a step beyond and had her just outright alter reality without the bad luck element. That aspect of her power was then quickly de-emphasized when Byrne left the title. Later, Kurt Busiek suggested that her strange powers were due to her being imbued with Chaos Magic at birth, so that's what led to her powers being so chaotic.

Years later, Brian Michael Bendis took over as the writer on *Avengers* with "Avengers Disassembled" and he went back to Byrne's theories (as well as Byrne's shocking revelation that Wanda's powers had created her two children and thus, they eventually ceased to exist) by revealing that Scarlet Witch had blocked the "death" of her children from her memory and once she was confronted with her past, she snapped and then used her reality-altering powers to attack the Avengers, killing Ant-Man, Vision, and Hawkeye. Doctor Strange showed up to help deal with her but then Magneto arrived and took his daughter to his home in Genosha and told everyone that he would deal with her. Still in shock, the Avengers let him go and then disbanded their team in the wake of all the damage caused by one of their most prominent team members.

Once the Avengers reformed, however (with Wolverine now a member of the team, alongside other new members Luke Cage, Spider-Man, and Spider-Woman), they decided to revisit the Scarlet Witch situation in the crossover event, "House of M," after Professor X came to them after trying to deal with Wanda in Genosha and realizing how dangerous she had become. They brought in the X-Men to discuss what to do with someone who could change reality on a whim and was clearly mentally unstable. Meanwhile, Wanda's brother, the former Avenger known as

Quicksilver, found out about the meeting and went to warn Wanda and his father, Magneto. When the Avengers and X-Men showed up, suddenly Wanda altered all of reality to a new world where mutants were in charge and Magneto (and his "House of M") was the most powerful person on the planet.

Eventually, Wolverine regained his memories and helped others to realize the truth and they fought their way to Magneto's palace and tried to get Wanda to change things back. They had presumed that Magneto had been the one who pushed her to alter reality, but it turns out that it was Quicksilver all along, as he told her the world would be better with mutants in charge. When the final battle came and it was clear that the world was not better, Wanda (clearly in a disturbed state) said three words that would change the X-Men forever, "No more mutants."

Instantly, millions of mutants on Earth lost their powers. Only Doctor Strange's quick actions saved a thousand or so mutants from losing their powers (including all of the heroes who were present at the battle, so nearly all of the most famous mutants, with Magneto, Professor X, Scarlet Witch, and Quicksilver notable exceptions). Scarlet Witch's actions would later be referred to as "Decimation" or "M-Day," the day that the mutant race changed forever. Eventually, it would be discovered that Wanda was manipulated by Doctor Doom when she sought out his help in restoring her children to life and she became possessed by a cosmic entity and that was why she was driven mad in "Avengers Disassembled" and "House of M."

72 The Kubert Brothers

Adam and Andy Kubert might be the only two X-Men artists who appeared in comic books before they were even comic book artists! The two artists, born in 1957 and 1962, respectively, each appeared in a short story in 1969's *DC Special #5* starring their father, Joe Kubert, about his life as a comic book artist. The whole issue was a special dedicated to Kubert's artwork, with a couple of new Kubert-drawn stories and a number of reprints of older Kubert stories. That a comic book in 1969, just a year after DC Comics even began crediting the artists on their comic books, was entirely devoted to the work of one of their artists lets you know how strong a legacy the Kubert brothers are following in with their comic book work.

Joe Kubert broke in to comics in the early 1940s when he was still just a teenager (there is a decent chance that Kubert's first comic book work appeared when he wasn't even 13 yet). He worked for a variety of companies before settling down at DC Comics in the mid-1950s. He would then work for DC Comics for the rest of his career. He helped relaunch the Hawkman character in the 1960s (he had drawn the Golden Age version of the character in the 1940s). However, he is best known for his work on DC Comics' war comics, including *Sgt. Rock*, a character he cocreated with longtime collaborator, writer/editor Robert Kanigher. Eventually, Kubert took over as editor on DC's war comics line from Kanigher and began to work more behind the scenes at DC Comics. In 1976, he opened up a school for aspiring comic book artists called originally Joe Kubert School of Cartoon and Graphic Art (now just called The Kubert School). A number of notable comic book artists have graduated from The Kubert School, including Stephen Bissettte, Amanda Conner, Rick Veitch, and Alex Maleev.

Two of the most notable alumni from The Kubert School just happened to be two of Kubert's sons, Adam and Andy. Since Kubert was in charge of DC's war comics, he helped his sons break in to comics, giving them lettering work when they were very young. Adam, actually, even appeared on the syndicated TV version of *What's My Line?* as the youngest letterer in comics. Both brothers got the chance to draw backup stories in DC war comics as they progressed in their careers. The brothers gained a lot more attention when they began collaborating. They first drew the miniseries *Adam Strange* for DC Comics in 1990. Andy penciled the book and Adam inked him. Two years later, they repeated that process for a Batman/Predator crossover comic that was a huge hit and won Adam an Eisner Award for Best Inker.

Then something happened that changed their careers forever. In 1992, *X-Men* artist Jim Lee left Marvel to cofound Image Comics, along with *Wolverine* artist Marc Silvestri and *Uncanny X-Men* artist Whilce Portacio. Suddenly, three of Marvel's prestige titles were now without artists. This opened up opportunities for both brothers to move up the ladder at Marvel. Andy took over *X-Men* and eventually Adam took over *Wolverine.* (Adam had already gotten an assignment on *Ghost Rider/Blaze: Spirits of Vengeance,* so he took a year to finish his run on that before he took over *Wolverine.* Mark Texeira was the initial replacement for Silvestri on *Wolverine.*) Adam later recalled, "Thank god for Image!" and Andy also once noted, "It was the best thing that ever happened to me."

Andy Kubert drew *X-Men* for the next six years, while Adam Kubert drew *Wolverine* from 1993 to '96 and then drew *Incredible Hulk* for a couple of years.

The thing that stood out about the Kuberts was their loyalty to Marvel. While their page rates did not initially go up when they took over their respective titles, the books were selling so well that they were getting very good royalties. Eventually, too, Marvel made it a priority to lock down the Kuberts and artists Mark Bagley and Ron Lim, as one of Marvel's biggest problems was that after the original Image Comics founders left, the Image guys would recruit Marvel's other hot young artists. Portacio's replacement on *Uncanny X-Men*, Brandon Peterson, also got wooed to Image, as did Lee's initial replacement on *X-Men*, Art Thibert. However, the Kuberts were happy where they were.

The Kuberts both worked for Marvel into the 21st century (Andy drew Wolverine's *Origin*, while Adam launched *Ultimate X-Men* after a stint on *Uncanny X-Men*) until they each signed a three-year deal with DC Comics in 2005, where Andy took over *Batman* and Adam took over *Action Comics*. Adam eventually returned to Marvel, while Andy has remained at DC Comics since 2005.

73 Attend a Comic Book Convention

In 1964, a New York fan named Bernie Bubnis had an idea to have a convention for comic book fans. Earlier that year, Bob Brosch and Jerry Bails had a gathering of fans in Detroit that sometimes gets referred to as the first comic book convention, but the Brosch/ Bails event was more of a general meeting of fans of comics, sci-fi, fantasy, and horror, and it wasn't specifically a convention. No, the best case for the first comic book convention was the July 1964 convention put together by Bubnis and two other fans who helped him organize it, Ron Fradkin and a still-teenaged Len Wein. Wein actually came up with the name for the event, calling it "Comicon."

The very first guests at the New York Comicon were Flo Steinberg (Stan Lee's secretary), Tom Gill (artist on the *Lone Ranger* comic strip), and, amazingly enough, Steve Ditko (co-creator of Spider-Man and Doctor Strange). Ditko even supplied a Spider-Man drawing for the convention brochure! The very first person to sign up for this New York Comicon? Why, none other than a young fan by the name of George R.R. Martin! Yep, years before he wrote the novels that became *Game of Thrones*, Martin was a big comic book fan that often had letters appear in early issues of different Marvel comics.

The success of the Brosch/Bails meet-up and the New York Comicon soon led to the first two regular comic book conventions. Bails and Shel Dorf launched the Detroit Triple Fair in 1965 (the three things making up the Triple Fair being fantasy literature, fantasy films, and comic book art) and Dave Kaler, executive secretary of the Academy of Comic-Book Fans and Collectors (ACBFC), followed up Comicon by launching the Academy Con in New York City in 1965. Soon, conventions began to pop up in cities all across the United States. In 1970, Shel Dorf launched the Golden State Comic-Con in San Diego. It soon evolved into San Diego Comic-Con International, which has become the most popular comic convention in the United States. (A recently revived New York Comic Con by Reed Exhibitions has been the closest rival to San Diego Comic-Con, with over 180,000 attendees to the con in 2016.)

In the early years of comic book conventions, the major appeal was both meeting the writers and artists behind the comic books that people loved as well as meeting other people who shared a love of comic books. Comic book creators were not public figures back in those days (this is what led Stan Lee to think a fun idea would be to release a record for Marvel fans so that they could hear the voices of Marvel's various writers and artists of the mid-1960s), so this would be one of the only times where fans could ever interact

X-Men fans dressed as Beast and Mystique pose on Day One of the 2014 San Diego Comic-Con. (Photo by Denis Poroy/Invision/AP Images)

with their heroes. Similarly, comic book stores were not common, so beside pen pals, there were not a lot of opportunities for comic book fans to interact with each other.

The 1965 Academy Con was noteworthy in that it was the first year that there was a comic book masquerade, where fans would dress in costumes based on their favorite comic book characters. That idea of fan-designed costumes (now referred to as "cosplay") has become a constant presence in comic book conventions today, with costumes more and more elaborate every year.

As time has gone by, however, comic book conventions became the ideal place for movie producers to promote their genre pictures. *Star Wars*, for instance, saw some of its earliest hype at a comic book convention. Once those films began to do well through promotion at comic book conventions, others followed suit. To the point where most comic book conventions are now more geared around television and film than they are about comic books, with Artists Alley (the section with the comic book creators) taking more of a backseat every year. However, even with them taking a backseat, the conventions are so huge that it still is a great place to meet all your favorite comic book creators.

In addition, comic book conventions are good places for aspiring comic book artists to show their work to representatives from comic book companies. Two of the most notable comic book artists for the X-Men titles in the early 1990s, Jim Lee and Rob Liefeld, both broke in to comics by showing their work to editors at comic book conventions (New York and San Francisco, respectively). If you're an X-Men fan, you really should try to attend at least one comic book convention in your life.

74 Utopia

Following the events of M-Day, when the Scarlet Witch decimated the mutant population of Earth through her reality-altering powers, the mutants of the world were suddenly more in danger than ever before. They were being threatened when there were millions of them in the world, now that there were just a thousand or so spread across the planet, they were in grave danger. One hundred ninety-eight mutants who kept their powers were welcomed to the Xavier

Institute for safe haven. The X-Men took in any mutant who wanted to get sanctuary, including some of their former enemies. With so few mutants left on Earth, there was little time to think in terms of "good" or "bad."

The United States Government also got involved, sending a squad of human-piloted Sentinels (led by James Rhodes, the former War Machine) to protect the residents of the Xavier Institute. The problem with that sort of "protection" is that it was awfully close to the residents of Xavier Institute being, in effect, prisoners in their own home. Only the main X-Men team, who cut the deal with the government, was allowed to freely go to and from the school.

The protection sadly became needed when the X-Men were transporting a large group of now de-powered students away from the school when they were attacked by anti-mutant zealots who blew up all of the buses with the de-powered students on them. It was one of the biggest X-Men-related tragedies ever.

Things got even worse when the first mutant birth since M-Day occurred. There was a race for the baby between the X-Men, the anti-mutant hate groups, Mister Sinister, and the mysterious mutant-eating Predator-X. While the X-Men were trying to find the baby, they were also doing experiments with future timelines to see if there were any futures where mutants came back into existence. They sent duplicates of Jamie Madrox into the future and when the dupes died, their information would return to the prime Jamie's mind. He learned that in one future, the one that Bishop came from, the baby was responsible for the horrible state of mutants in Bishop's time (when they were all kept in concentration camps) while in Cable's future, the baby was a messiah figure who brought the mutant race back to life.

Therefore, Bishop tried to kill the baby and used nanotechnology to turn the Sentinels against the X-Mansion, destroying it and giving him the opportunity to kill the child. Cable, though, was able to take the baby into the future to protect her. Bishop shot at him as he was leaving but missed and instead shot Professor X in the head, nearly killing him.

With the X-Mansion in shambles and the mutant race in bad shape, Cyclops decided to disband the X-Men. Soon, however, he and Emma Frost were called to San Francisco to help his old friend and teammate, Angel. It turned out that Lady Mastermind had brainwashed the entire city into believing it was the 1960s. Once the heroes saved the day, the mayor of San Francisco offered to host the X-Men in San Francisco, making it a safe haven for mutants in exchange for the X-Men serving as the official superheroes of the city. Cyclops agreed and the X-Men moved west.

Sadly, though, Norman Osborn had taken control of SHIELD after helping to turn back an invasion of Earth by the shape-shifting Skrulls. Osborn soon turned SHIELD into HAMMER and put together his own team of Avengers consisting of supervillains disguised as heroes (Venom as Spider-Man, Bullseye as Hawkeye, etc.). He then tried to form his own team of X-Men as well. He had formed a secretive group of seemingly like-minded people called the Cabal, which included Loki, Doctor Doom, and also Emma Frost and Namor (Frost kept her involvement a secret from Cyclops). So Frost and Namor were part of Osborn's new team of X-Men that were at odds with the "real" X-Men. Eventually, a series of anti-mutant protests led to a riot and a confrontation where Frost and Namor revealed that they were still on the side of the good guys.

When the dust settled, Cyclops' only out was to take the X-Men out of San Francisco entirely. Cyclops had Magneto's old base, Asteroid M, raised from the ocean (where it had crashed a few years earlier) and turned into an island. He then declared the island a sovereign mutant nation where all mutants could find sanctuary. Osborn chose to back down and accept it as a victory that he drove the X-Men out of the United States and could sell the public on the island being no less of a prison as when the Sentinels were guarding the X-Mansion. Whoever was right, Utopia (Cyclops' name for the island) was born.

75 Weapon X

Wolverine first appeared in a comic book in the final panel of *Incredible Hulk #180* (making the following issue his proper first appearance). The Hulk had wandered into Canada and gotten into a fight with the dark magic monster known as the Wendigo. The Canadian government felt that they had to get involved in the fight, so they decided to send "Weapon X" into the situation. The final panel has a caption stating, "Well, now you know what — er — who Weapon X is, faithful one. He's a living, raging power-house who's bound to knock you back on your emerald posterior."

That, then, was all that we knew about Weapon X for a number of years. It was just the codename that Wolverine was given by the Canadian government. This was specifically referenced in a number of other comics, like when Weapon Alpha (James Hudson) comes to take Wolverine back to Canada in *X-Men #109* (referencing the fact that Wolverine's superior told him that he couldn't leave in *Giant-Size X-Men #1* and obviously Wolverine did not listen to him). The first hint that there was a larger project at hand was when we learned that Alpha Flight and Wolverine both fell under the same program, a Department H, and that they had given Wolverine his adamantium skeleton.

Obviously, that was back when Wolverine's memories were not as much of a mess as they would become in his comic book career. Later, we learned that Wolverine had blocked out a lot of his past and that now "Weapon X" actually referred to the project itself, as revealed in Barry Windsor-Smith's classic *Marvel Comics Presents* story arc. So Wolverine was only called Weapon X because he came out of that project. Around the same time, we discovered that Wolverine had been part of a group called Team-X, which was formed using other people who were experimented on at the Weapon X project. The most notable members of Team-X were Logan, Victor Creed (Sabretooth), Maverick, and Wraith. They worked for the CIA as a sort of special forces team.

Later, in the pages of *X-Force*, we met Garrison Kane, the latest version of Weapon X. Kane and Deadpool were both revealed to have come from a Department K that was set within Department H. The experiments done on Deadpool, however, appear to be independent from whatever they were doing with Wolverine.

During his epic *New X-Men* run, Grant Morrison revealed that Weapon X was not Weapon X like the letter of the alphabet, but rather Weapon X like the Roman numeral for 10. It was revealed that Weapon X was just the 10th in a series of experiments that made up the Weapon Plus Program (the "plus" part of the program name, naturally, also looks like an X). The idea is that Captain America and his Super Soldier Serum were Weapon I and that all the other weapons were attempts to, if not replicate Captain America and the Super Soldier Serum, at least come up with something that could be comparable to their early successes with Weapon I. Weapon X was the first time that they decided that it made sense to use mutant test subjects. It was later revealed that the villainous John Sublime was working behind the scenes of the Weapon Plus Program. The mutant mercenary known as Fantomex was also a product of the Weapon Plus Program.

A second version of Weapon X was responsible for cloning Wolverine and coming up with the female clone that is now known as X-23. A third version of the group was started by Malcolm Colcord, who was one of the guards on Wolverine's original

Top Five Best Wolverine/Sabretooth Fights

5. *Uncanny X-Force #34*

   At the end of *Uncanny X-Force*, Sabretooth tricked Wolverine's son, Daken, into launching an all-out assault on X-Force, until Wolverine was forced to kill his own son. Sabretooth arranged it all just to laugh when Wolverine had to kill his own kid.

4. *Wolverine #10*

   In a flashback to one of his yearly visits to Wolverine on Wolverine's birthday so that he could prove to Wolverine that he could kill him at any moment, we see Wolverine finally stand up for himself and throw himself and Sabretooth off a mountain cliff after Sabretooth killed his girlfriend.

3. *Wolverine (Vol. 2) #55*

   While investigating whether or not there is a connection between all characters with similar mutant powers to Wolverine and Sabretooth, Sabretooth showed up and was almost feral. Wolverine held off on killing him and Sabretooth then killed one of the young mutants hanging out with Wolverine. So Wolverine then decapitated Sabretooth with a magical sword!

2. *Wolverine #90*

   The X-Men had been trying to rehabilitate Sabretooth for a while before Wolverine decided to fix things for them by just getting rid of Sabretooth (as Wolverine felt he could never be trusted). So they got into a fight and Wolverine proved himself the better fighter. He then holds Sabretooth's face between two of his claws and, as the issue ends—he pops the third claw! Sabretooth survived, just with massive brain damage.

1. *Uncanny X-Men #213*

   In just their second fight ever, Wolverine fought Sabretooth with a shocking sense of constraint. This was because the fight was really an attempt for Psylocke to read Sabretooth's mind to get information about the Marauders while he was too distracted by the fight with Wolverine.

Weapon X project. When Wolverine escaped, he was in a mindless rage due to the experiments performed on him and he slaughtered the guards on the project. Colcord was the only one to survive and even he only barely survived (he was badly scarred). Colcord reconfigured Weapon X as a project to hunt down mutants and eliminate them, while using a private strike force of mutants and mutates, like Garrison Kane, Marrow, Sabretooth, Sauron, Wild Child, and Aurora, led by a former SHIELD agent, Brett Jackson. Jackson and Colcord fought for control of the group. Once M-Day hit and mutants were no longer as much of a concern, the group shut down. They killed hundreds, if not thousands, of mutants before shutting down.

Recently, Weapon X was started again for a fourth time, this time with William Stryker (from "God Loves, Man Kills") as the head of the group. This new program was about experimenting on humans and turning them into mutant killing machines through Hulk and Wolverine DNA. Sabretooth and Wolverine from the alternate "Old Man Logan" reality have to team up to take them down, before they can build too many "Weapons of Mutant Destruction," like Weapon H, a mixture between the Hulk and Wolverine!

76 Arthur Adams

One of the most important comic book artists of the 1980s might never have been discovered had it not been for the need to clean out an office. Arthur "Art" Adams was a self-taught comic book artist who was trying to break into comics in the early '80s while he was still in high school. He was heavily influenced by two of the most acclaimed comic book artists of the time, Michael Golden (who later became Marvel's art director, and also happened to draw the first appearance of Rogue in *Avengers Annual #10*) and Walter Simonson (who later drew a long run on *X-Factor* when his wife, Louise Simonson, was writing the book). Adams was somewhat of a mix of those two artists' styles (more Golden than Simonson), which were tight lines and dynamic characters. Adams was also one of the first American artists to have a noticeable Manga influence in his artwork.

Adams would go to comic book conventions and also send in copies of his portfolio to comic book companies. Eventually, artist Joe Rubinstein (who did finishes and inks for Dave Cockrum during Cockrum's second stint on *Uncanny X-Men*, which allowed Cockrum to keep up with the monthly deadlines and then also did pencils and inks over Frank Miller's layouts on the *Wolverine* miniseries) recommended Adams to Marvel editors Denny O'Neil and Linda Grant. They gave him a story to draw for *Bizarre Adventures*...which was then canceled before Adams' story could ever see print. So Adams' big break didn't actually happen for another year or so!

The pages from the unpublished story ended up in the bottom of a drawer in Marvel editor Al Milgrom's office. Milgrom then decided to leave his editorial position to become a full-time free-lance writer and artist. When he was cleaning out his office for the new inhabitant, Carl Potts, Milgrom discovered Adams' pages. He showed them to Potts and Potts' assistant editor, Ann Nocenti. They hired Adams to draw a sample Defenders story.

Nocenti was just about to get promoted to the main editor on *Uncanny X-Men*. Before that, though, she first had a writing project of her own that she thought the young Adams (not yet 20 years old) would be perfect for (partially because all the other established Marvel artists that she asked had turned her down). The series was about an alien named Longshot who was an artificial being created by the evil Mojo, a creator from another dimension who used the slave people that he created as entertainment for his constantly filming cameras. Longshot helped lead an uprising against Mojo but was injured and lost his memory. He ended up on Earth, with Mojo sending some bad guys to get him. Longshot eventually regained his memories and the miniseries ended with Longshot continuing the rebellion in the Mojoverse.

Adams designed Longshot himself (using some early design aspects from Potts), using a number of interesting stylistic choices, like giving him pouches (a major design element on 1990s superheroes) and a mullet based on the lead singer from the pop band, Kajagoogoo. Adams was a very slow artist who was just learning how to do sequential work, so the first issue took eight months for him to complete. Working with Louise Simonson (who edited the series as a freelancer, as she had left her *X-Men* editing gig to become a freelance writer) and other advisers (including Jim Shooter), Adams' sequential work got better and better. The miniseries was a major hit.

When Nocenti moved over to become the editor of *Uncanny X-Men*, Chris Claremont wanted to work her *Longshot* characters into the series, including making Longshot a member of the team and Mojo a recurring villain. Claremont also wanted to use Adams on the *X-Men*. Adams couldn't really draw fast enough for a monthly series, so he began to do a series of annuals. In 1985, he drew both parts of a classic crossover event where the X-Men and New Mutants traveled to Asgard (where Loki planned to make Storm the Goddess of Thunder to replace Thor).

Adams has mostly worked as a cover artist in the years since, drawing the first two years of covers for *Classic X-Men* (a series that reprinted the early All-New, All-Different X-Men stories). He also drew a Wolverine promotional piece in the late 1980s that would be used on Marvel licensed products for many years afterward. Adams was one of the most notable artists of the era, as most of the superstar artists of the early 1990s (the guys who later founded Image Comics) were heavily influenced by Adams, despite him being barely older than most of them. Recently, Adams has gone back to being a regular cover artist for Marvel, drawing the covers for *X-Men Blue*.

77 Must Read: "To Have and Have Not"

One of the oddest things about the classic *Uncanny X-Men* two-parter, "To Have and Have Not" (we're using the title of the second part as the overall title of the story; the first part was titled, "Scarlet in Glory") in *Uncanny X-Men #172–173* (by Chris Claremont, Paul Smith, and Bob Wiacek) is that the story relies heavily on the then-recently released *Wolverine* miniseries by Claremont, Frank Miller, and Joe Rubinstein. It basically picks up right where that series left off, with the reader pretty much expected to know what happened in that series, plus the new character, Yukio, who was introduced in that series. Yet, even with those odd aspects, the story remains an absolute classic in the genre.

The story opens with the X-Men traveling to Japan to attend Wolverine's marriage to Mariko Yashada, who recently took over as the head of the Yashada Clan after Wolverine killed her evil father, Shingen, in the aforementioned *Wolverine* miniseries. While Wolverine was in Japan, Rogue, who was a former enemy of the X-Men as part of the Brotherhood of Evil Mutants, joined the team because she needed Xavier's help in dealing with her powers (her touch of someone else's exposed skin causes her to absorb other people's powers and personality). Rogue typically only temporarily borrowed people's powers and personality, but she had taken it too far with the superhero Ms. Marvel. Rogue ended up with her powers permanently, plus Ms. Marvel's personality was stuck in her head (that was the main reason that she needed Xavier's help). Wolverine was a good friend of Carol Danvers before she became Ms. Marvel, so he was not happy when Rogue showed up with the others.

Before he died, Shingen Yashada had promised his criminal empire to his son, the villainous Silver Samurai. However, when Wolverine killed Shingen, Mariko took over instead. Now Silver Samurai and his partner, the deadly Viper, wanted to kill his half-sister, Mariko, to take Clan Yashada back. Silver Samurai attacked the X-Men directly and they fought him off, but while they were distracted, Viper poisoned everyone's tea (except Mariko, who had gone to meet with her half-brother, not knowing that he was ready to kill her). Wolverine managed to keep Storm from drinking her tea, so she and Wolverine's friend from the *Wolverine* series, Yukio, head to save Mariko's life. They pull it off but in the process, Storm's powers go haywire and she almost dies. Yukio must take her in to protect her.

Meanwhile, the X-Men are all down for the count except Wolverine (due to his healing powers) and Rogue (due to Ms. Marvel's own healing powers). Rogue forced Wolverine to let her come with him to help track down and stop Silver Samurai and Viper. He reluctantly agreed. Mariko goes to keep watch over the X-Men in the hospital. After failing to find their prey, Wolverine realized that it was all a ruse to draw Wolverine away from their main target, the hospital where Mariko was alone with the incapacitated X-Men! The heroes rush back in time to head the bad guys off and Paul Smith then drew an iconic battle between Wolverine and Silver Samurai. In the end, though, Viper fired a deadly blast at Wolverine when Rogue jumped in front of the blast and took the fatal shot herself. Wolverine, moved by her sacrifice, gave her

The Uncanny
X-Men #173,
*part of "To
Have and Have
Not."* (Cover art
by Paul Smith)

a gentle kiss to allow her to absorb his healing powers so that she could live.

The next day was the wedding, and Cyclops showed up with his new girlfriend, Madelyne Pryor, who bizarrely looks just like his dead ex-girlfriend, Jean Grey. Everyone freaks out (and Madelyne also has a hard time with her boyfriend's friends, like when Kitty Pryde asked Madelyne to watch Lockheed, not knowing that he was Kitty's pet alien dragon!). Yukio had helped Storm cut loose while they were together and when Storm showed up at the wedding, she had dramatically cut her hair into a Mohawk and was now wearing a black leather outfit.

Sadly, the wedding was then called off when Mariko told Wolverine that he was not worthy of marrying her. This led to an epic panel at the end of Wolverine crying a single tear of loneliness, while we see that the brainwashing villain, Mastermind, was behind Mariko's sudden change of heart. (Tragically, Mariko and Wolverine never marry and Mariko dies a decade later. Suffering from being poisoned by a rival clan, Wolverine had to use his claws to put Mariko out of her misery.) The 2013 film, *The Wolverine*, was a basic adaptation of this classic story arc (Hugh Jackman read it and loved it so much that he pushed for it to be the next Wolverine film).

78 Excalibur

The launch of *Excalibur* in 1988 with the graphic novel *Excalibur: The Sword is Drawn* (which was followed by an ongoing series) achieved two major goals for Chris Claremont. One, he managed to find a new team for Nightcrawler and Kitty Pryde, who Claremont had written out of the X-Men in 1987 following the "Mutant Massacre" (Claremont was worried that other writers would try to take the characters for other titles if he didn't come up with a series for them to star in) and two, he managed to work on an ongoing series with the great British artist Alan Davis.

Davis had become a star artist over at Marvel UK, Marvel's British comic book line, working on *Captain Britain*, a character that Claremont had actually created for Marvel UK in the mid-1970s. Davis joined the book in the early 1980s with writer David Thorpe and then Alan Moore. Davis revamped Captain Britain's costume and when Moore joined the book, they brought back another one of Claremont's creations, Captain Britain's sister, Elisabeth, who was now the telepathic agent known as Psylocke. Moore and Davis created a number of excellent stories together before Davis launched a new Captain Britain series with writer Jamie Delano. Davis then took over the series as writer and artist and wrote it to the end of the series (with Psylocke filling in as Captain Britain and being blinded). The final issue, released at the end of 1985, promised that Captain Britain would soon continue as an American comic book. Obviously, it took a couple of years before that actually came to fruition.

Alan Davis had already broken into the American comic book market while still writing and drawing *Captain Britain*. He had become the regular artist on *Batman and the Outsiders* and then got the gig as the main artist on *Detective Comics* in 1986. However, throughout it all, Chris Claremont kept trying to get Davis to come to Marvel. Eventually, Davis finally agreed. Claremont kept Davis busy in 1987 while waiting for their new project to finally come out, so Davis drew the 1987 annuals for both *New Mutants* and *Uncanny X-Men* (between 1985 and 1988, *Uncanny X-Men Annual* was drawn by either Art Adams or Alan Davis for four straight years—wow), plus a couple of fill-in issues of *Uncanny X-Men*.

Finally, in early 1988, Claremont and Davis (with inkers Paul Neary and Mark Farmer) combined the two ideas (a new *X-Men* spinoff with an American version of Captain Britain) with a new superhero team called Excalibur, which was set in England, where Kitty Pryde (then known as Shadowcat) and Nightcrawler had gone to recuperate. Some villains show up looking for Rachel Summers, who had been written out of *Uncanny X-Men* in 1986, and Captain Britain and his girlfriend, the shape-shifting elemental known as

Meggan, ended up teaming up with Kitty and Nightcrawler to save Rachel. The five heroes decide to become a superhero team.

Excalibur was designed as a place where Claremont and Davis could come up with ideas that would be a bit wackier than Claremont's standard *X-Men* fare from that era. This was spotlighted by an epic story line called "The Cross-Time Caper," which lasted over a year from 1989 to 1990 in *Excalibur #12–24*. The team traveled throughout Marvel's Multiverse, getting into trouble in worlds very similar to their own, but just different enough to be bizarre.

Alan Davis left the series with the conclusion of the "The Cross-Time Caper." Claremont also left the book roughly half a year later. Davis intended to return to the book to write and draw it, but his return kept getting delayed, so the fill-in writer, Scott Lobdell (before he got the *Uncanny X-Men* gig) had to just keep doing one-off stories that would keep the book a blank slate for Davis. Finally, with *Excalibur #42*, Davis returned to the series full-time and he made it an even stranger and more humor-driven series. It was an excellent run, which introduced a few new members to the team in the Shi'ar warrior, Cerise, and Kylun, a young boy who was transported to another dimension and came back an adult warrior.

Once Davis left the book, Lobdell returned to make the book feel more like an X-Men title, including crossing it over with the 1993 "Fatal Attractions" crossover, the first time *Excalibur* was treated as an X-title officially. Warren Ellis then wrote an acclaimed run on the book, where he introduced the gruff British secret agent Peter Wisdom, who helped take the book into darker areas. Eventually, when the writers of *X-Men* wanted to bring Kitty Pryde and Nightcrawler back to the X-Men (plus Colossus, who had also joined the team), the book was canceled following *Excalibur #125*.

79 Schism

When Cyclops put out the call that Utopia was now an island sanctuary for any mutant who needed it, he also knew that he had, in effect, placed a giant target on their new home. Luckily, in their fight with Norman Osborn, Emma Frost had successfully recruited Namor to join the X-Men and Namor brought a lot of power to the team. Magneto then showed up (his powers had been restored by the High Evolutionary and the Celestials that had been sleeping outside of San Francisco, which had been established in Neil Gaiman's *Elementals* series that had launched a couple of years before the X-Men moved out West). With the X-Men having a number of powerhouse members, Cyclops was feeling pretty good about their ability to defend the island.

That belief was put to the test in the major crossover event "Second Coming," when Cable arrived in the present with Hope Summers, the baby that everyone had been fighting over in the "Messiah Complex," now grown to be a teenager. Cable had been on the run from Bishop for years but was now back to put Hope in the care of Cable's father, Cyclops, and the rest of the X-Men. However, a collective of X-Men villains chose this time to assassinate Hope, with the belief being that killing Hope would be cutting off the future of the mutant race.

The villains, led by Bastion (a magical fusion of two powerful Sentinels, the Master Mold and the futuristic Nimrod), launched a targeted attack on the X-Men, slowly but methodically eliminating all transportation that the X-Men had, as well as all mutant teleporters. Their plan began to be clear; they were going to pin the X-Men down on Utopia so that Hope would have nowhere to hide.

Cyclops assigned Rogue and Nightcrawler to be Hope's personal bodyguards. Bastion almost managed to kill Hope after beating Rogue mercilessly, but Nightcrawler managed to teleport her to safety, but not before being impaled by Bastion's arm (in a punch meant to crush Hope's skull). Eventually, Bastion surrounded Utopia with a force field that no one could break through. He then opened up a portal from the future and unleashed thousands of Nimrod Sentinels from the future.

Cyclops decided to send Cable and X-Force (Cyclops' secret black ops team of X-Men) into the future to stop the Sentinels' power supply. This move caused Cyclops to have to publicly admit that he had his own private murder squad, which did not sit well with many members of the X-Men (Wolverine would then launch his own, non-Cyclops directed, X-Force team). X-Force succeeded in the future, but Cable seemingly sacrificed himself to allow them to return to the present. With the Sentinels now gone, Hope's powers manifested—she could borrow other people's powers. She used the powers of a variety of X-Men to then kill Bastion and the remaining villains. She then seemed to manifest the Phoenix flames. While everyone freaked out for a moment, suddenly five new teen mutants popped up across the globe!

These mutants were recruited to the X-Men. However, Wolverine was growing disillusioned by the X-Men's bunker mentality on Utopia. It was like Cyclops was training these kids to be soldiers in his war and Wolverine did not like that. Then a newly formed Hellfire Club attacked the X-Men while they were taking a few of these new mutants to a museum. Only one of the young mutants, a shy 14-year-old girl named Oya, was conscious after the initial attack. She contacted Cyclops for directions and he told her to use her powers to kill the Hellfire Club attackers.

Wolverine was aghast at Cyclops teaching a kid to kill, but Cyclops explained that he had been trained by Professor X when he was a teen as well. So this was just about doing what needed to be done. Oya killed the guards, saving her friends' lives. The X-Men then launched a series of attacks on Sentinel bases (owned by the new Black King of the Hellfire Club) around the world, leaving just Cyclops, Wolverine, and the new teen mutants on Utopia. So when they were attacked by a Super-Sentinel, Cyclops was willing to fight the Super-Sentinel along with the young mutants. Wolverine wanted to just destroy Utopia rather than take the kids into the fight.

Once they defeated the Super-Sentinel (Hope and the other teen mutants did end up helping), Wolverine announced that he was leaving Utopia and he was going to reopen the school. He believed that these young mutants needed to be students, not soldiers. Roughly half the X-Men decided to go with Wolverine (including most of the young mutants) while half remained with Cyclops on Utopia. Wolverine reopened Xavier's as the Jean Grey School for Higher Learning.

80 Visit Uncannyxmen.net

When the internet was still in its infancy in the 1980s, the worldwide distributed discussion system known as Usenet was launched. Usenet was basically a giant message board, only it was decentralized. It was split into different newsgroups, all existing out there on various web servers, whether they were a private server, a university's server, or, most commonly, a commercial internet service provider's server. People began using Usenet in the early 1980s, but obviously early on, you had a very select group of people who would actually interact with others on Usenet. As it turned out, a nice chunk of that select group of people happened to be comic

Top Five Best X-Men Crossovers

5. **"X-Tinction Agenda"**
   In the island nation of Genosha, mutants are controlled by the
   ruling class. The various X-groups end up in the island when a
   number of their own are captured to be turned into servants. The
   heroes end up starting a revolution and winning back the country
   for mutants.

4. **"X-Cutioner's Song"**
   After Cable seemingly tries to assassinate Professor X, it turns out
   that it is all a plot by Stryfe (who did the actual shooting) to cause
   disarray that will allow him to kidnap Jean Grey and Cyclops, who
   he believed to be his parents. The X-Men must save them, while
   also stopping the side machinations of Apocalypse.

3. **"Age of Apocalypse"**
   Time travel went wrong and created an alternate reality where
   Apocalypse took over the world decades earlier and Magneto
   had to form the X-Men in honor of Charles Xavier. Bishop has to
   get them to help him change reality back to the way it should be
   before a fed-up humanity decides to just nuke all of the mutants.

2. **"Fall of the Mutants"**
   In a clever approach, this crossover told three parallel stories, all
   about death. The New Mutants deal with the first time that one of
   their members is killed, Angel became Apocalypse's Horseman
   of Death, and the X-Men sacrificed themselves to stop the evil
   Adversary from destroying our world.

1. **"Mutant Massacre"**
   The evil Marauders show up in the Morlock tunnels and start
   killing every Morlock that they can see. The X-Men enter the
   tunnels to save the Morlocks and suddenly find themselves in a
   vicious battle where not every member of the X-Men was able
   to get out of the fight on their own power. This dark story line
   changed the X-Men for good.

book fans. Talking about comic books on Usenet had become so popular by the early 1990s that it was used to disseminate the leaked ending of DC Comics' 1991 crossover event, "Armageddon 2001" (where one of DC's established heroes was going to be revealed to eventually become the villainous Monarch in the far-off year of 2001). Monarch was going to be Captain Atom initially, but after Usenet was used to spread that leaked information far and wide, DC abruptly changed tactics and instead Hawk (from Hawk and Dove) became Monarch.

One of the most popular comic book groups was, naturally, the X-Men newsgroup, which was titled rec.arts.comics.marvel. xbooks ("rec" stood for recreation or entertainment and the rest is self-explanatory). It was the place to be for behind-the-scenes information about the X-Men, as well as reviews of comic books. Scott Lobdell and other comic book creators would occasionally stop by to share information with the readers. The rec.arts.comics.marvel. xbooks FAQ (Frequently Asked Questions—the term "FAQ" originated in the Usenet) was legendary, since there was just so much information to learn about the X-Men for new fans.

Soon, though, the internet began to be opened to the masses. The proliferation of the World Wide Web made that possible. With the World Wide Web now around, the popularity of Usenet slowly decreased in essentially equal proportion. The issue, of course, is that there were not that many websites out there yet for comic book fans. In 1995, Jonah Weiland wanted to discuss the then-new DC miniseries, *Kingdom Come*, with other fans, but there was no place out there to actually do so. So Weiland created a Kingdom Come website. He then wanted to make it so that people knew of other websites out there that they could read, so he began to list Comic Book Resources for fans. That site then slowly evolved into one of the most popular comic book communities and news sites in the United States.

Similarly, then, when the X-Men movie opened in England in 2000, Dean Clayton wanted to read up on the history of the X-Men for the film. He found very little in the way of websites out there that had any real information about the X-Men. So he formed uncannyxmen.net. At first, it was not much different than other sites out there, but then he merged with another X-Men site, Peter Luzifer's "The Other Side of X" (which was a site about X-Men villain teams). They soon became the premier place on the web for the website equivalent of the old rec.arts.comics.marvel.xbooks FAQ, a not-for-profit site made up of contributors sharing an expertise in X-Men history.

Their most popular feature on the site are their character spotlight pages. These are detailed looks into the history of various members of the X-Men Universe. These spotlights take detail to a whole new level, as they are formatted in chronological order, citing each issue as you go along. For instance, taking, say, Nightcrawler as an example, you would see the following all before you would even hit *Giant-Size X-Men #1*, when Professor X recruited Nightcrawler to join the X-Men. You would see a description of Nightcrawler's birth (depicted in both *X-Men Unlimited #4* and *Uncanny X-Men #428*), a description of his childhood (depicted in *Excalibur #1*), a description of his young adulthood (depicted in *X-Men Annual #4* and *Marvel Comics Presents #103*) and then finally his meeting with Xavier (depicted in *Giant-Size X-Men #1*).

Continuing with Nightcrawler as an example, there would be also a checklist of notable events in Nightcrawler's life (for the fans who wants to collect all the major moments) and then an awesome costume gallery, showing his various looks over the years.

The site also has extensive recaps of various X-Men issues going back 50 years. This is not even counting all the other neat articles and columns, like "Mondays With Marts," an interview series with former *X-Men* editor Mike Marts. Uncannyxmen.net is the type of website that you could find yourself spending hours reading without even noticing that any time has passed. It's a wonderful comic book resource.

81 Generation X

When it comes to comic book continuity, one of the trickiest aspects of continuity is the concept of the sliding time scale. The idea is a very logical one, which is to say that you pick a general time that the Marvel Universe began and then everything that has taken place since *Fantastic Four #1* has taken place in that time. You then just scale everything within that time (whether it be 10 years or 15 years) and just try to avoid locking yourself into any specific dates (hence why Reed Richards and Ben Grimm don't often talk about their shared history fighting in World War II).

While the sliding time scale is the best way to go, it leads to a problem when you introduce new generations of heroes. The reason why this is tricky is because writers typically want these younger heroes to grow, but if they grow, then they would inherently cause the heroes who were older when they were young to then have to age as well. You can't very well keep Cyclops in his late twenties while also aging the members of the New Mutants (the teenagers Xavier made into his new class in the early 1980s) into their twenties as well. It just makes things very awkward, continuity-wise. However, in 1994, Marvel decided to double down on that issue by introducing a third generation of X-Men students with *Generation X*.

The logic behind the book was just as sound in 1994 as it was in 1980, when John Byrne and Chris Claremont wanted to introduce a new class of mutant students at Xavier's. When Stan Lee and Jack Kirby launched the X-Men originally, the X-Men were students of

Xavier's School for Gifted Youngsters. Eventually, they graduated and after a while they were replaced by the All-New, All-Different X-Men. These characters, however, were not students like the original X-Men. So eventually, Byrne and Claremont thought it would be a good idea to have a new class of students. That didn't come to pass, though, until 1983, when *New Mutants* launched, starring a new group of students at Xavier's. Over time, though, just like how the original X-Men graduated, so, too, did the New Mutants move on to become the paramilitary strike force known as X-Force.

So in 1994, there were no young people at Xavier's. Except, of course, for Jubilee. Jubilee was an odd little part of the X-Men. She was a runaway who followed the X-Men back to Australia and hid in their base for a few months. When the Reavers ambushed Wolverine and crucified him on a giant X, Jubilee took the opportunity to help Wolverine escape. They became traveling companions (for years, writers have always liked to team Wolverine up with young female heroes, as it's a great contrast between the rugged older Wolverine and the upbeat young female heroes) and when the X-Men reformed, Jubilee was along for the ride but really didn't have a role on the team.

Then the "Phalanx Covenant" happened, and these evil aliens known as the Phalanx showed up and kidnapped a number of teen mutants so that they could test their assimilation abilities on them, as they were not yet able to assimilate older mutants. Banshee, Emma Frost, Sabretooth and Jubilee showed up to free these young mutants. Once the crisis was passed, Professor X decided to reopen Emma Frost's old school for mutants as a new offshoot of Xavier's and give her a chance to redeem herself by making her the headmaster, with former X-Men member Banshee as her coheadmaster.

The new team was a diverse group of young mutants, with strange and different powers: Jubilee, Asian American mutant who projects exploding "fireworks"; Husk, younger sister of X-Force's Cannonball, could tear her skin off to gain new powers; M, a powerful mutant from Monaco with a variety of powers; Skin, a Hispanic mutant whose skin could stretch (but would always sag); Chamber, a telekinetic and telepathic mutants whose powers blew open a hole in his chest; Synch, a black mutant who could copy the powers of mutants near him; and Penance, a mute mutant who was covered in razor-sharp armor.

The book was written by Scott Lobdell and drawn by award-winning artist Chris Bachalo, who had worked on Vertigo books for DC before coming to Marvel. Bachalo's striking artwork (he was inked by Mark Buckingham) and Lobdell's charming characterizations made the book a hit. Then Lobdell and Bachalo left the series and it eventually petered out and was canceled after *Generation X #75*. Most of the cast has either been killed or ended up in limbo. Marvel recently launched a new series, where Jubilee serves as a mentor to a group of oddball younger mutants. It sadly only lasted a little more than a year.

82 Marc Silvestri

Marc Silvestri became the artist on *Uncanny X-Men* at a strange time in the history of the book. After John Romita Jr. left the series with *Uncanny X-Men #211*, the book had a remarkable stretch of eight straight issues with only a single artist doing two issues in a row (Jackson Guice drew *#216–217* and even there, he had a different inker on each issue). So while John Romita Jr. was the clear heir apparent when he took over *Uncanny X-Men* from Paul Smith, the succession from Romita Jr. was far less evident. In fact, it was such an abrupt decision that Silvestri was pulled off a four-issue miniseries with a single issue left to go!

Marc Silvestri broke in to the comic book industry in the early 1980s. He did so at a comic book convention, like many other comic book creators. However, very few comic book creators have ever quite pulled off what Silvestri did. He and his brother showed up for a portfolio review at the 1981 Chicago Comic Con, but then things took a turn. Silvestri later recalled, "[DC Comics editor] Joe Orlando paid for my brother not taking no for an answer. The line for portfolio reviews got cut off and we went to Joe's room to show him my stuff. He was very patient—not to mention kind for not calling security. He liked most of what he saw and a week later I was working for DC and not in jail for holding a comic editor against his will."

Silvestri then spent the early 1980s working on short stories for DC Comics. He transitioned to Marvel Comics and in 1986 he got his biggest break to date. He became the regular artist on *Web of Spider-Man*, which was the third Spider-Man monthly at the time and had not originally had a steady creative team during its first year. Paired with writer David Michelinie and inker Kyle Baker, the idea was to show Peter Parker traveling the world with reporter Joy Mercado, covering stories for *Now* magazine (a sister publication to the *Daily Bugle*). Then, a couple of issues in, there was a story about the "Troubles" in Northern Island and after Marvel received a bomb threat at their offices, they re-wrote the story to eliminate any political aspects and Michelinie and Silvestri were now off the book.

Silvestri moved on to a high-profile gig, a miniseries called *Avengers vs. X-Men*, written by *Avengers* writer, Roger Stern, which was set to see Magneto return to villainy as the Avengers fought against the X-men to prove that Magneto was still secretly evil. However, after three issues were finished and the fourth was all set to be drawn, Marvel decided that they did not want Magneto to return to villainy. Silvestri had already drawn the first three issues, but since the fourth was going to need to be rewritten, they instead

X-Men vs.
Avengers #1
(Cover art by Marc
Silvestri)

had Silvestri move over to the main *Uncanny X-Men* title. He drew *Uncanny X-Men #219*, but his official run started with *Uncanny X-Men #221*.

Silvestri worked with longtime Marvel inker Dan Green, who had also worked with John Romita Jr. earlier on the series. Silvestri's work was marked by a compelling loose quality to it that really worked well when it came to action. His characters felt like that they were constantly in motion. Meanwhile, his character designs were distinct. You could always identify a Silvestri page just by the faces that the women make.

As noted earlier, Silvestri joined *Uncanny X-Men* at a strange time in the book's history, as Marvel began to expand their release schedule so that there would be a few months with double shipments made. Suddenly, instead of the normal 12 issues a year, there were now 15. Silvestri tried his best to draw as many as he could, but ultimately he was sort of paired with an alternate artist, Rick Leonardi, who would fill-in the issues that Silvestri didn't have time to draw. This increased schedule ultimately led to Silvestri leaving *Uncanny X-Men* to become the regular artist on *Wolverine*. Silvestri later noted, "The thought of moving over to Wolverine—a single character book featuring one of my favorite characters—was a relief! I was like, 'I'm ready to go.' That turned out to be a great switch for me. I'm happy it happened."

Silvestri worked with writer Larry Hama on *Wolverine* for the next two years until Silvestri left Marvel to cofound Image Comics. Silvestri's title for Image, *Cyberforce*, actually began life as an attempt by Silvestri to do an *X-Men* spinoff. That's why Cyblade from *Cyberforce* is essentially just Psylocke from the *X-Men*. Silvestri would later return to draw the finale of Grant Morrison's *New X-Men* run.

83 Avengers vs. X-Men

In a story line soon after they moved to San Francisco, the X-Men fought against a new team called the Sisterhood, led by a seemingly resurrected Madelyne Pryor. When Emma Frost was trapped, she was visited by the spirit of Jean Grey, who warned Emma to "prepare." Frost thought of that warning when Hope Summers' powers kicked in at the end of "Second Coming" and she started to have fire around her just like the Phoenix. At that same point, however, five more mutants showed up alive around the country. This led to an obvious dilemma—if Hope was destined to bring the Phoenix Force, but she could also theoretically bring mutants back to Earth, how should the X-Men "prepare?" Prepare to stop Hope from merging with the Phoenix Force or prepare her to merge with it?

When the Phoenix Force was spotted in deep outer space, heading for Earth, the Avengers and the X-Men clearly had two different answers to those questions. The Avengers wanted to make sure that Hope did not merge with the Phoenix Force, while Cyclops wanted to make sure that she did. Wolverine, now the headmaster of the Jean Grey School for Higher Learning, had a third solution—just kill Hope so she couldn't ever merge with the cosmic force. On this point, at least, the Avengers and X-Men were on the same page. After the Avengers won the first battle against the X-Men (before the X-Men escaped through Magik's teleportation through Limbo) the Avengers stranded Wolverine in the middle of nowhere to keep him from killing Hope. Wolverine, being Wolverine, managed to escape and confronted Hope, who convinced him not to kill her.

Meanwhile, as the Phoenix Force came closer to Earth, Beast (now a member of the Avengers after leaving the X-Men following a number of confrontations with Cyclops) and Iron Man built a machine that could possibly destroy the Phoenix Force. When the Phoenix Force was as close as the moon, the Avengers headed out there to destroy it and the X-Men tried to stop them. In the end, the machine did not destroy the Phoenix Force but instead split it into five pieces, which each possessed one member of the X-Men. Cyclops, Emma Frost, Namor, Colossus, and Magik all became possessed by the Phoenix Force.

The "Phoenix Five" began to use their great power to help the world. They traveled the world, feeding the hungry, healing the sick, and providing free energy to everyone on Earth. However, despite their good deeds, everyone knows that it is only a matter of time until that power corrupted them, just like it has routinely done throughout the history of the Phoenix Force. So the Avengers tried to stop them. Their battles against them went poorly, but they were able to take Hope from where the X-Men had her locked up on Utopia and hid her with the Scarlet Witch in the hidden mystical city of K'un L'un. Cyclops then decided that it was time for there to be "no more Avengers."

The Phoenix Five then traveled the globe, capturing every Avenger they could get their hands on. The Avengers who were free were hiding in Black Panther's kingdom of Wakanda. When Namor found out about this, he decided to unleash a tsunami on Wakanda. He destroyed much of the country. The remaining Avengers all took on Namor and defeated him. His power, though, just went to the other four members of the Phoenix Five. In the aftermath of the attack, the Black Panther annulled his marriage to Storm, since she had not condemned the Phoenix Five until just now.

In an epic battle, Spider-Man was able to stand up to Colossus and Magik long enough on his own to trick them into attacking each other. Their energies then went to Cyclops and Emma Frost. After a battle against Hope and Scarlet Witch, Cyclops realized that there was only one way that he could capture Hope—he needed to have Emma's Phoenix power. So Cyclops betrayed her trust and took her Phoenix powers. He then transformed into Dark Phoenix. Professor X tried to stop him, but Dark Phoenix Cyclops didn't care and shockingly killed his old mentor in front of everyone.

Finally, Hope stepped up, with the help of Scarlet Witch, and she absorbed the Phoenix Force from Cyclops, and through the assistance of Scarlet Witch, the Phoenix Force was dispersed once more, among all of the mutants on Earth. This activated the dormant mutant genes out there and so mutants were back to numbering in the millions around the world. Cyclops accepted his arrest gladly, knowing that the mutant race had been saved. Captain America then decided to form a new Avengers team made up of mutants and humans.

84 Ultimate X-Men

The idea of doing alternate-reality versions of comic book characters to gain a new audience was not a new one in 2000. Marvel had done a number of comic book series like this. The idea was always a good one. It was getting increasingly difficult to explain to new readers all of the various continuity points of Spider-Man or the X-Men, so it made sense to give new readers (particularly younger readers) a continuity-free reboot that they could enjoy without knowing 40 years of continuity. The problem, though, was that these comics always felt like they didn't "matter." They were always treated like throwaway comics, with little top talent involved, so fans learned to ignore them. In fact, when Marvel editor-in-chief Bob Harras came up with the idea for another continuity-free line of comics, the Ultimate Universe, he planned on just using the same general pool of talent as always. Then, however, Harras was removed as Marvel's editor-in-chief before the line could launch. New editor-in-chief Joe Quesada decided to totally revamp the Ultimate line.

Quesada brought in up-and-coming writers Brian Michael Bendis and Mark Millar to be in charge of the line. Quesada convinced superstar *Spider-Man* artist Mark Bagley to at least draw the first arc on *Ultimate Spider-Man*. Similarly, longtime *X-Men* artists the Kubert brothers would draw the first *Ultimate X-Men* arc. Marvel put a lot of promotion behind this new line of comics (plus special cardstock covers to make them stand out even more) and the line's launch was a huge success. Their Ultimate titles were soon some of Marvel's highest-selling titles! Only Grant Morrison's *New X-Men* sold better than *Ultimate X-Men* in the early 2000s.

The concept was to do a fresh reboot and try to make the series feel like it was a movie, so it would appeal to a fan of the movies that came into a comic book store and wanted to try something new. Thus, the lineup was basically that of the recent X-Men films, so it was Professor X, Cyclops, Jean Grey, Storm, Iceman, Beast, and Colossus (who was gay in this continuity). Wolverine, naturally, showed up to join the team in the first arc. However, this time he was a double agent sent by Magneto to murder Professor X!

Mark Millar had a radically different approach to the X-Men, as he came up with the idea of the X-Men being, in effect, a pacifist organization. However, while the organization was a pacifist one, that did not mean that the X-Men were a cheery bunch. They were slightly darker than their original counterparts in most ways. Millar famously noted the problem that had always plagued attempts to get younger audiences to read comic books again is that they were being pitched as though Cartoon Network was the audience, while it should have been *Buffy the Vampire Slayer* as the audience. In other words, kids didn't want to read comics that were plainly designed for them—they wanted to pick up books that seemed like they were designed for an older audience.

One of the most shocking moments in Millar's run was when Wolverine, who had basically reformed upon joining the X-Men, in part because of him falling in love with Jean Grey, decided to kill Cyclops on a mission to eliminate Cyclops as a rival to his affection for Jean. Cyclops managed to survive.

When Millar left the book after three years, Brian Michael Bendis came on board for a year, working with artist David Finch. The initial idea was for *X-Men* director Bryan Singer to follow up Bendis' run with a year-long run of his own. That never ended up happening, so instead, Brian K. Vaughan and Robert Kirkman each had stints on the title.

A problem with the Ultimate line was that as time went by, the main Marvel Universe just kept on adapting elements of the Ultimate Universe (Kurt Busiek once noted that it was annoying to be writing *Avengers* when Marvel was pushing the Ultimate version of the Avengers, dubbed "the Ultimates," as the "cool" Avengers) until there really wasn't that great of a difference between the two universes, except, of course, that the Ultimate Universe now had just as much continuity built up as the Marvel Universe. So in 2009, Jeph Loeb and David Finch did "Ultimatum," where Magneto tried to destroy the world. Most of the X-Men, including Professor X, Cyclops, and Wolverine, were killed.

Marvel tried a relaunched *Ultimate X-Men* series with a new team, including Wolverine's son, James Hudson, but ultimately the Ultimate Universe was destroyed in 2015, with the surviving characters (including James Hudson and Miles Morales, the Spider-Man who took over in the Ultimate Universe after Peter Parker was killed) merging into the main Marvel Universe.

85 Iceman

There is a very specific type of comic book character that ages really poorly, and that is the class clown of the group who is younger than everyone else. Those characters fit in fine at first, but the problem is that if the series continues for long enough, then other characters are going to be introduced who are younger than that "young" character, so they can no longer get by on being the youngest and once you're no longer the youngest of the group, then suddenly the whole "class clown" angle begins to look more pathetic than endearing. That was the problem that Human Torch had with the Fantastic Four as the years went by and it was definitely an issue with Iceman (Bobby Drake) in the X-Men.

When the X-Men debuted in 1963's *X-Men #1*, Iceman was a year younger than his next-youngest teammate and he was all about being the group jokester. When he debuted, he did not yet have the superpowers that he is now known for. He looked like a snowman more than anything else. Within a few issues, however, Jack Kirby honed the character's look, giving Iceman the now famous clear solid ice look in *X-Men #8* that he has basically maintained ever since. In addition, starting with *X-Men #9*, Iceman began using ice slides to travel, which became one of the most distinctive visual aspects of the character over the years, the cool-looking ice slides that he made to travel around.

When the original X-Men left the team upon the introduction of the All-New, All-Different X-Men, Iceman ended up as a member of the Champions, a new Los Angeles–based team along with his good friend Warren Worthington, the Angel. Throughout that series, Iceman struggled with being taken seriously, which tended to be a recurring theme with him over the years. In fact, when the Champions broke up, Bobby quit being a superhero to become an accountant!

Eventually, he was wooed back to superheroing by Warren and their fellow friend Hank McCoy, the bouncing boisterous blue-furred Beast, who had just become the leader of the Defenders. Iceman and Angel joined up with the Defenders and when that team ended, Jean Grey turned out to be alive, so they all reunited to form X-Factor.

When X-Factor eventually merged back into the X-Men, Bobby was a bit lost in the shuffle. Toward the end of his time on X-Factor, he had gained a girlfriend, named Opal Tanaka.

Top Five Best Wolverine/Colossus Fastball Specials

5. *X-Men #100*
This was the first time that they tried out their new maneuver, with Colossus throwing Wolverine at the bad guy.

4. *X-Men #114*
This is the first time that John Byrne/Terry Austin drew the fastball special and it saw Wolverine getting thrown at a pterodactyl, which is super awesome.

3. *X-Men #137*
In the zero gravity of the moon, Wolverine and Colossus flipped the play, as Wolverine threw Colossus at Phoenix.

2. *X-Men #142*
In one of the most famous comic book death sequences of all time, future Colossus and future Wolverine try one last fastball special against a Sentinel (it does not go well).

1. *Astonishing X-Men #6*
Colossus had just been revealed to have never actually died. The bad guy who kept Colossus prisoner was escaping on a space-ship with a hostage. The only way to stop him was clear to both Colossus and Wolverine, so much so that all Wolverine had to say was "two words" and Colossus knew what those two words were—fastball special.

However, the relationship fizzled out when he rejoined the X-Men. During this time, Bobby had his body taken over by Emma Frost, who showed him that he could do much more with his ice powers than he'd ever considered. This was a recurring theme with Iceman for years, so much so that it got pretty annoying over time, as Iceman kept going on and on about how disappointed he was that he couldn't tap into his powers like Emma Frost had been able to do so when she had taken over his body.

Meanwhile, during this period, Bobby also began to act rather sullenly. He went on a road trip with Rogue and they visited his folks who treated Bobby like anti-mutant bigots. The whole situation seemed like they were heading toward Bobby realizing that he was actually gay, but nothing ever came of it. A popular debate among X-Men fans at the time was whether Bobby was going to be revealed to be gay.

However, nothing was done with the idea for the next 20 years. Instead, a common topic in Iceman stories was just how repressed Bobby was. In one *Astonishing X-Men* story, he ended up accidentally causing giant ice monsters to show up that he did not know he was doing, because he had repressed the memory so much. Bobby had some major issues with repression.

During Brian Michael Bendis' run on the X-Men titles, he revealed that the Iceman from the past was gay. This led to a confrontation between the two Icemen in Bendis' last issue on the series. Finally, the adult Iceman acknowledged that he was gay and that he had just hidden it so deep within himself that he had always repressed it. He felt that being a mutant already made him so different that he didn't want to be even more different still.

The adult Iceman is now dealing with the effects of coming out as an adult. He has received his first ongoing series, where writer Sina Grace deals with the not-so-smooth transition Iceman has been making to being an out superhero, especially when his bigoted family (who were already ashamed of him for being a mutant) did not react so well. Still, Bobby's sense of humor has somehow remained intact.

86 Madrox and the Second X-Factor Team

In the early 1970s, Marvel launched their fourth major superhero team, the Defenders, which starred four of Marvel's most significant solo heroes—Doctor Strange, Hulk, Namor, and Silver Surfer. The series lasted about 15 issues and had a few revivals over the years. (This included a short-lived 1990s series, *Secret Defenders*, which had Doctor Strange using Tarot cards to choose different heroes for each mission. Shockingly, Wolverine was selected to be part of the first team in that series.)

However, when Marvel debuted their slate of Netflix TV series, they chose the name "Defenders" to serve as the name of the team that Daredevil, Jessica Jones, Luke Cage, and Iron Fist formed after each of their individual series ended. Marvel then launched a new *Defenders* comic book series starring those characters. "Defenders" is a cool name and it wasn't being used, so it was repurposed for something much different than its original concept. That's precisely what happened when the original cast of *X-Factor* left that series.

X-Factor debuted as a reunion of the original X-Men. After a while, they reunited with the rest of the X-Men, and after 70 issues, they were gone. Marvel now had a name that had served them perfectly well as a series name and no team to use in the title. So they looked at Freedom Force. Freedom Force was the name that the Brotherhood of Evil Mutants used when they were pardoned by the United States government in exchange for becoming a strike force under the direction of the United States. So Marvel took that concept and used it with a new team in 1991's *X-Factor #71*.

Leading into the combined X-Men series, there were a number of mutants who were present at Muir Isle when they were taken under the control of Shadow King. Most of those mutants rejoined the newly reformed X-Men. The characters that weren't used, though, joined a new government-sponsored mutant team, which was taking over the name X-Factor. Those included Guido, the super-strong bodyguard of singer Lila Cheney; Polaris, the former X-Man who had been used as a nexus for the Shadow King to spread his evil; and Jamie Madrox (who had been working on Muir Isle as Moira MacTaggert's lab assistant), a hero who could make duplicates of himself. They were joined by two mutants from Genosha, the mutant nation that the X-Men had just helped free from oppression. Havok and Wolfsbane had stayed behind to help with rebuilding. They joined this newly formed mutant team, with former X-Man (and brother to Cyclops) Havok, becoming the team leader.

Written by Peter David, the series was offbeat and often hilarious. (Guido chose "Strong Guy" as his superhero name as, well, every team had a Strong Guy in it, right?) It was also heavily character driven. Former Avenger Quicksilver ended up joining the team, as well, and Peter David ended up coining a description of Quicksilver's irritability that people have stolen for years. The idea is, "Don't you get annoyed if you're stuck on a slow-moving ATM line? Well, that's what every moment of Quicksilver's life is like. Now do you get why he is always so irritable?"

The book was unique among the X-Titles, but that caused problems when it came time to doing crossovers. For sales reasons, the X-Books all had to cross over, but the problem was that all of those crossovers interfered with Peter David's long-running plot-lines in the series. He kept getting interrupted by new crossovers until he just quit. The book then became a straightforward action series until it ended in 1998.

Years later, Peter David returned to write a miniseries with Jamie Madrox working now as a detective. People always say, "If there's interest, this miniseries can become an ongoing," but it never actually happens. This time around, though, *MadroX* bucked the odds and it was picked up as an ongoing series. David had the detective agency be named X-Factor Investigations, so the name *X-Factor* was used for the new series and it lasted another *10 years*, with the series having the same acclaimed combination of clever humor and in-depth character work as David's first try.

Madrox was rejoined by his old friends, Wolfsbane and Strong Guy, plus new friends Siryn, M, Rictor and Shatterstar (two former X-Force teammates who officially became a couple in this series after hints of a gay relationship between them kept popping up in *X-Force* during the 1990s), and Layla Miller, a little girl whose power is to "know stuff." She was trapped in the future at one point and when she returned, she was an adult. She then married Madrox. After the series ended in 2014, Madrox was then killed off from the deadly effects of the Terrigen Mists on mutants.

87 Must Read: "Old Man Logan"

Mark Millar had himself quite a decade in the early 21st century for Marvel Comics. Beginning with *Ultimate X-Men* and *Ultimates*, Millar finished his run on *Ultimate X-Men* and, in short succession, launched "Marvel Knights: Spider-Man," a year-long story arc where Spider-Man's Aunt May is kidnapped and he has to fight his way through the Marvel Universe to find her (the series introduced a brand-new Venom) and "Enemy of the State," a year-long story in the pages of *Wolverine*, where Wolverine is captured and killed by the Hand, who then bring him back to life as a brainwashed agent of the Hand and Hydra, who are working together to take down SHIELD and take over the world. Wolverine eventually breaks free of their control and teams up with SHIELD to hunt down and kill every member of Hydra and the Hand alive. Fresh off of those successes, Millar then wrote one of Marvel's most successful crossover events of all-time, "Civil War," working with artist Steve McNiven. In 2008, Millar reunited with McNiven for another classic storyline, this time going into the future to detail the life of "Old Man Logan."

Millar's work for Marvel was generally notable in how dark it often got. For instance, in his run on *Fantastic Four* with artist Bryan Hitch that directly preceded "Old Man Logan" (the future version of Wolverine even cameos in that *Fantastic Four* story), he introduced the Marquis of Death, who made Doctor Doom look like a choir boy in comparison. However, even with that in mind, "Old Man Logan" (which ran in *Wolverine #66–72*, plus a conclusion in *Wolverine Giant-Size Old Man Logan #1*) was a dark story. It opened in a world where the United States has been divvied up amongst various supervillains. Logan (who has long retired as Wolverine) lives with his wife and children in a section ruled by the Hulk Gang (this section was initially given to the Abomination but then the Hulk took it over from him). The Hulk Gang is made up of the inbred grandchildren of Bruce Banner's Hulk and Banner's cousin, She-Hulk. Logan needs money to pay off the Hulk Gang, so when Clint Barton (the former Avenger known as Hawkeye) shows up needing some protection on a ride across the country to deliver a "package," Logan agrees to go on the dangerous mission with the now-blind archer (Logan assumes that they are delivering drugs).

The rest of the story arc mostly involves them driving across the country and seeing the various problems that have happened over the years as the supervillains have taken over. Eventually, we learn why Logan retired from being Wolverine and the answer is truly disturbing. On the night that the villains of the country teamed up for one synchronized attack across the country, an army of 40 supervillains attacked the X-Mansion. Wolverine managed to kill them all. When the dust settled, he discovered that the villainous master of illusions, Mysterio, had actually disguised all of Wolverine's X-Men teammates as supervillains and Wolverine had just slaughtered all of his friends and teammates. The incident caused him to snap. He would have killed himself, but since he can't be killed, he instead killed off his superhero identity.

When they arrive at their destination, Logan realizes that Hawkeye had him deliver a supply of Super Soldier Serum so that new Captain Americas could be made to fight back against the evil of the world. However, the president of the United States, the Red Skull (who keeps the costume and shield of Captain America, who he killed years earlier), had actually made the order in an attempt to draw the Resistance to him. He has Hawkeye and Logan killed, but Logan recovers and decapitates the Skull with Captain America's shield.

Logan returns home to discover that his family has been murdered anyway, as the Hulk Gang didn't feel like waiting for him to return. For the first time since "the Incident," Logan unleashes his claws and he slaughters the Hulk Gang as well as their patriarch, Bruce Banner. Logan finds an infant, Bruce Banner Jr., and decides to raise the kid himself and see if he can find some good out of all of this.

Years later, during 2015's "Secret Wars," where alternate timelines collided together, the Old Man Logan universe collided with the regular Marvel Universe. When everything else had gone back to normal, Old Man Logan somehow ended up trapped in the main Marvel Universe, during present day. He has to adjust to a world where all of his friends are still alive. He has served as a member of the X-Men ever since. The 2016 Hugh Jackman film, *Logan*, was roughly based on the plot of "Old Man Logan."

88 Angel/Archangel

In 1978, one of the great ad campaigns of all-time debuted, with the promotions of the then-upcoming film, *Superman*. The trailer for the film and all of the commercials for it included no scenes of Superman actually flying. The poster for the film was simply the Superman insignia and the legendary tagline, "You'll believe that a man can fly." Now, obviously, the main thing being conveyed through these advertisements was that the special effects were going to be so good that you will legitimately believe that a man is flying. However, it also speaks to the simple fact that, once upon a time, the idea of a flying man was, in and of itself, pretty incredible. That helps to explain the relatively blasé power set of Warren Worthington III, Angel of the original X-Men, whose power was that he had wings and could fly.

In so many ways, Warren was a nightmare for writers to take on, as he was good-looking, confident, rich, and without a particularly cool power. What, exactly, was the hook with this guy? He already had everything! Amazingly enough, though, the first member of the X-Men to get their own solo feature actually was the Angel! After the X-Men regular series stopped printing new stories, Angel appeared in a solo story (fighting against his uncle, who had murdered Warren's father to try to steal the Worthington fortune) that appeared in, of all places, a backup in *Ka-Za #2–3* and then a backup in *Marvel Tales #30* (*Marvel Tales* was a series that mostly reprinted old Marvel Comics). The most interesting thing about this story is who wrote it—it was penned by none other than Jerry Siegel, the cocreator of Superman, who had been on the outs with DC Comics after he and Joe Shuster took another crack at trying to get the copyright to their creation back from DC.

When the All-New, All-Different X-Men showed up and pushed the old X-Men out the door, Angel quickly ended up in a new series. Initially, Marvel editor-in-chief Len Wein was thinking about a comic book starring Angel and his old friend Iceman hitting the back roads of the United States, sort of like the popular TV series, *Route 66*. Instead, they formed two-fifths of a new superhero team set in Los Angeles called the Champions. Angel then briefly returned to the X-Men for a spell during "The Dark Phoenix Saga," during a period where John Byrne planned to surreptitiously bring back all of the original X-Men (as those were the X-Men that he had grown up on as a kid). His presence on the team was mostly used to contrast against Wolverine, as Angel just couldn't fathom how the X-Men would be okay with being on the team with a guy who looks like he would stab you just as soon as look at you! Ultimately, Angel couldn't take it anymore and quit for the second time.

He then joined the Defenders with Iceman, as their old friend, Beast, had become the leader of the Defenders. When the Defenders broke up, Warren ended up founding X-Factor with his fellow original X-Men teammates (they were all thrilled to see Jean Grey alive again).

During his time on X-Factor, the team got involved in the "Mutant Massacre" and Angel tragically had his wings badly damaged. They had to be amputated. A depressed Warren considered killing himself. Then his private plane crashed and everyone assumed that he had committed suicide. Instead, he had been taken in by Apocalypse, who offered him new wings if he became Death of Apocalypse's Four Horseman. Warren agreed and his skin was dyed blue and he was given new, metal wings that would shoot out razor-sharp feathers.

His teammates broke down the control Apocalypse had over Warren and he became a hero again, but his wings had a mind of their own. He began to call himself Archangel now. He was a lot more powerful than he was before. He began to date his new X-Men teammate Psylocke (they were both born rich, so they had a lot in common). Over the years, though, he slowly but surely reverted to his original form, with his wings "molting" and his skin returning to its natural color.

However, it turns out that the Archangel side of him is always in there and can be turned on at a moment's notice, with his wings turning into metal blades and his desire to kill returning. This was exploited when Apocalypse was killed and Warren discovered that he could be turned into a repository for Apocalypse! He slowly turned evil and his girlfriend, Psylocke, was forced to kill him. He was then reborn as a new Angel, without memories of his past. He still can turn into Archangel, however.

89 X-Statix

No title better symbolized Marvel's new "let the acclaimed creators do what they want to do" approach in the early 2000s than when they handed over the keys to *X-Force* to Peter Milligan (best known for the bizarre adventures of *Shade, the Changing Man* for Vertigo, which was mostly drawn by *Generation X* artist, Chris Bachalo) and Mike Allred (best known at the time for his quirky independent comic book series, *Madman*). *X-Force* was mostly known as a paramilitary strike force led by Cable and, most recently, it had undergone a revamp when acclaimed writer Warren Ellis was brought on board to come up with new directions for three of the lower-rung X-Titles—*X-Force*, *X-Man*, and *Generation X*.

He came up with new directions and then he would select writers to follow him on the revamped books. X-Force was revamped as a black ops title (with Ian Edgington following Ellis) starring British secret agent, Peter Wisdom, plus longtime X-Force members Domino, Cannonball, Proudstar, Bedlam, and Meltdown. In the final issue of that run, *X-Force #115*, it appeared as though all of the team members except Domino had been killed in an explosion! The next issue, *X-Force #116*, started a completely new take on X-Force, one that was so out of this world that Marvel ultimately turned on it!

When you become a black ops team for a year, a funny thing happens; people just assume that you've given up your team name, so a new group of heroes began to call themselves X-Force. These heroes were reality stars. Everywhere they went, they were recorded by the mysterious artificial being known as Doop. (Doop might have been created as part of some strange Cold War project decades earlier, and he spoke in a strange language that few people could decipher.)

In the first issue, the team leader, known as Zeitgeist, reflected on his dark life. He had the ability to secrete a dangerous chemical from his mouth. When his powers manifested themselves, he had been making out with a girl. She was badly injured and it haunted him for years. He worked out a deal with a billionaire, Spike Freeman, to fund a reality series starring a group of superheroes (with a sinister Coach directing them on missions and cleaning up their messes). Zeitgeist hated the rest of the team, who he felt were pathetic. When Spike came to him with a plan for their next mission where everyone on the team except Zeitgeist and new member, Anarchist (who shot corrosive blasts), would die, Zeitgeist went along with it. Instead, Zeitgeist died along with the rest of the team (only Anarchist and the teleporting U-Go-Girl survived, plus Doop, but he always survived). As he died, he finally remembered the name of the girl whose injury had haunted him for so many years.

That, in a nutshell, was *X-Force*. It was a parody of reality shows, but it was also a dark look at superheroes. Milligan and Allred would come up with ridiculous names for superheroes but then give them deeply personalized backgrounds and make fans love them despite their ridiculous setups, like Phat, a young white teen who made appropriating black culture his thing. When he didn't get enough attention, he and his teammate, Vivisector, pretended to be a gay couple. They then realized that they were both actually gay!

The main center of the team were three members, Anarchist, U-Go-Girl, and Zeitgeist's replacement as leader, Mister Sensitive (who preferred to be called the Orphan), who was so sensitive to the world around him that Professor X had to build him a sensory-deprivation suit (the sensitivity made him a skilled fighter). The relationship between the three carried the book, especially a classic arc at the end of the first volume of *X-Force* where Death literally tells them that one of them will die and they each try to make sure that it is them and not their friends (U-Go-Girl was the one who died).

The book was then relaunched as *X-Statix*, to better show just how different it was than the original *X-Force*. New team members included the teleporting Venus Dee Milo (she literally replaced U-Go Girl as both the team teleporter and as the Orphan's girlfriend) and Dead Girl who was, you know, dead. Milligan, then, went too far with a story line that Marvel caused him to squash. He thought that since people always come back to life in the Marvel Universe, what if Princess Diana came back to life in the Marvel Universe? The Royal Family was not pleased and it was re-written to be a popular pop star from another country. X-Statix didn't last long after the aborted Princess Diana arc. It ended with *X-Statix #26*, where, appropriately enough, everyone but Doop was killed.

90 Shi'ar Empire

Early on in their run together on *X-Men*, Chris Claremont and Dave Cockrum showed that Professor X was getting mysterious messages from some being from some other world and/or dimension. As time went by, he eventually discovered that it was an alien named Lilandra. Lilandra was from the Shi'ar Empire. She needed the help of somebody because her older brother, D'Ken Neramani, the Emperor of the Shi'ar Empire, had gone insane and was trying to control the M'Kraan Crystal, the powerful relic which had the power to alter the entire universe. This was how the X-Men first got called to outer space, a place where they would soon find themselves very familiar.

At the time, Dave Cockrum had planned on selling a book about an interstellar group of pirates. When it became clear that book was as likely to happen as *Outsiders*, the other series he tried to pitch to DC Comics (the one where a few of the members, like Nightcrawler and Storm, ultimately were reworked into becoming members of the All-New, All-Different X-Men), Cockrum decided to just work the pirates into the X-Men series. Dubbed the Starjammers, they were pirates from different worlds who teamed up to fight against the Shi'ar Empire under D'Ken Neramani's rule (D'Ken had killed the wife of Corsair, the leader of the

Starjammers). They agreed to team up with Lilandra to help take down her brother. They also teamed up with the X-Men when the X-Men came through a Star Gate to help turn the tide against D'Ken (as coincidence might have it, Corsair also turned out to be the long-thought-to-be-dead father of Cyclops).

The biggest advantage that the Shi'ar Empire has at any given time is their remarkable Imperial Guard. It consisted of heroes from all the different planets that make up the Shi'ar Empire (so very few members of the team are actually Shi'ar themselves—Shi'ar people

Top Five Oddest Secondary Mutations by X-Men Characters

5. Masque
The whole hook with the Morlock known as Masque is that he could change anyone else's appearance, but he was stuck looking hideous. That changed after his secondary mutation allowed him to become beautiful.

4. Husk
Husk's powers had always been that she tears off a layer of skin and each layer underneath had a different power. However, her secondary mutation revealed that each peel was also affecting her brain a little. She began to spiral out.

3. Havok
Havok's main power is that he can shoot energy blasts based on him collecting "cosmic energy." In a similar way (by "similar," we mean, of course, "not at all similar"), he also is a nexus of all realities—all alternate reality Havoks are apparently connected.

2. Gambit
During a battle with the bad guys, Gambit accidentally had a card blow up in his face, blinding him. He then gained the ability to tell the future when blind…for some reason. His regular vision later returned.

1. Angel
Angel had one of the most prominent secondary mutations, and it also doesn't really fit with anything else. He could now heal people with his blood…because that's a thing that flying people do?

are distinguished by their avian-like qualities). It was intended by Cockrum to be a stand-in for the series he had drawn before leaving DC Comics for Marvel, the Legion of Super-Heroes. The super-strong Gladiator was the stand-in for Superboy, the telepathic Oracle was the stand-in for Saturn Girl, Fang was the stand-in for Timber Wolf, and so on and so forth.

Ultimately, mostly through the help of Phoenix on the X-Men, the heroes were able to stop D'Ken and save the universe. Lilandra was then named the replacement for her brother as the head of the Shi'ar Empire. Majestrix (or Empress, if you prefer) Lilandra was grateful for the aid that Professor X and the X-Men gave her and she and Xavier became lovers.

As one of the most stable empires in the Marvel Universe, the Shi'ar Empire played a major role in universal politics. This sometimes, though, led to them having to make terrible decisions. After Phoenix turned into Dark Phoenix, it was Lilandra and the Shi'ar Empire that determined that Phoenix needed to be killed. Even though she was dating the head of the X-Men, she had to do what was best for her people. Luckily for her, Phoenix decided to kill herself.

When Professor X was possessed by one of the aliens known as the Brood, who use people's bodies to harvest their young, it was Shi'ar technology that allowed Xavier to survive by cloning his body and transferring his consciousness to his new body. This meant, for a while, that Xavier could actually walk again! After Xavier was then badly beaten around *X-Men #200*, he decided to head off into outer space with Lilandra while Magneto watched Xavier's school for him. The X-Men later headed off to save the Shi'ar Empire when it turned out that the shape-shifting Skrulls had taken the place of Xavier and had taken control of the Shi'ar Empire through Lilandra (they had to team up with one of their old enemies, Lilandra's younger sister, Deathbird, to save the day).

The Shi'ar Empire was then involved in a war with the Kree Empire. The Shi'ar ended up winning it when a Nega Bomb was dropped on the Kree's throne world of Hala, killing billions of people. The Nega Bomb had been stolen by a conspiracy led by the Kree's own leader (he wanted to kick-start the evolution of the Kree race—the survivors out of the billions of the dead would evolve to become more powerful), so the Shi'ar did not actively kill billions of people, but the fact that they were willing to do so is quite hardcore.

In recent years, Lilandra was killed and briefly, Corsair's long-lost son, Vulcan, took over as Emperor. Vulcan was killed by Black Bolt of the Inhumans (representing the Kree). Gladiator, of the Imperial Guard, has been the leader of the Shi'ar ever since.

91 All-New X-Men

As you might imagine, following the conclusion of the Avengers vs. X-Men battle, the X-Men were in disarray. Cyclops had been arrested and was seen by many as a martyr-like figure, because he had pushed for the world to accept the Phoenix Force and it turned out that the Phoenix Force had, in fact, brought the return of the mutant race to Earth, just like Cyclops had hoped that it would. He was then freed by a few members of the X-Men still loyal to him— Magneto, Magik, and Emma Frost (although Frost and Cyclops were no longer dating over his whole "knocking her out to steal her Phoenix powers to add to his own" situation from Avengers vs. X-Men). They formed their own renegade team of X-Men that traveled the world through Magik's teleportation to rescue and recruit mutants that they found being oppressed.

The X-Men who had remained with Cyclops on Utopia after the great Schism event all left Utopia, either to go off on their own or (as most of them did) to head to the Jean Grey School for Higher Learning, where they hooked up with Wolverine's team of X-Men. These X-Men followed the news of Cyclops' new X-Men team with great distress.

Beast, in particular, took the actions of Cyclops very hard. He and Cyclops had been clashing for many years over what Beast felt were reckless and dangerous plans of action by Cyclops, who he felt had lost some of his moral center (the final straw was when Beast found out about Cyclops' formation of a special black ops X-Force team that Cyclops was using to eliminate threats to the X-Men before they became threats). So for Beast to learn that Cyclops had gone on to become possessed by the Phoenix Force and actually killed their former teacher, Professor X, and that Cyclops was now more of a renegade than ever before? It was too much for Beast to handle.

When Iceman made an offhand remark that Cyclops' younger self would never tolerate his current actions, Beast decided to one-up Cyclops in the reckless actions department by actually using a time machine to bring the original X-Men from the past into the present, so that the younger version of Cyclops could help Beast convince the adult Cyclops to turn himself in.

Everyone seemed to agree that the old X-Men being here in the present was a bad idea, but the classic X-Men disagreed. They wanted to fix their future. Jean Grey, though, is shocked to learn of what happened to her before she died and her telepathy kick-starts much sooner than it did in her normal timeline. Once the X-Men have decided to stay in the present, Kitty Pryde agreed to become their mentor, as sort of their own version of Professor X.

The adult Cyclops, meanwhile, had opened up his own hidden school for mutants called the New Xavier School for the Gifted. After a clash with the Jean Grey School, Kitty actually decided to take the original X-Men out of the Jean Grey School and shockingly decided to go stay at Cyclops' school, Cyclops having convinced her that his is the better spot for the teens to stay. Around this time, Wolverine's female clone, X-23, also ended up joining the young X-Men under Kitty's leadership. She flirted with Cyclops but ultimately enters in to a relationship with Angel.

The team got into some trouble when they were attacked by the Shi'ar, who saw the return of Jean Grey as an opportunity to punish her for the actions of the Dark Phoenix, which they never got a chance to do the first time around (because Phoenix killed itself). The X-Men, naturally, argued that it was unfair to punish Jean Grey for the actions of her future self and ultimately they avoided punishment for Jean. Jean, however, was struggling with having access to telepathy so much earlier. She didn't know how to properly use her powers. For instance, she kept on reading other people's minds without their permission, something her adult self would never do. It was during one of these instances that Jean realized that Iceman was gay. Showing her immaturity, she cruelly outed him.

Eventually, Beast came to realize that his actions were not good for the timeline, especially when he learned that he had helped to destabilize Marvel's very Multiverse through his rash use of time travel. Cyclops also apologized for his actions and ultimately all of the X-Men came back together for a march on Washington, D.C., for mutant rights.

Recently, the original X-Men have formed a new team together under the tutelage of their former nemesis, Magneto. They star in *X-Men Blue* (while Kitty Pryde leads the main X-Men in *X-Men Gold*).

92 John Romita Jr.

It's clear that if you had to pick one artist to symbolize Marvel Comics for the 1960s, it would be Jack Kirby. Once Kirby left in 1970, however, it would be up in the air as to which artists would symbolize Marvel Comics in the years since. One of the best bets, though, would have to be John Romita Jr., who literally worked nonstop at Marvel from 1978 until 2014, one of the most impressive continual employments at a single comic book company in comic book history. Very few artists have ever remained an in-demand artist for 36 years period, let alone 36 years at a single company! And Romita Jr. is still going strong (just for a different company now)!

Romita Jr., naturally, is the son of John Romita, the artist who took over from Steve Ditko on *Amazing Spider-Man*. Romita is the artist that the world now largely associates with Spider-Man, as the version of Spider-Man who would appear on Marvel licensed products from the late 1960s through the late 1980s would be John Romita's Spider-Man. Romita then became Marvel's art director from 1973 through the late 1980s (his wife, Virginia, also worked for Marvel as their traffic manager throughout most of that time). During this period, the senior Romita designed some of the most famous costumes of the era, including Wolverine, Luke Cage, and the Punisher.

After graduating college, Romita Jr. got his first regular gig at Marvel in 1978, when he became the artist on David Michelinie and Bob Layton's acclaimed run on *Iron Man* (Layton would do finishes over Romita Jr.'s breakdowns). Romita Jr. got the chance to draw the classic "Demon in a Bottle" story line, where Tony

Stark dealt with alcoholism, which was a rare subject for comic books in the late 1970s. While working on *Iron Man*, Romita Jr. was also the artist who developed Dazzler for Marvel. Romita Jr. drew the first couple of issues of her ongoing series (while working on two other regular books—speed has always been a hallmark of Romita Jr.'s work).

Romita Jr.'s work on *Iron Man* gained him enough attention that he was given one of Marvel's top books, *Amazing Spider-Man*, while continuing his work on *Iron Man*. Romita Jr. (who got to work with his father on a couple of issues of *Amazing Spider-Man*) paired with writer Roger Stern for an acclaimed run that introduced a new major villain for Spider-Man, the Hobgoblin, as well as saw Spider-Man somehow find a way to stop the unstoppable Juggernaut.

In 1983, Romita Jr. became the first new artist to take over *Uncanny X-Men* after it had become Marvel's top-selling comic book series. Up until this point, while drawing *Uncanny X-Men* was a good assignment to have, you didn't have to worry about screwing up Marvel's top book. Romita Jr. came aboard while still drawing *Amazing Spider-Man*. That plan quickly changed and he started to devote himself solely to *Uncanny X-Men*. He did not let the sales down. He drew the book regularly from *#175* through *#211* and sales kept on going up. He was taken off of the book to launch the flagship book of Marvel's New Universe, *Star Brand*, which was written by Marvel's editor-in-chief, Jim Shooter.

When his *Star Brand* run ended, Romita Jr. teamed up with his *Uncanny X-Men* editor Ann Nocenti on *Daredevil*. This run was a major turning point in Romita Jr.'s career. You see, in the first decade of his career, Romita Jr. only did breakdowns, not full pencils. That allowed him to work faster, but the work that you saw had a greater influence from his inkers than a normal penciled page (Dan Green was his main finisher on *Uncanny X-Men*). On *Daredevil*, Romita Jr. did full pencils, and Romita Jr.'s full pencils

Uncanny X-Men #207 (Cover art by John Romita Jr. and Dan Panosian)

look a lot different, stylistically, than his earlier work. So Romita Jr. really has two distinct periods, basically pre-1988 and post-1988.

Romita Jr. returned to *Uncanny X-Men* in 1992 with *Uncanny X-Men #300*. As a sign of how big Romita Jr.'s career has been at Marvel, he has drawn *Uncanny X-Men #200* and *#300*, plus *Amazing Spider-Man #500* and *#600*. Not many artists can say that they drew four different anniversary issues like that. Romita Jr. temporarily left *Uncanny X-Men* to do a Batman/Punisher graphic novel, but he did not return. He worked on Punisher comics, instead. Then he had a long run on a few different Spider-Man series, first with Howard Mackie and then later, J. Michael

Straczynski. He returned to the X-Men world with an acclaimed run on *Wolverine* with writer Mark Millar in 2004. In 2014, he moved to DC Comics, where he has been drawing ever since (most recently drawing the *Suicide Squad* ongoing series).

93 Listen to *Jay and Miles X-Plain the X-Men*

Less than two years after Superman made his debut in *Action Comics #1*, he made his debut on *The Adventures of Superman* radio show in February 1940. At the time, the most popular form of entertainment in people's homes were radio programs (television did not become popular until the end of the decade) and *The Adventures of Superman* was one of the biggest radio shows on the planet. *The Adventures of Superman* was responsible for introducing Jimmy Olsen, Perry White, the *Daily Planet*, and kryptonite to the Superman mythos.

An interesting thing about the popularity of *The Adventures of Superman* is that it is a clear case of simply serving whichever form of technology is most current. For instance, a decade later, *The Adventures of Superman* was a hit television series as well. Had Superman debuted in 1951, it's likely that it would have first been a television series. If Superman had launched in 2015, there is a good chance that Superman would have first been adapted to some sort of web-based series, like perhaps a podcast. Podcasts are, after all, the modern day versions of the classic radio shows. They are an increasingly popular form of entertainment. Luckily for X-Men fans, within the world of podcasts, there is a great one that is all about the X-Men. It is called *Jay and Miles X-Plain the X-Men*.

Their full tagline on their website (www.xplainthexmen.com) is, hilariously, "Jay and Miles X-Plain the X-Men. Because it's about time someone did." In a lot of ways, their podcast is the audio equivalent to this here book you're holding in your hands (or on your screen). Former married couple Jay Rachel Edidin and Miles Stokes launched their podcast in 2014. Edidin had been an editor at Dark Horse Comics for seven years before going freelance in 2013. Stokes was (and is still) the director of technology at the same company. The two were big X-Men fans and they decided to collaborate on a podcast that would take an informed, critical, and, of course, occasionally lighthearted look at the convoluted history of the X-Men.

The show generally set itself up around story lines in chronological order, but for each story line, there are natural tangents to discuss about that story line. Like, for instance, if you discuss the first appearances of the Brotherhood of Evil Mutants, you're probably going to want to talk about Scarlet Witch and Quicksilver's later departure to join the Avengers or the revelation that they were the birth kids of Magneto (or perhaps the later revelation that they actually weren't Magneto's kids after all).

Choosing an episode truly at random, in their spotlight on the X-Men's time in Australia (after they were briefly believed to be dead after "The Fall of the Mutants," the X-Men opened up shop in Australia, where an Aboriginal mutant named Gateway helped them teleport around the globe so that they could remain hidden in the outback of Australia), here were their talking points for the episode: Gateway's probable origin—Wintry mix—Miles's definitive X-era—*Uncanny X-Men #228-231*—O.Z. Chase—Vladimir Zaitzev—The Reavers (No, not those Reavers)—Bonebreaker—Skullcrusher—Pretty Boy—Children—Jessan Hoan (Tyger Tiger)—Gateway—Teamwork (again)—The Siege Perilous—Cooterman's Creek—Jay's favorite mythic figure (and long-term career goal)—The best brother in the Marvel Universe—A really sad team-up—Favorite X-science moments—Where to donate comic books.

As you can see, every X-Men story is connected to different stories and they all lead down different and interesting paths. It makes for a fascinating listening environment, and, of course, the main thing is that it's a fun way to learn new things about the X-Men in a laid-back setting. They have a few cool running gags, like how the cold open of the show will be Miles or Jay describing a period in comic book history in the most convoluted way possible, then the other one will shout, "What?" and then the show will begin.

Of course, they also have much more than just discussions about the history of the X-Men. They also have plenty of creator interviews, live events, and all sorts of other fun stuff. Their 100th episode was a great interview with the legendary Chris Claremont, which was a delight.

Going into the end of 2017, they had just gotten close to the end of the Chris Claremont run on *X-Men*, which would be around 1991. So, in 165 episodes, they had covered about 28 years' worth of X-Men comics. However, starting with 1991, there is a huge explosion in X-Men-related titles (particularly with the second official X-Men title that launched that year). In the past, they have spent plenty of time addressing X-Men tie-in books, so they will have so much material for future episodes. We're lucky to have them.

94 Joe Madureira

There are many versions of how Wally Pipp came to get a day off from his regular job as the first baseman for the New York Yankees on June 2, 1925. Some say he asked for the day off because he was hung over or suffering the after-effects of being beaned in the head by a pitch a few days earlier. Some say that he was simply benched by a manager trying to make some sort of move to improve a struggling baseball team. Whatever the reason, young Lou Gehrig took over as first baseman for the New York Yankees that day and then played every game that the Yankees played for the next 14 years, 2,130 consecutive games in all. You never know what will happen when you take time off from a gig.

That was the annoying lesson that John Romita Jr. learned when Marvel asked him to draw a crossover graphic novel featuring Batman and Punisher. Romita Jr. needed a month off of his regular gig on *Uncanny X-Men* (his second stint on the book) to draw the graphic novel. Just a year earlier, Romita Jr. had been approached by Jim Lee to leave Marvel to join Lee at Image Comics. Romita Jr. turned him down out of his loyalty to Marvel Comics. Well, when Romita Jr. was ready to return to *Uncanny X-Men* after this time off, he learned that he had been replaced by the artist who had been filling in for him. That artist? Joe Madureira.

Romita Jr. was angry and he had every right to be, but that does not take away from the fact that Joe Madureira soon became one of the hottest comic book artists in the business. Madureira was 16 years old when he got a gig working as an intern at Marvel while still attending the High School of Art and Design in New York City. Madureira was given the chance to draw a short story for *Marvel Comics Presents*, which appeared when he was still just 16 years old.

Going into 1993, Marvel was in a strange position, artists-wise. They had lost their most famous artists in 1992, with Jim Lee, Marc Silvestri, Rob Liefeld, and more having left to found Image Comics. The issue they discovered was that the artists they chose to replace those artists would also be poached by Image Comics. Art Thibert, Brandon Peterson, Greg Capullo, Tony Daniel—it seemed like every artist that they developed, Image would take out from under them. It was getting to the point where they basically had the Kubert brothers and John Romita Jr. as their only major X-Men artists.

Madureira had been doing some assignments here and there during 1992 and 1993. One of the pieces of art that he did around this time that got seen by the most people was a Pizza Hut advertisement that he did in early 1993 to tie in with the fact that Pizza Hut sold videotape copies of *X-Men: The Animated Series*. Eventually, Madureira started to get some fill-in assignments on main titles, including a notable two-issue stint on *Excalibur* in 1992, which guest starred the X-Men, so Marvel got to see what Madureira could do with the X-Men. Madureira also drew Deadpool's first solo miniseries in 1993 (and later drew some Marvel trading cards featuring characters from the *Deadpool* and *X-Force* series).

When he filled in for John Romita Jr., *X-Men* editor Bob Harras decided to renege on his promise to Romita Jr. and just keep Madureira on board the title. Madureira's art was a breath of fresh air. It was heavily inspired by the work of another artist who broke in at a young age, Art Adams. However, Madureira was also heavily influenced by Manga artwork. He was one of the first major mainstream artists who tried to evoke the feeling of Manga artwork. Other artists had obviously been influenced by Manga (Frank Miller, Arthur Adams, and Keith Giffen, to name three prominent examples), but not quite as clearly as Madureira, who used loose lines rather than the classic tight lines of the Jim Lee style of artists.

Soon after he became the regular artist on *Uncanny X-Men*, Marvel did the "Age of Apocalypse" crossover and Madureira got to cut loose by being the main designer of what the alternate-reality X-Men would look like. Around this same time, he was spreading out and doing video game art for the X-Men vs. Capcom video game.

In 1997, after four years of one of the most popular artists in the business, Madureira finally left Marvel to go do a creator-owned series for Image Comics called *Battle Chasers*. He only did nine issues. For the most part, Madureira has been working in video game art for the past 20 years.

95 Northstar

In *Uncanny X-Men #322*, Juggernaut landed in New York City, having been thrown there by some mysterious person or force. When he awoke, the X-Men fought him until he let them know that he was there to warn them. When they asked him who he was trying to warn them about, he said simply, "Onslaught."

Onslaught turned out to be a psionic being formed by the darkest thoughts of Professor X and Magneto. However, when *Uncanny X-Men #322* was written, Scott Lobdell had no idea who or what Onslaught was. Similarly, in *X-Men #109* (by Chris Claremont, John Byrne, and Terry Austin), when Weapon Alpha failed to bring Wolverine in to the Canadian government and then threatened to bring "Alpha Flight" with him next time, neither Claremont nor Byrne had any idea who Alpha Flight was!

Top Five Saddest Deaths in the Pages of X-Men Comics

5. Senator Robert Kelly

Senator Robert Kelly had long been one of the biggest anti-mutant voices in the United States government. After the X-Men save his life, though, he comes around and begins to teach tolerance…and then is promptly murdered by one of his old supporters, who felt betrayed.

4. Squid Boy

Sammy the Squid Boy was a young mutant who had befriended Juggernaut when Juggernaut had gone undercover as a member of the X-Men as part of a plot by the Brotherhood. Juggernaut had reformed for real and he planned on taking the Brotherhood down, but when Sammy saw him, he wouldn't believe him. He then had to watch Sammy killed in front of him.

3. Colossus

Beast found a possible cure for the Legacy Virus, but planned to keep working. The reason being that it only worked if a mutant activated their powers after injecting the serum, and then the activation would kill the mutant who was injected. Colossus, though, could not wait and chose to sacrifice himself. As he died on the floor, snippets from his first appearance appeared in the final page, in a touching moment.

2. Phoenix

Jean Grey had seemingly gotten too out of control with the Phoenix power that she had gained (later, it would be revealed that it was really the Phoenix Force taking the form of Jean Grey) and, in her Dark Phoenix form, she destroyed a whole planet. Now fighting for her life, she realized that she could no longer control her changes, so she chose to kill herself while she could.

1. Illyana Rasputin

Illyana Rasputin had been artificially aged into a teenager for a while, where she became Kitty Pryde's best friend. Then she ended up getting turned back to a preteen. At the same time, though, she contracted the deadly Legacy Virus. So the whole X-Men team had to sit around and wait while watching a little girl die and none of their powers could do anything to save her.

A year later, however, the X-Men were set to fight Alpha Flight in a snowy Canadian airport. Canadian John Byrne had to come up with an entire team for that issue and he came through with flying colors. Alpha Flight was made up of Shaman, Snowbird, Sasquatch, Aurora, and Northstar (paired, of course, with the aforementioned Weapon Alpha, who was now calling himself Vindicator). Not only did Byrne come up with names, costumes, and superpowers for Alpha Flight, but in a quick introduction on the bottom of the issue's first splash page, Byrne also gave them all real life names and some basic information about their life (like how Dr. Walter Langkowski, the alter ego of Sasquatch, was a professional football player before he became a professor of biophysics). However, those quick descriptions were all the thought that Byrne gave to Alpha Flight. They were just meant to be a one-off threat, a chance to wrap up the previous Weapon Alpha story where he promised to return for Wolverine.

Fans, though, wanted to see more. They wanted Alpha Flight to get their own series. Finally, three years after they debuted, John Byrne agreed to write and draw an *Alpha Flight* ongoing series, figuring that if anyone was going to do it, it might as well be the guy who invented them all. It was at this point that Byrne actually sat down and came up with distinct personalities for each of the team members and it was at this point that Byrne decided that Northstar was going to be gay.

Openly gay characters were not allowed at Marvel at the time, which was a problem that Claremont and Byrne had encountered earlier with Mystique and Destiny, who were intended to be a lesbian couple. Byrne, though, just made a point to make it as obvious as he could with Northstar without ever explicitly saying that he was gay. Four years later, Byrne would use the same approach when he introduced Captain Maggie Sawyer in his run on *Superman*. Like Northstar, you would have to be pretty oblivious to not get that Sawyer was meant to be gay.

When Byrne left *Alpha Flight*, incoming writer Bill Mantlo wanted to further explore Northstar's sexuality by having him die of AIDS. It was clearly a well-intentioned idea by Mantlo, but it was also pretty ill-considered. The one gay superhero and he wanted to kill him off from AIDS? Jim Shooter would not allow it and instead, Northstar was revealed to be descended from Asgardian elves. Yes, they came about as close as they could to making the first gay superhero a literal fairy.

In 1992, Scott Lobdell was writing *Alpha Flight* and he managed to get a story approved where Northstar would adopt a young infant who was infected with AIDS from her mother. A retired Canadian superhero, Major Maple Leaf, got angry at how the media was treating the news as a nice public interest story when they treated his son's death from AIDS like his son was a deviant. So he got into an old-fashioned superhero brawl with Northstar where he told Northstar he couldn't possibly understand what he was going through, and Northstar shouted, "I am gay!" Marvel was unprepared for how much backlash that they received, especially from conservative department stores that threatened to pull all X-Men action figures because they didn't want kids to play with a gay action figure (Northstar did not even have an action figure). Marvel, to their demerit, then pulled back dramatically for the rest of the 1990s with Northstar..

In 2002, Northstar joined the X-Men (he had joined briefly in 2001, but just for a single mission). He became a longtime member of the X-Men (only taking a brief break when he was murdered by Wolverine in 2004—he got better). In 2012, with a lot of media coverage, Northstar married his boyfriend in front of all his fellow X-Men in *Astonishing X-Men #50*.

96 Inhumans vs. X-Men

In 2000, the first X-Men film came out. Marvel was thrilled about it and heavily promoted the movie. However, starting in 2008, Marvel had their own Marvel Studios and suddenly they were in direct competition with films based on characters that they otherwise owned! When Disney purchased Marvel, the problem only intensified. Marvel did not like that they did not own the film and TV rights to such major characters as the X-Men. Not only that, but it was a specific detriment to Marvel to not have mutants or something similar to mutants in their TV and films, since the whole "mutant as minority" take is so compelling. This, then, led Marvel to the Inhumans.

In 2014, Marvel had a crossover named "Infinity." The series was about all of Marvel's most powerful heroes heading into outer space to team up with the all the other major alien empires to take on a powerful race of alien invaders. Meanwhile, Thanos chose the absence of the heroes as a perfect time to attack Earth to eliminate his son, who Thanos knew was an Inhuman. Thanos came to Black Bolt on Attilan to offer him a deal. Thanos would leave the Inhumans alone if Black Bolt would kill every Inhuman the same age as Thanos' son. Instead, Black Bolt evacuated all Inhumans and blew up Attilan, as well as the Terrigen crystals that Inhumans had used for millennia to give themselves superpowers, thus keeping the crystals away from Thanos and also taking away any leverage Thanos had to force Black Bolt to kill any single Inhuman.

What Black Bolt did not know is that now that the crystals had exploded, they turned into a gigantic Terrigen Mist cloud that traveled around the globe. The reason that is significant is that millennia ago, before the Inhumans had cut themselves off from human society, that had openly intermingled with other Homo sapiens. In the years that passed, those Homo sapiens naturally continued to propagate the human race on Earth. The issue is, though, that there was enough Inhuman DNA mixed into the world's population from back in those early days that a millennia later, people who thought that they were normal humans were actually part Inhuman! Thus, when they were exposed to the Terrigen Mists, they would suddenly develop a cocoon around them and when they left their cocoon, they would have superpowers!

People, naturally enough, then began to distrust these NuHumans, especially the fact that they could be anyone. Essentially, with the NuHumans, Marvel completely co-opted the "mutant as minority" metaphor from the X-Men. On the Marvel TV series, *Agents of SHIELD*, they actively have been doing plots involving the government treating NuHumans like the government used to treat mutants in the comics. In the comics, characters like Ms. Marvel and Squirrel Girl would have been mutants in the old days but were now NuHumans (Squirrel Girl literally was a mutant originally!).

There was an extra twist, though, that turned the conflict from simply the insult of being replaced to actual injury. As it turned out, the Terrigen Mists, while harmless to humans and empowering to NuHumans, was deadly for mutants. Mutants exposed to the Terrigen Mists would contract a disease called M-Pox that was highly fatal and, even if they survived, would sterilize them. The various X-Men groups, led by Storm, Magneto, and Cyclops, each tried to negotiate with the Inhumans, with the X-Men and Inhumans agreeing to try to evacuate any mutants ahead of the cloud's travel. Cyclops, though, began to act more and more aggressive, including telling the world what the Terrigen Mists were doing to mutants, which caused a riot in Madrid before the cloud arrived there. One of the NuHumans put everyone in the town to sleep, including Storm and her X-Men. This was treated as an act of war by Cyclops. He pushed the fight with the Inhumans and seemed to goad Black Bolt into killing him! As it turned out, Emma Frost had been faking Cyclops' existence up until his "death." The real Cyclops had died of Terrigen exposure weeks ago. Emma wanted to make him a martyr for the anti-Inhumans cause.

So this led to an actual Inhumans vs. X-Men war, but in the end, Medusa of the Inhumans agreed to destroy the Terrigen Mists for the good of the mutant race. The Inhumans Royal Family then decided to leave Earth to explore more about their heritage and find a possible alternative to the Terrigen Mists. Emma Frost became an outcast when people found out about not just what she did with Cyclops, but when the fighting was just about over, Emma had such anger toward the Inhumans that she took over Magneto's mind and had him slaughter a bunch of Inhumans.

97 Chuck Austen

In 2001, there was a strange hierarchy in the three major X-Men titles. Grant Morrison was writing *New X-Men*, which was the clear leader of the X-Men line. Morrison basically had his pick of the X-Men and chose most of the more notable X-Men for his team (Cyclops, Jean Grey, Professor X, Emma Frost, Wolverine, and Beast) while Chris Claremont launched a new series, *X-Treme X-Men*, and also had his pick of the leftover X-Men, choosing Storm, Psylocke, Bishop, Gambit, and Rogue for his team (along with characters no one would have wanted, like Sage and the new Thunderbird). That left *Uncanny X-Men*, where Joe Casey was allowed to use Wolverine pulling double duty, but otherwise was dealing with the dregs of the X-Men—Archangel, Iceman, Nightcrawler, and Chamber. Casey soon just decided to go a whole other direction on *Uncanny X-Men*.

Part of the problem was that Casey lost his original artist, Ian Churchill, before their first story even finished. Casey turned to his *Wildcats* collaborator, Sean Phillips, to come on board. Sean Phillips is an excellent artist and Joe Casey is a great writer, but their take on the X-Men was a lot different than what Marvel was likely expecting from the book. Casey's serious contemplations on the human condition did not seem to fit in with the X-Men line, even when Casey tried his best to adapt with a story arc with more action in it where former X-Man Banshee got tricked into forming a sort of fascist version of the X-Men called the X-Corps. So just over a year after starting, Casey was out as the writer of *Uncanny X-Men*.

Marvel replaced Casey with Chuck Austen. Austen had been a comic book artist in the 1980s (he even worked on Alan Moore's *Miracleman!*), who did a popular pornographic comic book series about the sexual misadventures of a group of college students called *Strips*. He then left the world of comic books during the 1990s to work in animation, before returning at the start of the 21st century. He had done a decently received *War Machine* series for Marvel and he got a crack at following up Casey. Where Casey's *Uncanny X-Men* was reflective, Austen's was intentionally going for action. His initial arc, working with Ron Garney, was a typical superhero action adventure.

Once he settled in, though, Austen would routinely make the oddest decisions with his stories. He revealed that mutants cannot contract AIDS, for some bizarre reason. He later recalled that he thought that had been established already (it had not). He even doubled down on the "mutants cannot contract AIDS" bit a few issues after establishing it by having Angel visit a hospital, where a doctor confirmed the fact.

He wrote a special 25 cent issue of *Uncanny X-Men* that was designed to draw in casual fans from the second X-Men film that had just come out. The story was about the Church of Humanity planning on installing Nightcrawler as the Roman Catholic Pope (disguising his appearance with an image inducer) and then, using special Communion wafers that would cause people to disintegrate, they would make it seem like the Rapture had occurred. They would then reveal Nightcrawler's true visage and make people believe he was the Anti-Christ, which would destroy the Catholic Church and lead to mutants being hunted down as demons. Austen didn't bother to check whether the Rapture was even part of Catholic dogma (it is not).

Next, Austen wrote his most infamous story line, "The Draco," which revealed that Nightcrawler's father was a demonic-looking mutant named Azazel (this was part of some bit where Austen suggested that all biblical stories of demons and angels were just early mutants). Azazel, you see, was trapped in another dimension and wanted to get out of it. So his plan was to go to Earth and mate with Earth women and create teleporting babies, who would then grow up and he would recruit them so that they could all work together and free him from the other dimension. Yes, he traveled to the other dimension to mate with women so they could grow up and teleport him...out of the dimension that he was already traveling out of to mate with the women. If you understand how that doesn't make any sense, you're already one step ahead of Austen.

Austen wrote a number of other terrible stories (like "She Lies With Angels," where Angel and Husk declared their love for each other and have sex...in the sky...above her mother), but somehow managed to remain on *Uncanny X-Men* (and *X-Men* afterward) for a shocking four-year run! We can say this much, he at least certainly made his mark on the X-Men…if you're going to be bad, you might as well be the worst.

98 Must Read: "Gifted"

During his stint on *New X-Men*, Grant Morrison introduced a number of major changes to the X-Men. He expanded the mutant population, he had the X-Men stop wearing colorful costumes, he had Beast mutate further into a beast, he killed off Magneto and Jean Grey and he had Cyclops and Emma Frost begin a relationship. Within a few years of his final issue, though, nearly all of his changes were overturned by other writers. Heck, with just the first arc on *Astonishing X-Men*, one of Morrison's changes was already reversed.

Astonishing X-Men was launched as the new face of the X-Men franchise following the conclusion of Morrison's *New X-Men* run. The creative team was famous screenwriter Joss Whedon, who had just finished work on his acclaimed *Buffy the Vampire Slayer* series, as well as its spinoff, *Angel*, and award-winning comic book artist John Cassaday, who was still working on the Wildstorm series, *Planetary*, with writer Warren Ellis. (The idea was that Cassaday would switch back and forth between the two series, with lengthy breaks between arcs on both books. As it turned out, it took five and a half years for Cassaday to finish the last eight issues of *Planetary*.)

Whedon continued the Emma Frost and Cyclops relationship from Morrison's run, but in the first arc on the series, titled "Gifted," Whedon quickly reversed course on the uniform debate. Cyclops decided that the X-Men had to put together a squad that could reassure the public by being outright superheroes. So Cyclops recruited Kitty Pryde to return to the X-Men, since she was so good at being the public face of the X-Men. Whedon had generally worked well with young, strong-willed female heroes (the most famous one being, of course, Buffy the Vampire Slayer), so he clearly took a real shine to Kitty Pryde and made sure to feature her heavily in the series.

After the team made their big, public debut as superheroes, with their bright costumes, the team was shocked to learn that a scientist, Dr. Kavita Rao, had apparently developed a "cure" for being a mutant! Since Beast had only recently suffered a secondary mutation, the idea of going back to being a human had a lot of appeal for him. He was interested enough that he went to visit Rao, with whom he had worked in the past. She happily gave him a sample of the cure for him to study. He brought it back to the X-Mansion, which did not sit well with Wolverine, who was informed by Emma Frost that Beast was giving off signs that he was interested in perhaps taking such a cure. Wolverine and Beast fought over the idea of whether it was okay to "give up" on being a mutant. However, things changed dramatically when Beast discovered whose body the serum had been tested on.

The next issue, the X-Men went to break into Genetech, the company that produced the cure, looking for their dead teammate whose body was being used to develop the cure. In an example of a clever case of dealing with spoilers, John Cassaday specifically drew a fake page showing the X-Men meeting a resurrected Jean Grey that Marvel then "leaked" to the public. That helped to throw people off of the scent of the real hero making their return in a major shocker—it turned out that the mutant being held by Genetech was not Jean Grey but rather the Russian mutant known as Colossus! He had seemingly died a few years earlier while trying to find a cure for the deadly Legacy Virus (he succeeded).

As it turned out, Colossus was a prisoner of an alien named Ord. It was Ord's technology that allowed Rao to create a mutant cure, using Colossus' body to help test the serum. When the X-Men showed up to take Ord down, they were shocked to discover that SHIELD was there to keep them from doing so. As it turned out, SHIELD had a secret side division called SWORD, which dealt with alien invasions of Earth. The head of SWORD, agent Abigail Brand, had cut a deal with Ord, who saw a vision that his planet, Breakworld, was going to be destroyed by a mutant. Brand allowed him to capture Colossus and keep him captive to avoid that confrontation, while also allowing him to help develop a mutant cure.

Ord, though, ended up trying to escape from Earth with a sample of the cure and a young mutant with terribly destructive nightmare powers. Wolverine and Colossus teamed up for one of their famous "Fastball Specials" and stopped him. It was a well-written and beautifully drawn opening arc that ended up winning the Eisner Award for Best Continuing Series.

99 X-Men Licensing

When you have a piece of intellectual property that people enjoy, they tend to want to see that property in as many different contexts as possible. For instance, if you have a kid who likes Spider-Man, he or she would probably want a Spider-Man backpack as well as Spider-Man shirts and a Spider-Man bedsheet. Things like that. That's where the licensing department comes in. And in the 1990s, the X-Men were licensed like almost no other comic book property had ever been licensed before (with the notable exceptions of

Batman in 1966 and 1989 and the Teenage Mutant Ninja Turtles circa 1990).

We mentioned earlier how the X-Men were heavily licensed into a variety of video games throughout the '90s, and the X-Men toy line made so much money for ToyBiz that they ended up in control of Marvel Entertainment as a whole. (Marvel's X-Men toy line had been so thorough in turning practically every X-Men character into a toy that Scott Lobdell and Joe Madureira actually invented two characters before their run on *Uncanny X-Men* was finished called Spat and Gravel, mercenaries where the one partner, Spat, was a woman who was aging backward and so looked like a little girl and the other partner, Grovel, was a giant reptilian creature. Lobdell and Madureira created them, in part, to come up with two characters who would never be turned into action figures... within a year, they had been made into action figures.)

Another area where licensing was very successful was in trading card lines. Baseball cards were booming in the late '80s and early '90s, so Marvel got into doing trading card series featuring both Marvel characters and specifically X-Men characters. Jim Lee famously drew every card in the 1991 set. Trading cards did so well that Marvel actually bought a trading card company, Fleer, just so they could produce their own Marvel trading cards. (Sadly for Marvel, the trading card bubble burst at around the same time as the comic book bubble, so Marvel trading cards soon ceased to exist.)

Really, though, there were so many X-Men-licensed products that it would almost be easier to try to name which products did not have some sort of X-Men license. Ice cream pops? You better believe that there were some absolutely haunting popsicles with what looks to sort of be Wolverine's face on them. Pasta? You bet, as Chef Boyardee made a number of canned pastas with X-Men-shaped pasta pieces soaked in "tomato sauce." Inflatable balloon hammers where the hole where you blow the air in is right on Wolverine's crotch? Was there ever any doubt?

There was an interesting side effect to the X-Men-licensing craze that occurred in the early 2000s. The classic version of Wolverine had been ingrained in people's minds, but at the same time, Hugh Jackman's Wolverine was also well known. Adding to the mix was the Wolverine from the hit new comic book series, *Ultimate X-Men*. Each Wolverine looked different from each other. So Marvel determined that they had to pick a single one to make their official licensed Wolverine. They chose the *Ultimate X-Men* version of Wolverine, since he was the closest in the middle between classic yellow-costume Wolverine and just regular Hugh Jackman Wolverine. In 2003, Marvel actually had Wolverine change his look in all of his comics to match the official licensed look so that the licensing for the character would be extra simple. (You'll notice if you read Grant Morrison's *New X-Men* run that Wolverine abruptly changes his look midway through the series, gaining a soul patch on his chin and everything.)

In recent years, though, a dramatic shift has taken place in X-Men licensing. You see, one thing that was very important about X-Men licensing in the '90s was that there weren't any X-Men films yet. Once the X-Men films came out, other rights kicked in with them as well. Since the X-Men films made the characters more popular than they already were, then Fox's deal with Marvel is that Fox gets a sizable chunk out of any licensed X-Men material released close to a Fox X-Men film release (which is basically always, since Fox is constantly making new X-Men films). Thus, Marvel cut back on making licensed products featuring the X-Men.

As Marvel executive editor Tom Brevoort once explained, "If you had two things, and on one you earned 100 percent of the revenues from the efforts that you put into making it, and the other you earned a much smaller percentage for the same amount of time and effort, you'd be more likely to concentrate more heavily on the first, wouldn't you?" The X-Men were even removed from shirts that reprinted classic covers including the X-Men (like the cover of *Secret Wars #1*). With Disney presumably purchasing Fox, though, X-Men licensing might be making a major comeback very soon!

100 Visit the X-Mansion

When it comes down to it, your options of visiting famous superhero movie sets are pretty slim. You can't go visit Superman's Fortress of Solitude. You can't go to visit Batman's Batcave. You can go visit the buildings used for the *Daily Bugle* and *Daily Planet*, respective offices in *Spider-Man* and *Superman*, but they look nothing like those places anymore. This likely explains just how popular the Batmobile from the 1966 *Batman* TV series is. That is because you can actually physically touch it and, in most instances when it appears as part of exhibitions about the program, you can even sit inside it. That gives you an immersive feeling that you are hard-pressed to find anywhere else. One of those rare other places is the X-Mansion from the X-Men films, which you can visit any time you are in British Columbia!

In 1906, the lieutenant governor of British Columbia was a man named James Dunsmuir, who was rich due to his family's coal-mining business. Dunsmuir was fiercely anti-union, and while he was alive, his collieries never once unionized. Likely understanding that he would need to have some political clout if he wanted to assure his anti-union stance would hold, he got involved in the politics of British Columbia. (Those connections likely led to him

Top Five Best Wolverine/Hulk fights

5. *Wolverine/Hulk: Six Hours #4*

Wolverine needs some of Hulk's blood for a serum that could save a child's life. The six hours they had before the kid died were almost up, so Wolverine picked a fight intentionally, figuring in the fight he would get some blood for the serum.

4. *Savage Wolverine #5*

A threat to the Earth itself had been calling people to its Savage Land prison with telepathy to get it free. When the Hulk was drawn to the prison, Wolverine had to fight the Hulk and do anything he could (including stabbing the Hulk in the head) to get him to not free the villain.

3. *World War Hulk: X-Men #2*

Hulk had returned from his exile by the Illuminati to get revenge on the men who sent him into outer space (and, at the time, Hulk believed that they sabotaged his ship), which included Professor X. The rest of the X-Men tried to stop the Hulk, but the Hulk was stronger and more clever than ever and he pounded Wolverine's head repeatedly to give him a ton of mini-concussions.

2. *Incredible Hulk #181*

Their very first fight was one of their best. They ended up having to briefly team up against the Wendigo, but Wolverine quickly showed how resilient he was by holding his own with the Hulk in a man-to-man combat situation!

1. *Incredible Hulk #340*

The Hulk and Wolverine were on separate missions heading in opposite directions when they happened to cross paths in the road. The Hulk couldn't leave well enough alone and they engaged in a brutal fight, beautifully depicted by burgeoning comic book superstar artist Todd McFarlane (just months away from his move to *Amazing Spider-Man*, where he changed Spider-Man's look forever).

being able to call in the militia to get his workers to go back to work. Remember, we are just here to admire his house, not the man himself.)

He had a mansion built in southern Vancouver to evoke his Scottish ancestry by making it Scottish Baronial architecture, which basically means it was designed to look like a castle. The home (which they dubbed "Hatley Park," just like all the great houses in England, like Downton Abbey) was lived in by the Dunsmuir family until the last of them died out in 1937. It was then sold to the Government of Canada, who then sold most of the land around the estate. During World War II, England worked out plans for the King and Queen and their two daughters, Elizabeth and Margaret, to move into Hatley Park if they had to evacuate from England. Luckily, that never had to happen. It was then used as a military college until 1995, when it became a Canadian National Historic Site.

Most importantly for our purposes, of course, it became the X-Mansion in the X-Men film series beginning with *X2*. It also appeared in *X-Men: The Last Stand*, *X-Men: Days of Future Past*, *Deadpool*, and *X-Men: Apocalypse*. The mansion is open to the public and most of the estate is free admission, although you do have to pay a few dollars if you want to visit the beautiful gardens on the estate.

If you're going to travel to Vancouver, there are a couple of X-Men related activities that you can partake in on the way to Hatley Park. If you're flying, you can be sure to download and watch the television series *Magnum P.I.* on your devices on the flight. *Magnum P.I.* has a strange place in X-Men history. During Chris Claremont's run on *New Mutants*, it was the one show that the whole team could agree to watch (the boys liked the action and the girls liked to watch Tom Selleck, even Wolfsbane, who noted that it was improper to think such thoughts) and for the rest of the series, there were recurring references made to the show. Even today, you will occasionally see one of the members of the *New Mutants* make a reference to the series, even though it's obviously now anachronistic that they would be watching a show that went off the air in 1988. But, hey, that's what reruns are for!

When you get to Vancouver, with all of their many parks, you should also make sure to play some baseball before you head off to Hatley Park (it is possible that you might even be allowed to play on the massive park grounds, but better not to risk it). Baseball has played a very important role in the history of the X-Men, as it has long been the go-to choice for a team sport that the team members can play together. They first played baseball all the way back in *X-Men #110*, with Wolverine popping his claws to try to keep Colossus from making it to second base on a hit (Colossus just turned into organic steel and barreled ahead). The X-Men played baseball in the 20th anniversary of the All-New, All-Different X-Men in *Uncanny X-Men #325* and again when Chris Claremont returned to *Uncanny X-Men* for his final stint on the book in *Uncanny X-Men #444*. Most recently, in *X-Men Gold #1*, they played baseball but saw it cause some controversy when it turned out that the artist on the book, Ardian Syaf, hid references to a political controversy back in his native Indonesia on Colossus' shirt while playing the game. Since the controversy revolved around possible anti-Christian protests, many people were offended. Marvel reprinted the issue with the references removed and then fired Syaf.

Acknowledgments

I'd like to thank my uncanny wife, Meredith, as well as my astonishing parents, Eugene and Kathleen, and my extraordinary siblings and their significant others, Matthew (and Kristie), James (and Jenn), and Jean (and Jesse)! Plus, I would never have known this much about comic books had it not been for Robert Williams and Squiggy's Dugout.

I'd also like to thank my editors at CBR and ValNet—Albert Ching, Stephen Gerding, Kevin Melrose, Rob Levin, Steve Paugh, Ben Kendrick, and Rob Keyes (plus, as always, CBR's founder, Jonah Weiland).

Also, thanks to my editor at Triumph Books, Jesse Jordan, who made this experience a delight. The same can be said for my literary agent, Rick Broadhead.

Finally, thanks to all my readers over the years that have helped out with suggestions and topics and comments at one point or another. One of my goals has always been to write stuff that I think interests me, as if it interests me, I imagine it might interest others. Similarly, then, when others come up with ideas, that's usually a sign that it might be a good topic to talk about, so I greatly appreciate all the feedback this past decade plus.